THE MIDDLE WEST

THE
MIDDLE
WEST

Its Meaning
in American Culture

James R. Shortridge

UNIVERSITY PRESS OF KANSAS

© 1989 by the University Press of Kansas

Published by the University Press of Kansas (Lawrence, Kansas
66045), which was organized by the Kansas Board of Regents and is
operated and funded by Emporia State University, Fort Hays State
University, Kansas State University, Pittsburg State University,
the University of Kansas, and Wichita State University

Library of Congress Cataloging-in-Publication Data

Shortridge, James R., 1944–
    The Middle West : its meaning in American culture/James R.
    Shortridge.
       p. cm.
    Bibliography: p.
    Includes index.
    ISBN 0–7006–0475–8 (pbk.)
      1. Middle West – Civilization. 2. Middle West – Social conditions.
    3. Anthropo-geography – Middle West.   4. Regionalism – Middle West.
    I. Title.
F351.S5 1989   88–29991
977 – dc19   CIP

Printed in the United States of America
10 9 8 7 6 5 4 3 2

The paper used in this publication meets the minimum requirements
of the American National Standard for Permanence of Paper for
Printed Library Materials Z39.48–1984.

To the memory of Clark and Bertha Knorpp,
who provided a window into
an older Middle West

Contents

List of Illustrations, Maps, and Tables

Illustrations

Maps

Tables

. . . unless you are at home in the metaphor, unless you have had your proper poetical education in the metaphor, you are not safe anywhere. . . . You are not safe in science; you are not safe in history.

— *Robert Frost, "Education by Poetry"*

Preface

This book is unconventional geography. Although understanding regions has always been a central concern for geographers, the traditional approach has been grounded in natural and social science. A "scientific" approach to regional analysis has much to recommend it, but it falls embarrassingly short of being able to capture important intangibles of place: meaning, essence, and character.

As a discipline, geography now contains a small group of scholars who call themselves humanists. They note how social-science-minded geographers have emphasized the somewhat sterile, theoretical term *space* at the expense of the equally important but emotion-laden and particularistic term *place.* They debate alternative philosophies to positivism, including phenomenology and existentialism. So far, though, the humanist movement is mostly prescriptive. Geographers see the need to use humanities materials but are poorly equipped to handle them. We know formal hypothesis testing and statistical methods; but we are unfamiliar with and thus somewhat afraid of the subject matter and critical approaches used in the analysis of novels, poetry, and the arts in general.

In this study I attempt to deal directly with the subjective aspects of a place. My subject is that amorphous region known as the Middle West. Although as a sixth-generation Missourian I grew up immersed in Middle-western lore, my curiosity about the place did not begin until I first left it to attend college in New Hampshire. The making of comparisons between New Hampshire and Missouri probably influenced my choice of geography as a career; a desire to understand the underlying character of the Middle West has lingered ever since.

This study was initiated in 1979/80 with release time provided by a fellowship from the John Simon Guggenheim Memorial Foundation and a sabbatical leave from the University of Kansas. I spent the year at Dartmouth College, and I am grateful to the staffs of the Department of Geography and Baker Library there for providing an ideal work environment during that period. Professors Blanche Gelphant and Robert McGrath, whose classes I audited, helped me to understand more about how humanists approach their work. Within my own discipline I have drawn inspiration from the writings of Carl O. Sauer, John K. Wright, and J. B. Jackson. Conversations with my students Michael Caron and Roger Stump also were influential in turning my interests toward subjective materials. The support of Walter M. Kollmorgen, Peirce Lewis, James J. Parsons, and Wilbur Zelinsky helped to initiate this project; that of my wife, Barbara, enabled it to come to fruition. Earlier versions of materials in chapters 2, 3, and 5 have been published in the *Annals* of the Association of American Geographers.

1

Contradictory Images

Dorothy, Toto, Aunt Em and Uncle Henry from L. Frank Baum's *The Wizard of Oz* are among the most enduring characters in American fiction. One reason is symbolic, for they encapsulate values and flavor from America's heartland, a paradoxical place known as the Middle West. This region has intrigued writers from its inception. It was a mixing ground for Yankees and Southerners, its experience has been tied closely to that of America in general, and it frequently is proclaimed to be the nation's real birthplace and cultural core. Such powerful associations ought to have produced a clear regional identity, but none exists. To some the Middle West is a place of idealism and democratic temperament, but to others it is bland, materialistic, and conservative. The overall enigmatic and contradictory regional character remains largely unexplored.

This book is a historical probe into the "idea" of the Middle West. It explores the personality and image of the region, including what the label Middle West originally meant to Americans and how this meaning has changed over time. I will argue for a close and continuing association between Middle-western identity and the concept of pastoralism. The region has come to stand as a symbol for this important aspect of American culture and thereby has derived a measure of prestige. Concurrently, however, the fitting of a simplified, anachronistic image to an increasingly complex region has produced a host of contradictions, distortions, and misunderstandings.

Baum provides a useful point of departure for all this, because his imagery, first written in 1900, is typical of much of the twentieth-century literature and raises some issues and dilemmas

1

that are basic to Middle-western identity. Consider Dorothy, for example: polite, friendly, and bright-eyed, she wears her hair in braids, is a little naïve, and lives on a farm. Her Aunt Em and Uncle Henry are simple, hard-working religious folk. They wear practical clothing, raise chickens and hogs, and are so trusting of authority that they give up Toto when a fussy schoolteacher claims it is the law. The farmstead also is stereotypical: it sits amidst a flat, nearly treeless plain; Kansas is vast and fertile but also bleak. This Middle-western scene contrasts vividly with Oz, the land "over the rainbow." Oz is lush and wondrous in all ways, a point that was made graphically in the 1939 Judy Garland version of the tale by a switch from black-and-white to color photography. Still, for all its fascination, Oz is as full of danger and deceit as it is of opportunity, and Dorothy eventually opts to return home.

Farming is the dominant image in Baum's Middle West, as it has been in the accounts of journalists throughout this century. The image contrasts not only with the sophisticated, exotic Oz (an allusion to the East Coast states?), but with the predominantly urban reality of the modern Middle West.[1] Much has been written about the values attached to this rural image. For most observers it has suggested wholesomeness and self-sufficiency, but others have seen in it a narrow conservatism and a dependency on outside business and governmental interests. Fertile land can reward or even encourage hard work, and seasonal variability may foster planning and resiliency. On the other hand, a harsh environment and isolation on the farm might lead to an embittered, parochial society. Contradictory images of this sort have plagued the Middle West throughout much of its history. They create an uncertain identity, and uncertainty, in turn, inhibits the development of regional pride. Natives of the South, New York, and the Pacific Northwest are said to defend their regions over all objections, whereas Middle-western folk tend to waver between neutrality and outright defensiveness.

The inherent contradiction in a region that is said to be the nation's heartland and yet is afflicted with insecurity forms one of the springboards for this study. Equally intriguing, and possibly related, is the apparent lack of a historical core for Middle-western culture. Most major American regions have obvious roots. New England owes much of its temperament even today to its puritan heritage; the Southwest, to its Spanish-Catholic and Indian traditions; and the South, to its ruralism and period of independence. The Middle West is more complex. Its early settlers came from Yankee, Middle Atlantic, and Southern cultural traditions on the eastern seaboard, as well as from Germany, Scandinavia, Ireland, and Eastern Europe. The agriculture of the region is divided among corn, wheat, and dairy farming, ranching, and other traditions. Some sections are highly urbanized; others are very rural.

The more one thinks about the Middle West, the more muddled the regional identity seems to become. Most writers today define the area as the twelve states extending westward from Ohio to Kansas and then northward to the Canadian border, but many exceptions exist. To some writers the place lies entirely west of the Mississippi River, but others locate it entirely east of that river (maps 1.1, 1.2).

The origin of the regional label might be expected to provide insights into its culture and location, but this question, too, is answered only vaguely in either the popular or the scholarly literature. Most writers imply that the Middle West is defined essentially by its relationship to the West. The connection derives from our nation's persistent definition of the West as a near wilderness, sparsely occupied by a somewhat unstable society. The West, in other words, represented the settlement frontier at least as much as it did a fixed location. The Ohio Valley was once considered the West, but as time passed, a new regional term was needed for what had become a mature society. Many writers assume that the West was then subdivided into "Far" and "Middle" West components. The former label retained the traditional pioneer and wilderness traits, whereas the latter referred to the second stage of settlement, a land of small towns and a stable, prosperous agricultural economy.

If this line of reasoning is correct, the phrase "Middle West" likely would have had its origins in Ohio, the first extensive area

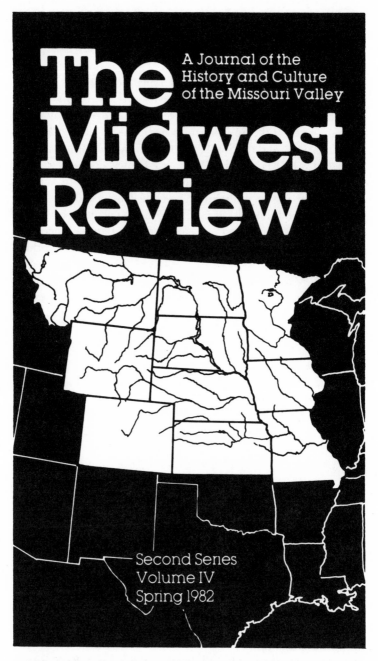

A Journal of the
History and Culture
of the Missouri Valley

The Midwest Review

Second Series
Volume IV
Spring 1982

Map 1.1. A View of the Middle West from Nebraska. Reprinted by permission from *The Midwest Review*, published annually by Wayne State College, Wayne, Nebraska.

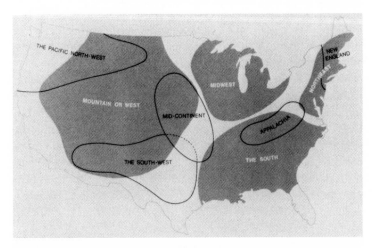

Map 1.2. A View of the Middle West and Other Major Regions from Ohio. Reprinted by permission from John A. Jakle, Stanley Brunn, and Curtis C. Roseman, *Human Spatial Behavior: A Social Geography* (North Scituate, Mass.: Duxbury Press, 1976), p. 62 (reissued in 1985 by Waveland Press). The map originally appeared in another form in Kevin R. Cox and Georgia Zannaras, "Descriptive Perceptions of Macro Spaces: Concepts, a Methodology, and Applications" (Columbus: Ohio State University, Department of Geography, discussion paper no. 17, 1970), p. 19.

of good farming land settled beyond the seaboard colonies. The time, perhaps, would have been the 1830s. As the settlement process continued, "Middle West" would gradually have chased "West" across the country. The eastern portion of the Great Plains would have become Middle-western late in the century, but there the diffusion process would have stopped. The same arid and mountainous conditions that prohibited a densely settled farming society would also have prohibited the expansion of the term Middle West — somewhere around the 100th meridian or the Front Range of the Rockies. As a corollary to this line of thought, one might expect a local attachment to the term Middle West (as well as to Midwest, its more recent shortened form) to vary with the length of usage. Ohioans would revere the phrases; Kansans would be only moderately attached to them.

Culture regions traditionally are studied by measuring the presence or absence of religious, dialectal, or various other culture elements. These studies, although straightforward and useful, cannot adequately measure the essences and moods that make up a region's character; they cannot convey the often subtle differences between the way a people see themselves and how outsiders may view them. Questionnaire surveys can provide information on currently perceived images of places, but data on past attitudes are more fugitive. For this study, I rely heavily on the perceptions recorded in articles, advertisements, political cartoons, and editorials drawn from popular magazines of the type indexed in *Readers' Guide to Periodical Literature.*

To a careful reader the tone and words of popular writings can reveal distinctions between established and new ideas, as well as between majority and minority views; they can disclose the tensions that separate regional cultures. I have gathered impressions, moods, and images from this literature between the 1820s and the present; I have integrated them with ideas from novelists, other humanists, and the scholarly literature in general; and I have sorted them out by time and place. The following presentation is arranged chronologically; but within each period, the focus is geographic. I try to discern how Middle Westerners have seen themselves and to what extent these views were in conflict with images of them held in the East and elsewhere. The goal is not only to understand the Middle West as a cultural idea but also to reveal the important interplay that has occurred between this regional culture and that of the United States as a whole.

An extended study of the popular literature has convinced me that widely held assumptions about the origins and meaning of Middle-western culture are in error. As I suggested at the outset, much of the meaning of Middle West as a regional label seems to revolve around its identification with American pastoralism. Pastoralism, the concept of an ideal middle kingdom suspended between uncivilized wilderness and urban-industrial evils, was applied to the original American colonies by many European writers and soon became an important part of the new country's self-image. Over time, this pastoralist face of the United States has become regionalized. I will demonstrate that the term Middle West initially was coined to describe a particular pastoral setting but that this regional name then quickly came to symbolize Arcadian idealism in a more general sense. This identification is the unwavering fact of Middle-western existence—a root identity equivalent to New England's puritanism. It has failed to produce a simple unified regional image, however, because values associated with pastoralism have changed, the rural character of the Middle West itself has lessened, and the physical area said to be Middle Western has been modified. The basic pattern is thus something of a paradox—continuity yet change; and this melange is a key to the cultural confusion that has characterized the region throughout much of its history.

In chapter 2, I trace the early history of the Middle West label, including its original cultural and regional associations. The term came into being, not in relationship to "Far" West, as is commonly believed, but as part of a north-south ordering of space on the plains frontier. The place was Kansas-Nebraska, not Ohio, and the time was the 1880s. The term Middle West was used to differentiate the comparatively settled and stable "middle" states both from the frontier "North West" in the Dakotas and from the culturally different "South West" in Texas and Indian Territory.

After about 1902, contemporary writers began to use the term Middle West in an expanded sense, adding to Kansas and Nebraska the states of the northern plains (North and South Dakota, Minnesota, Iowa, Missouri) and of the upper Ohio Valley (Wisconsin, Illinois, Indiana, Michigan, Ohio). This enlargement of territory was probably initiated by a need for new regional names. Neither the "Old Northwest," in the Ohio Valley, nor the "New Northwest," in the Dakotas, was adequate or appropriate by then, given the rise of a third Northwest on the Pacific Coast. Middle West was a vague territorial description whose origins were quickly forgotten but whose associations with pastoral imagery were highly regarded by the general public. By 1912 the new labeling process had become universal, and the Middle West had acquired a twelve-state definition.

People in the newly expanded version of the Middle West reached a pinnacle of self-confidence in the 1910s. Americans at that time placed a high value on the pastoral traits of morality, independence, and egalitarianism; and they saw the Middle West as a symbol for these ideals. Moreover, people all across the nation thought of the Middle West as the favored region in an analogy that linked sections of the country with stages in the human life cycle. Whereas the West was seen as brash and youthful, and the East was viewed as stodgy and old, the Middle West escaped the problems of both extremes. It was still young enough to have ideals and energy, yet it was not so old as to be ossified by decay, class stratification, and overcrowding. Agriculture there was stable, which guaranteed prosperity, while the development of industry and culture seemed to ensure a glorious future. Writers both in and outside the region agreed that the Middle West had replaced the East as the standard by which to gauge other sections of the nation. It was the heartland, the vital core, and as such, it was almost beyond criticism. I describe this flowering of self-confidence in chapter 3.

In the decade after World War I, Middle Westerners were able to maintain their agricultural might and to add to it tremendous urban and industrial growth, particularly in the Great Lakes states. Given the flexibility with which the regional label had been employed during the first several decades of its existence, one might assume that people would again change its definition to accommodate this new reality. The popular perception of the Middle West would now focus on a marriage of industry and agriculture and would probably stress that this combination represented not only the region but also America in general: the region would still epitomize the nation.

The popular literature that I analyze in chapter 4 reveals some support for the hybrid view of agriculture and industry in harmony, but this was distinctly a minority opinion and was confined largely to descriptions of Michigan and Ohio. For some reason, writers who assessed the Middle West as a whole stuck almost exclusively with rural themes. Some of the journalists maintained the totally positive assessments of earlier times, but others thought that conservatism had begun to replace progressive idealism, a sign perhaps that the yeoman society was aging. Old-fashioned, even culturally backward, ideas were often seen to exist along with the traditional pastoral friendliness and honesty. The Middle West was still rural America, but either the nature of rural society or the nation's collective opinion of it had changed for the worse. Middle Westerners themselves seemed unsure initially about how to react to these circumstances, but one can detect during the 1920s a gradual replacement of self-confidence with self-doubt.

The failure of people to modify their perception of the Middle West as a rural society in the post-1920 decade raises some major questions for regional and national cultural identity. Certainly the inertness was not because the new industrial scene lacked allure, for descriptions of Detroit and Cleveland during this time are rife with their praise of new technological achievement and prosperity. The automobile industry, in fact, was employed widely as a symbol for modern American vigor and enterprise.

I will argue that the failure of journalists to incorporate the new Detroit image of the 1920s into the established view of the Middle West is an example of what may be a general need for Americans to regionalize — that is, compartmentalize — national myths in order to avoid a confrontation with the contradictions inherent in these myths. Pastoralism is the principal myth in question, of course. Even though sections of the United States had long been urbanized, this reality apparently did not threaten national pastoral ideals so long as farming remained dominant in at least one major region. Were the Middle West to abandon its rural ways, however, the vital supply of wholesomeness and integrity that presumably was being pumped into the national being would surely be threatened. Popular literature strongly suggests that Americans first began to delude themselves in this way during the 1920s. They equated the Middle West with unchanging pastoral values, and regional descriptions began to incorporate nostalgic praise for "traditional" values. Journalists made a compromise with reality. For example, Detroit's urban-industrial success was not incorporated into the regional model, presumably because its urban imagery was so strong that it would have threatened pastoral themes. Reporters only partially acknowledged the growing complexity of the region; at most they interrupted their steady flow of stories about farming villages with occasional datelines from small manufacturing cities such as Dubuque, Iowa; Peoria, Illinois; or William Allen White's Emporia, Kansas.

The fusion between pastoralism and the Middle West eventually strained the traditional twelve-state definition of the region. Until the 1950s the solution was simply to ignore the urban reality of the Great Lakes states. Gradually, however, as the gap between image and reality grew ever wider, the American public modified its physical definition of Middle West. As I argue in chapter 5, the core of what is considered the Middle West now has shifted to the west. It has returned to its birthplace on the Kansas-Nebraska plains, to an area that is still rural in at least a relative sense. This shift suggests that modern Americans still place tremendous stock in pastoral concepts. In order to preserve the purity of an image, an entire region has been relocated.

This study of Middle-western culture also includes an internal look at the society. I switch the focus in chapter 6 to state-level popular literature in order to determine variations in the intensity of Middle-western affiliation or feeling. Despite the results of perceptual surveys that show a Kansas-Nebraska focus for today's Middle West, the defining cultural traits actually describe Iowa better. Small towns dominate in both places, but the extent of rural prosperity differs considerably. A demanding yet rewarding physical environment is quintessentially Middle Western, but in the western plains, demand often exceeds reward. The disaster of the Dust Bowl was probably a factor in the original perceived migration of the cultural core of the Middle West eastward from the plains; similarly, perhaps the 1930s had to recede from memory before Americans could shift the imagery back to the west.

The southern limits for the Middle West are easiest to define. Kentucky is rarely associated with the region, a fact that is probably rooted in the cultural boundary set up along the Ohio River in 1787 by the antislavery and other provisions of the Northwest Ordinance. A second clear boundary cuts horizontally across central Oklahoma and separates the land rushes initiated from Kansas and from Texas, respectively, by peoples who had recently been bitterly divided by civil war. Missouri is a great mixing ground, a place that was initially Southern in culture but that is not totally at ease with any regional label today. St. Louis remains particularly ambiguous in this regard.

The pastoral definition of the Middle West has long created identity problems for people in the Great Lakes states. In Michigan, the most extreme case, the label of Middle West is almost never used as a descriptor. Lumber and mining, not agriculture, dominate accounts of Michigan's early history; the automobile industry and tourism, its recent past. Wisconsin and Minnesota share Michigan's heritage of lumbering, mining, and tourism; and Ohio, Wisconsin, and Illinois mirror its heavy industry side. Well-developed agricultural images, however, make all of these other states fit the pastoral Middle West better than does Michigan. Wisconsin owes much of its Middle-western identification to its self-proclaimed status as "America's dairyland." Minnesota, with its combination of rich agriculture and large cities that have escaped urban decay, is the epitome of the old Middle-western utopian dream of the 1910s before the industrial portion of the cultural definition was excised.

What conclusions can be drawn from the knowledge that Middle-western identity is fused with the identity of pastoralism and that this fusion is still so pervasive as to force the physical relocation of the region? A key is to recognize that the Middle West is but one of three major regional labels that have been popularly linked to specific traits of national culture. I argue in chapter 7 that the East is associated with America's technological might and the West with its youthful vigor and freedom. This compartmentalism of values has provided a tangible symbol for each trait, an identity for each region, and a means to avoid contradictions among the three cultural myths.

As Americans placed increasing emphasis on their role as the world's technology leader after World War I, the importance accorded to pastoralism and the Middle West necessarily declined. Recent popular literature suggests that this neglect may have ended. Knowledge that technological advancements have come at a high cost to the integrity of family, community, and environmental relationships has fostered new interest in Middle-western pastoralism. The region is increasingly being seen as one of the few "genuine" places left in the country. Unpleasant facts that are inconsistent with this view, such as the parochialism and materialism proclaimed by Sinclair Lewis in the 1920s, now have receded into the past. The restoration of an imagined golden age may be under way, whereby Walt Disney's version of Main Street will overtake the earlier characterization by Lewis.

2

The Origins and Expansion of the Regional Name

D. W. Meinig has argued that regions are best understood as dynamic processes, part of a "continuous shaping" of human culture. Simply put, he has said, "Places are created by history."[1] This straightforward approach is not easy to implement in the case of the Middle West, for the label is inherently vague and, as such, has been applied in different places and in different ways. Although this vagueness has provided useful flexibility, it frustrates a search for origins. As I have come to discover, the entire region has been relocated two times in the last century. Moreover, the lack of a strict identification has prompted the occasional use of the term far outside the traditional twelve-state context. A survey in 1980 revealed that some Americans think of Utah as the Middle West, and current telephone books for San Francisco and the Odessa-Midland, Texas, area list local businesses that employ the label.[2] All three cases are at least somewhat logical. Utah sits literally in the middle of the western half of the country; San Francisco is near the middle of the West Coast; and Odessa-Midland is in the middle of West Texas. The towns of Midwest, Wyoming, and Midwest City, Oklahoma, have created still other clusterings of the name.

I began a search for the origins of the Middle West with the assumption that the California, Oklahoma, Texas, Utah, and Wyoming versions of the term had histories separate from the principal usage. My concentration was on the popular literature generated in and about the nation's midsection, with initial emphasis on Ohio during the early nineteenth century. This Ohio premise has been implied by virtually all writers since the time of Frederick Jackson Turner. Following him, they saw the West as evanescent: "The wilderness disappears, the 'West' proper passes on to a new frontier, and in the former area, a new society . . . gradually . . . assimilates itself to the type of the older social conditions of the East."[3] Historians have assumed that the West was then divided into "Far" and "Middle" components, with Ohio as a logical birthplace for the latter.[4] As suggested, my search has revealed that a transition from West to Middle West did indeed occur, but not in the place, manner, or time predicted by the Ohio model.

THE WEST AND THE NORTHWEST DURING THE NINETEENTH CENTURY

Readers of travel accounts and other literature of the early nineteenth century from the Ohio Valley find rich descriptions of frontier life and then of the transition to more complex communities.[5] Throughout this period, however, and even into the last decades of that century, the words Middle West were never used to describe the place, either in its early or in its later phases of development. Ohio was referred to alternately as the West or the Northwest, and these regional allegiances persisted throughout the century. The name Northwest derived from the Northwest Ordinance of 1787, which organized and imposed a common set of laws on the region north of the Ohio River. When needed, the term Northwest provided a more precise regional designation than did simply the West, but authors generally used the two terms interchangeably. Cleveland, Ohio, named its first university Western Reserve in 1826; Evanston, Illinois, opted for Northwestern in 1851. Popular magazines from Cincinnati and St. Louis used *Western* in their names.

The commonly accepted cultural definition of the West in this country—an ebullient but somewhat raw and unsophisticated society—fit the Ohio Valley well during the early decades of the nineteenth century. For example, Timothy Flint, a Cincinnati editor, described writers and speakers from that region as possessing typical Western traits: "a vigor, an energy, a recklessness of manner and form, but a racy freshness of matter, which smacks strongly of our peculiar character and position." He also reminded readers of the other side of the image: Westerners as "backwood's ignoramusses" in the eyes of East Coast writers.[6]

Descriptions that paralleled those of Flint continued throughout the 1840s. Then, just after midcentury, a few observers began to comment on a growing gap that they perceived between reality in the Ohio Valley and the stereotypical images brought to mind by its label of being Western. A writer noted in 1853, for example, that his "object embraces the western portion of the United States, if so transitory a name can still be applied to its great central region, watered by the Ohio River and its tributaries." Two problems were involved. Not only had the Ohio Valley matured so that the Western stereotype was no longer appropriate, but the rapid expansion of settlement beyond the Mississippi had created new Wests. Another 1853 article usurped the label Northwest from the former Northwest Territory and applied it without apology to Minnesota, Iowa, Wisconsin, and Nebraska. Such usage became commonplace shortly, leaving the northern Ohio Valley the somewhat musty title of Old Northwest. Other regional names were available, including "central," "interior," and "Great Lakes" states, but none of these became established.[7]

The want of a new regional name for the Old Northwest at this time is somewhat surprising. Perhaps it had to do with the scale of regional generalization that was being employed. Judging from the contemporary popular literature, the primary regional labels at midcentury were three: East, South, and West.[8] The South was seen by Easterners and Westerners alike as a world apart, but kinship and commercial ties led to much comparing and contrasting of East and West. Just as Westerners made little distinction between Boston, New York, and Philadelphia, Easterners easily lumped Ohio with Minnesota and even with Oregon and Texas.[9] Either specific state names or Old Northwest apparently sufficed for the rare times when a more detailed regionalization was required. A new name had to await increased popu lations on the frontier, accompanying boosterism, and, most importantly, heightened perceptions of differences between parts of the West.

A MIDDLE WEST ON THE PLAINS

The earliest usage of the term Middle West that I have uncovered is from 1827, when Timothy Flint observed in passing that religious awakenings had been prevalent "in the middle western states: chiefly in Tennessee."[10] The context suggests that Flint was employing a north-south ordering of space, not an east-west one. In other words, Tennessee was middle western in contrast, not with Missouri or some other far-western place, but with the Northwest (e.g., Ohio and Indiana) and the Southwest (e.g., Alabama and Mississippi). Flint's term never caught on as a regional name, probably because slavery and other issues shortly caused Americans to view Tennessee more as a part of the South than of the West, but his usage anticipated the way in which the Middle West was to emerge in its modern context.

More than seventy years elapsed between the first use of the term Middle West and the second. The location of the region changed, too, shifting more than six hundred miles west from Tennessee to Kansas and Nebraska. A central-plains location seems odd unless the Tennessee situation is remembered. This time it is clear that space was being ordered in a north-south sequence. Kansas, Nebraska, and, to a much lesser extent, Iowa and Missouri were being distinguished from two regions that had become widely recognized by the 1890s: the Northwest—that is, Minnesota and the Dakotas — and the Southwest, or Texas and Indian Territory.[11]

The origins of this plains definition of Middle West are almost certainly older than the two instances from 1898 that I have been able to document; they perhaps date back to the 1880s. Both of the 1898 studies appeared in major journals, and each of the authors used the term in a familiar fashion. Neither of them felt a need to define the location or the meaning of the label precisely, and neither set the phrase within quotation marks or otherwise indicated that it was tentative or recently coined.

In retrospect, the birth of the phrase Middle West seems natural both in time and in space. After the Civil War, settlement was rapid all over the trans-Mississippi region, thus increasing public awareness of differentiation of place. The term West might still apply in some broad contexts, but it had become woefully inadequate to describe such contrasting locales as Colorado mining towns and quiet Hispanic villages or the humid-land farms of Oregon and of Mormon irrigation society.

With settlement, considerable contrasts had become apparent even within the plains region east of the Rockies. Partly this was a product of latitudinal expansion. Whereas during the 1840s and 1850s, West generally had referred only to a relatively narrow band between the Ohio River and the Great Lakes, the plains stretched over twenty-three degrees of latitude. Cultural differences were strong as well. Texas and the Indian Territory were Southern in heritage; the rest of the plains were northern. Furthermore, the pioneer period had just begun in Dakota Territory, whereas it was nearly completed in Kansas and much of Nebraska. The term Middle West in the 1880s thus described a distinctive and specific place: a rapidly maturing, mainstream American, rural society in Kansas and Nebraska.

The initial cluster of cultural traits associated with the new Middle West in the central plains was long and varied, but it was remarkably consistent from writer to writer. People there were self-reliant and independent, kind, open, and thrifty. They were pragmatic, and industrious, and they took pride in their work; yet they were also idealistic, moral, and humble. Other traits, particularly extravagance and exploitiveness, were mentioned regularly, too, but as being no longer characteristic of the region.[12] According to a typical correspondent from Nebraska, even "the Garden of Eden was not more purely pastoral . . . [and the settlers were] worthy specimens of a worthy type,—plain, sensible, honest men, who have never begged any odds in the game of life, and whose strongest wish seems to be to stand square with their fellows."[13]

The traits that were said to be Middle Western read today like an idealization of rural life, but contemporary observers regarded them as fact, not as philosophy. They were the direct products of experiences, especially of a prolonged drought and economic depression that had gripped the central plains for a decade, beginning in the winter of 1887/88 and lasting until 1897. These hard times not only altered the regional economy; they also profoundly influenced the emerging Middle-western temperament. In retrospect, the depression seems to have been the catalyst that forced a coming of age, turning the area culturally from the West into the Middle West. Charles Harger, a respected journalist from Abilene, Kansas, described the impact of the depression:

> The West was many years paying the debt incurred by its overweening ambition and its indiscreet speculations. The period of depression, beginning in 1888, covered eight years. In it were learned lessons of saving, of thrift, of endurance. They were lessons that the West needed to learn. Partly because it was very difficult to borrow, few new debts were incurred. Partly because creditors were pressing, old scores were reduced as much as possible. It was a time of severe business methods, of caustic criticisms from friends in the East, of sackcloth and ashes for those who could not meet the hastily assumed debts.[14]

Harger and other contemporary observers agreed that the hard lessons of the prolonged depression became deeply etched into the Middle-western character. Weak-willed settlers left the region. Those who stayed and weathered the bad years were humbled but at the same time gained confidence in themselves. Unfettered speculation was replaced by a clear-eyed, pragmatic approach to life. Typical of the general commentary were these words of Franklin Matthews, a visiting New York journalist writing in *Harper's Weekly*:

> It was interesting to watch the effect of this [return to] prosperity upon the farmers. So far as I could observe and learn

there was little elation. The carnival at Manhattan was the only case of open rejoicing that I heard of in the State of Kansas. The joy that came to the thousands upon thousands of homes . . . is the kind that expresses itself oftenest in tears. With the money that they made last year the farmers purchased the necessities they had gone without, and the luxuries that their wives and daughters craved, and then they went home ready to face the problems of this and the coming years with renewed courage, longing for more years of plenty, but prepared, with their surplus earnings and their experience in economy and improved methods of farming, to meet fearlessly another drought of one or even more years.[15]

The economic depression helped to foster a sense of regional identity and independence for the Middle West, in part by bringing people together and forcing cooperation to temper frontier individualism. The experience also broke many of the financial ties that bound the region to the East. Much Eastern capital had been invested in Kansas and Nebraska prior to 1887. Some of it had come as loans from family, some as support for the Free State movements prior to the Civil War, but most had been pure business investments. The money encouraged large-scale speculation in land, town sites, railroads, and nearly every other aspect of life that accompanied the settlement of the prairie in the two postwar decades. Some fortunes were made from this speculation, but when hard times in the early 1890s produced defaults on loans, the two regions blamed each other for the troubles. Prairie farmers were irresponsible spendthrifts in Eastern eyes; Easterners were selfish, unfeeling exploiters from the Western perspective. The financial troubles quickly became a regional political issue, spawning debates over free silver, protective tariffs, and populist reforms in general. They even created the first hero for the new Middle West, Nebraska's William Jennings Bryan.[16]

The financial crisis affected familial as well as financial ties, dividing peoples who had already begun to drift apart. Kansans and Nebraskans who had been Eastern born and thus were "full

of Eastern thought, energy, method, and sympathies" were replaced by a generation who had known only the prairies. "To
such people the West is home," wrote a Kansan; "Western ways
and Western ideas are inbred."[17]

EXPANSION FROM
THE KANSAS-NEBRASKA CORE

The identification of a distinct place called the Middle West in
Kansas and Nebraska is not difficult to understand, once the initial rationale for naming is known. The social and political rift
between the East and the central plains during the 1890s was the
immediate factor. In probing the causes for this rift, contemporary observers uncovered a host of traits that distinguished their
region from both the East and the mountain West, traits that had
been previously overlooked in the view of the country as being
tripartite (East, South, West). Much more complex is the second
stage of Middle-western existence, from about 1902 through 1912,
in which the regional label took wing, almost literally, and was
applied with increasing frequency to both the Old Northwest and
the New Northwest in addition to the central-plains hearth. By
1912 this remarkable change was complete, even to the extent
that the cultural core for the region had migrated to Iowa and
northern Illinois, with Chicago serving as an unofficial capital.

One can begin to understand this territorial expansion by noting the euphoric descriptions of Kansas and Nebraska society at
the turn of the century. The concern seemed to transcend the local achievements, by focusing on the general blossoming of rural
culture in the United States. Hardships had been overcome, and
the people were better for having endured some suffering. Now
a stable agricultural democracy had been established, and a great
future awaited. The story is an old one. It has obvious parallels
both with the Old Testament struggle to enter Canaan and with
Rousseau's vision of pastoral bliss. Similar scenes of hardship and
survival had been played out in Ohio and Indiana, but the plains
were special. There the struggle against climate, grasshoppers,

and economic depression was substantial. More significantly, this was the first rural area to develop since the Civil War. As such, it was symbolic, a demonstration that a third great section of the nation was emerging, the great midsection, a region that could perhaps lead the country beyond the old North-South schism created by slavery. Lincoln himself had expressed this larger idea as early as 1862:

> The great interior region, bounded east by the Alleghenies, north by the British dominions, west by the Rocky mountains, and south by the line along which the culture of corn and cotton meets . . . already has above ten millions of people, and will have fifty millions within fifty years, if not prevented by any political folly or mistake. . . . A glance at the map shows that, territorially speaking, it is the great body of the republic. . . . In the production of provisions, grains, grasses, and all which proceed from them this great interior region is naturally one of the most important in the world.[18]

The Middle West of Kansas and Nebraska thus was a demonstration of democratic rural development, one that was certainly not original in the country, but one that occurred against considerable obstacles and at a momentous time. For a brief period it crystallized the whole complex of an emergent agricultural society, with its attendant traits of vigor and morality. Localizing this complex also helped to make it tangible. As I will elaborate on in the next chapter, such a society was so omnipresent in American thought during the early nineteenth century that it lacked definition other than simply being a part of national culture. As the United States became more complex regionally, especially after the Civil War, it seems that the Middle West evolved rapidly from its status as the momentary incarnation of the idealized rural society into a permanent label and symbol for the idealization itself. The problems of its original literal meaning and of its being a regional, rather than a philosophical, label impeded the process but little.

Popular literature reveals that the process of territorial expansion for the Middle West took about a decade. Before about 1902 the label referred exclusively to the Kansas-Nebraska region. Over the next several years, the use of the term increased, but writers applied it to widely varied assemblages of territory. In general, two views predominated. One group of writers retained the old Kansas-Nebraska definition; another group expanded the term to include not only the central plains but also the lands northward to the Dakotas and eastward all the way to Buffalo and Pittsburgh. Confusion lessened after 1912. The restricted definition gradually was abandoned, and the enlarged version triumphed over other phrases such as prairies and the Central West. Middle West became the accepted name for most of the nation's midsection.

The changing definition of the Middle West is mirrored in the prolific writings of Charles Harger, the newspaper editor from Kansas whom I quoted previously. The earliest Harger piece that I have found used the label Middle West in 1898 as though it were an understood, familiar one for the Kansas-Nebraska area. Although he frequently employed the more general term West as a descriptive phrase for his region, Middle West was chosen for this article's title. The next article by Harger that I found, which was written four years later, described the same region, but he did not use Middle West as a label; instead he relied on the words West and prairie. Middle West returned in the title of a Harger piece in 1903, but by then the author lacked confidence in its meaning: the term was placed within quotation marks, and Harger admitted for the first time that the territory it described could be defined only "somewhat vaguely."[19]

Harger's hesitant and qualified use of the term Middle West to describe the limited Kansas-Nebraska region after 1902 was typical of the time. As we have seen, another definition of Middle West, greatly enlarged, had gained currency. The novelist Booth Tarkington was one of the first to employ this new meaning, labeling his home state of Indiana as being in the midst of a Middle West that extended from Omaha to Buffalo. This version of the region was given prominent expression in 1904 by Henry Loomis Nelson, a former editor of *Harper's Weekly*. Nelson clearly distinguished between the Middle West, which he defined as the Old Northwest Territory, and the West, which he defined as the trans-Mississippi region. He neatly excised Kansas and Nebraska, the essence of the original Middle West.[20]

The presence of two interpretations for a single regional phrase apparently was a product of alternative assumptions about the literal meaning of the term. Nelson, for example, made it clear that to him the term was not part of a Northwest–Middle West–Southwest sequence:

> We are accustomed to speak of the Middle West as if there were an eastern West and a western West, and, somewhat subtilely [sic], we are right. The appellation . . . possesses spiritual, intellectual, and material truth. . . . In the old Northwest Territory we find the part for which we are look-ing, the middle West, the edges of which are spattered with influences from the regions back of it and in front of it. It is not as western as it was; it is not eastern, and its people are grateful for both blessings, as they would call them. It is western to the Bostonian and the New Yorker, and it is far-eastern to the man of the plains.[21]

How could two definitions coexist for a single regional phrase? A clue, perhaps, lies in the rather ephemeral nature of Northwest as a name for Minnesota and the Dakotas. As early as the 1880s, Pacific Northwest was being promoted as a regional label by en-trepreneurs in Oregon and Washington.[22] The term Northwest soon came to be associated more with the Pacific region than with Minnesota. This new usage, in turn, altered the Northwest–Middle West–Southwest triad. Later, when the term Southwest was expanded from Texas westward to California, a second re-minder of the Middle West's origins was blunted. In this way the original clear, compact definition of Middle West seems to have been lost. The phrase kept its association with idealized rural traits, but it became vague in location and therefore flexible enough to be applied to new territories.

Place of birth or residence may have determined which definition of the Middle West a person adopted. I found nine writers from the 1902–11 period who outlined in at least a general way what states constituted the Middle West. Four of these nine resided west of the Mississippi River, and all four defined the region in the traditional Kansas-Nebraska manner. Four other writers were from the eastern seaboard. One of them used the traditional definition, but the other three made the Middle West largely equivalent to the Old Northwest Territory. The ninth writer, the novelist Booth Tarkington, from intermediately located Indiana, appropriately combined the two definitions.[23] If this small sample of popular writers provides an accurate guide, the old associations of Middle West with the central plains were not deeply ingrained. Westerners continued to recognize them, but elsewhere at least a few people had already appropriated the term to stand as a general mediator between East and West.

The transition from one regional definition for Middle West to another was not smooth. In fact, usage during the 1902–11 period suggests that the phrase might easily have disappeared entirely as a regional label. Although most Americans knew the term, it was used far less frequently than other labels either for the Kansas-Nebraska territory or for the enlarged area of the Old Northwest and the upper Mississippi Valley. The term Middle West was more popular than Interior, Prairie States, and Plains, but West remained the most widely accepted term for the entire trans-Appalachian area. The relative strength of these regional phrases is indicated by their frequency in the titles of articles in popular journals about the area between the Alleghenies and the Rockies. The word West appeared twenty-four times between 1902 and 1912 in titles listed in *Readers' Guide to Periodical Literature*, Middle West three times, Prairie(s) twice, and Corn Belt and Plains once each.

Middle West came into its own as a major regional term about 1912. Without any recorded debate, the American public merged the two Middle Wests of the previous decade into one. To be sure, one could still find disagreements as to the exact boundaries of the region, and an occasional Western writer still employed the limited Kansas-Nebraska definition, but in general, twelve states came to be recognized as Middle Western. Kansas and Nebraska were included, along with the five states of the Old Northwest (Illinois, Indiana, Michigan, Ohio, Wisconsin) and Minnesota and the Dakotas from the New Northwest. Iowa and Missouri completed the set.[24]

The term also gained general acceptance at this time. Among the titles of popular articles on the nation's interior that were listed in *Readers' Guide*, Middle West appeared twenty times between 1912 and 1920, whereas West was employed only six times, a dramatic reversal from the previous decade. Prairies, the only other regional term to be mentioned, appeared just once. Other indicators of general acceptance for the name Middle West include the introduction of a shortened version, Midwest, in 1918, and a concurrent decline in placing the name within quotation marks.[25]

The wholesale adoption of Middle West to describe the two Northwests after 1912 is intriguing. Certainly the clumsiness of having two Northwests in the interior and a third on the Pacific Coast was a factor in the transformation, as was the convenient vagueness of the new label. Northwesterners from Ohio to North Dakota, the people who would have been most aware of the crisis involved in names, apparently found in the emerging social and economic definition of Middle West an appropriate solution to their dilemma. The leaders in publicizing the enlarged definition of the Middle West were nearly all from these mislabeled states. An early landmark was a series of four articles that appeared in *Century Magazine* in 1912, entitled simply "The Middle West," by Edward A. Ross, an Iowa-born sociologist who taught at the University of Wisconsin. His series, which focused on the nature of Middle-western society, was frequently praised by other writers and seems to have formed a turning point in the solidification of the regional name, its location, and its regional image. These definitions and traits were restated six years later in a comprehensive, appealing manner by an Indiana writer, Meredith Nicholson. His six-part series in *Scribner's Magazine* firmly fixed in the American mind the basic ideas that the upper Mississippi Valley was the Middle West and that Chicago was its core city. Sherwood Anderson called Winesburg, Ohio, Middle Western in 1919, and Sinclair Lewis did the same to Gopher Prairie, Minnesota, in 1920. Even Charles Harger, the Kansas journalist who had championed the old, narrow, plains definition, finally yielded to the new perception.[26]

From the early nineteenth century onward, few people ever questioned the vast potential of the land that was to become known as the Middle West. For the region to emerge as distinct from the West, however, this potential had to be realized. People there had to convince themselves and others that they formed, to use Lincoln's terminology, "the great body of the republic," not only "territorially speaking," but in economic and cultural terms as well.[27] This process was well under way by about 1910, and concurrently, a regional name had evolved. The Middle West went from being a purely locational description for the central plains to a general label for all parts of the interior that were characterized by a prosperous rural economy. It was, simply, a suitable phrase with appropriate cultural associations that happened to be current at the time when a general descriptor was needed.

3

America's Heartland

The ascendancy of the term Middle West as the label for a vast section of the American interior after about 1912 corresponds to an expansion of the perceived importance of that region to American society. The literature from that time exudes an incredible sense of optimism and destiny about the region. A mature agricultural economy was the cultural and economic mainstay, but railroads, steel mills, meat packers, and other industries thrived also, while new universities, libraries, art museums, and political reforms provided a feeling of intellectual accomplishment. By about 1915, development and self-confidence had reached such a stage that the Middle West had become the standard by which to judge the rest of the nation. It was, in the words of one commentator, "more evenly American in tone than any like population in the East."[1]

Contemporary assertions of agricultural might and industrial development for the region had solid bases in fact, but the principal explanations for Middle-western ascendancy in the early twentieth century were cultural. They revolved round comparisons between the East, the Middle West, and the West, comparisons that produced long lists of complimentary traits for the Middle West. Two broad themes encompass the major arguments: one involves pastoralism—the yeoman-farmer ideal; the other is an association of the West, the Middle West, and the East, respectively, with youth, maturity, and old age.

THE PASTORAL THEME

The pastoral ideal—a haven midway between the corruptions of urban civilization and the dangerous, untamed wilderness—has been a symbol, a dream, and even a definition for America since the age of discovery. By the early nineteenth century, however, it had become obvious that pastoralism could not be applied to the country uniformly. Instead of a land of egalitarian rural prosperity, the East was characterized by abandoned farms and growing industry; in the South, a distorted agrarianism based on an ordered feudal society was dominant. After 1850, writers began to equate the image of the yeoman-farmer with the West in general, but this association, too, proved only temporary. Although the vision of democratic rural communities was a powerful force in a host of ill-advised settlement schemes on the dry High Plains, the Great Basin, and elsewhere, climatic limitations gradually forced American society to acknowledge that most of the Far West must remain as near wilderness.[2]

The realization that the West could no longer serve as a metaphor for pastoralism took place about 1900. This date, of course, corresponds to the emergence of Middle West as a regional name. The two concepts — pastoralism and the Middle West — which initially were similar in several respects, rapidly intertwined and soon became virtually synonymous. Together, they possessed immense power. In his pioneering work on regional symbols, for example, Henry Nash Smith concluded that the public saw in this growing agricultural society "a poetic idea that defined the promise of American life." The Middle West was the "Garden of the World," he said, a place that "embraced a cluster of metaphors expressing fecundity, growth, increase, and blissful labor in the earth, all centering about the heroic figure of the idealized frontier farmer armed with that supreme agrarian weapon, the sacred plow."[3]

The power of this pastoral imagery can be measured by how rapidly it came to dominate definitions of the Middle West after 1900. So natural was the tendency to see the region as the "middle" ground both figuratively and literally between the urbanized East and the western wilderness that the original regional meaning employed in Kansas and Nebraska was first ignored and then forgotten. A pastoral interpretation of Middle-western culture quickly became universal. For the first fifteen years of this century, in fact, neither outside commentators nor local writers expressed any doubt that reality might differ from the imagery. One result was a remarkably consistent set of cultural values.

The most nearly complete statements of early Middle-western pastoralism can be found in articles by Charles Harger, Edward Ross, and Meredith Nicholson, but the basic sentiments appear in hundreds of contemporary sources. The words vary little from what Hector Crèvecoeur or Thomas Jefferson had written more than a century before in describing the eastern seaboard. Most writers began with a statement on the richness of the land and the resultant prosperity of the farmers. Geographer Albert P. Brigham, for example, was an overwhelmed visitor:

> The writer thought he knew somewhat about the prairies and had even ventured a small way into print, but it was mainly from car window and book. But when there are five, or ten, or twelve feet of black earth under the foot and when the eye rests on yellow fields of corn all the way to the horizon, the prairie gathers solidity in the consciousness. One sees why the "poor white trash" is so rare as to be the exception, proving the proud dictum of the prairie dweller,— of such "we have none."[4]

Prosperity was attributed not only to the richness of the land but also to the industry of the people. Bountiful rural life fostered independence and self-reliance, and these traits in turn produced other characteristics of yeomen: an egalitarian society (usually contrasted with a class-bound Eastern hierarchy), a natural aristocracy in which any man might rise to important leadership roles (following the model of Lincoln), and social progress on a wide variety of fronts. With no one beholden to any other person, true democracy could flourish.

The foundation for all of these glories was farmers, a group that demonstrated for a visiting Harvard professor of economics a "manifest superiority . . . physically, intellectually, and morally" over the average town dweller. The moral quality, especially, was stressed. Although some commentators thought that the slavery issue had given the Middle West its moral conscience, most considered morality to be an integral part of the corpus of yeoman traits. Farming one's own rich land produced strength of character and a strong moral commitment to education, to women's rights, and to temperance. In the realm of politics, this commitment produced the initiative, the recall, and a spirit of nonpartisanship. It was the product of people's thinking of the general good, of independent folk's throwing off the power of vested-interest groups.[5]

The moral tone of Middle-western life acted as a deterrent to ostentation and arrogance, according to observers. Success was measured by competency in one's business and family life, not in terms of money or family name. Many writers perceived that this idea of success had disappeared in the East in the face of industrialization; again, they saw the rural Middle West as the epitome of virtue. The idea is expressed through a series of adjectives that were used routinely to describe Middle-western people: open, kind, humble, honest, genuine, wholesome, sincere, and hospitable. The New York journalist Stephen Dale, for example, observed:

> There is a notable absence of pretense, a willingness to be thought poor if they are poor and an equal willingness to be known as rich when rich. . . . There is a marked absence . . . of that temper and spirit of "smartness" and flippancy so noticeable in the East. . . . Every man who approaches a stranger is taken to be honest until he proves himself to be otherwise.[6]

THE THEME OF MATURITY

In part, the pastoral interpretation of the Middle West appealed to observers because it provided a clear means of separating this section from the industrializing and increasingly ethnically diverse East. Regional differentiation was even clearer with the second major Middle-western theme, a comparison of regions of the country with the human life cycle. The terminology was straightforward—youth, maturity, old age; it suggested vivid cultural images that the writers deemed appropriate. Its usage rivaled pastoralism in importance; in fact, the two themes often intermingled.

The country long had recognized a distinction between the mature East and the youthful West. The central plains clearly belonged to the latter category throughout the 1880s, and the Kansas newspaperman and novelist Edgar W. Howe still employed the analogy of youth as late as 1892.[7] He was about the last writer to do so, however, for as we have seen, after the depression of the 1890s, observers sensed that the area had changed. Although the region retained certain youthful or Western traits, particularly "resourcefulness, independence, optimism, and public spirit," other such traits had vanished.[8] Thriftlessness had disappeared, for example, along with recklessness, selfishness, and radicalism. The boomer philosophy "that the opportunities of the land that bore him were permanent and inexhaustible" was replaced by a more respectful attitude toward resources.[9] Negative aspects of youthfulness were virtually never associated with the label Middle West. In fact, the emergence of the region as a popular concept seems to have depended on the acceptance of the theme of maturity.

The life-cycle argument also had great appeal to Middle Westerners and others who were frustrated with the arrogance and patronizing air they perceived in the East.[10] In this interpretation, the Middle West was the land of the here and now, with growing importance in industry and agriculture; the East was in decline. It was much the same way that the American colonists had once viewed the Old World. New England no longer possessed "the primal American spirit," according to the Middlewestern sociologist Edward Ross. He noted changing agricultural and manufacturing situations and then went beyond:

> In the rougher parts of New England to-day one finds old towns that touched their zenith eighty years ago. The elite of the young people have regularly migrated. . . . Aside from the aliens that here and there have seeped in, the inhabitants are of the blood of those *who always stayed behind*. In such districts the children are, in general, so listless

that they have to be incited to play. . . . Neverworks loaf all day about the grocery, the feed store, or the livery-stable. In villages still bearing traces of the famed New England neatness, loose clapboards, unpruned trees, cluttered-up door-yards, broken windows, unpainted houses, leaning fences, and crazy buggies testify to the sagging of the community below its former plane.[11]

Like many others, Ross extended the migration argument with nativist statements. He emphasized the great numbers of South and East European immigrants that had come to Eastern cities, "a population so alien, so ignorant, and so helpless, that it takes refuge in the first industrial harbors or bays it finds." Middle-western people, in contrast, were "more evenly American in tone."[12] The glaring inconsistency whereby emigration produced the brightest of people in one instance and the most "helpless" in another was never noticed.

The distinction between maturity and old age encompassed many cultural traits. Most writers spoke about the Middle West as an egalitarian society. Although some interpreted this in yeoman terms, others implied that an explanation existed in the life cycle. One writer, for example, exhorted the Middle West to enjoy its open friendliness while it lasted, saying that "not until the town has grown rich and arrogant do the clique and the class appear."[13] Self-satisfaction, dilettantism, corruption, and the loss of idealism were other factors linked to old age and therefore to the East. Opposing traits, such as progressivism, pragmatism, and idealism, were the glory of the younger Middle West.[14]

The most popular conception of the Middle West that used the life-cycle analogy was the characterization of the region as being simultaneously youthful and mature. Proponents of this view stated that agriculture had reached maturity. Tried-and-true varieties of crops and livestock and farming methods ensured a steady prosperity. Other aspects of the culture were still youthful, however; they kept alive the progressive, confident spirit. Literature was in this category, along with higher education, music, and other fine arts. Manufacturing, however, was the most commonly cited example of youthfulness.[15] Chicago was the focus: a "lusty, young giant among the world's cities."[16] Its personification as a youth gave power not only to Carl Sandburg's famous 1916 poem but also to the region as a whole. It was a place, he concluded:

> Laughing the stormy, husky, brawling laughter of Youth, half-naked, sweating, proud to be Hog Butcher, Tool Maker, Stacker of Wheat, Player with Railroads and Freight Handler to the Nation.[17]

THE MIDDLE WEST AS AMERICA

As the themes of pastoralism and maturity became closely identified with the Middle West during the early years of the twentieth century, they gradually engendered a third major theme to characterize the region. The Middle West came to symbolize the nation and to be seen as the most American part of America. Up until the early 1900s, writers had used the East as the standard by which to judge American society; but attitudes began to change about 1904. By about 1912, corresponding with the incorporation of the Old and the New Northwests into the Middle West, writers generally acknowledged that the East and the Middle West had switched cultural roles.

Some examples illustrate the change from peripheral to mainstream status. At the turn of the century, observers both from within the region and from without began to stress the growing sophistication of the Middle West. Their strident tone, however, made it clear that the general American populace had not yet accepted this view. Pastoral imagery dominated, and a minority of Eastern commentators still pictured the typical Middle Westerner in frontier stereotypes. In 1903, for example, one writer described the typical farmer as "a lean, gawky, bewhiskered creature, ignorant of all topics that lie outside the sphere of farms and crops."[18] Another article opened with the claim that "much unneeded sympathy is expended by persons of tender feelings upon the woman of the prairies." She is not "a martyr, undergoing severe trials," the author pleaded; rather, she leads a "healthful, happy, prosperous life."[19] The novelist Booth Tarkington summarized the mood by reporting on a conversation he had heard on Long Island: "I have decided that my sons must go to Harvard . . . because at Princeton or Yale . . . they might be thrown in with Westerners."[20]

Continued prosperity throughout the first decade of the twentieth century led to the rapid decline of such lingering elements of frontier imagery. Regional self-confidence among Middle Westerners was high, the economy was becoming increasingly diversified, and outside commentators soon began to note that the region "stands sturdily with a smile on its face, confident that it ranks as an equal in the development and growth of a great nation."[21] Shortly thereafter the Middle West was seen as being more than "an equal" of the East. According to a *Scribner's* article published in 1908, it possessed "more pride of individual opinion and less reliance on tradition and corporate habits [than the East]. So [now] the East is more fairly judged by the West than the West is by the East . . . [and] the national spirit is more strongly developed in the West than in any other part of the country."[22] Descriptions of "fished-out communities" in the East and the rising proportion there of immigrants from southern and eastern Europe completed the regional transference of the American core of self images.[23] An editorial in the *Independent* put it thus: "One finds . . . in the Middle West today a larger proportion of men and women whose ideas, habits, and institutions are essentially those of Colonial America, and of England, than can be found now in the East."[24]

THE CULTURAL IMAGE CHALLENGED
AND REAFFIRMED

Charles Harger, that most prolific of commentators on the early Middle West, summed up the prevailing view of the nation's interior during the 1900–20 period when he exclaimed: "Was there ever on earth such a kingdom of plenty as is presented by the

Middle West of America? . . . Its youth is past; its old age has not begun. It is in the sturdy, healthy, full-blooded heyday of its strength."[25] Pastoralism, maturity, and the national core—the driving forces of this image—were all immensely flattering concepts, and writers easily melded the associated cultural traits. Even the names of region and themes coalesced. Was it not somehow destined that the "Middle" West should come to life already in "middle" age and be permanently characterized by a "middle" (i.e., pastoral) landscape?

Harger's contemporaries repeated the image countless times. Additional factors that might underlie the region's progressivism and strength of character were sometimes suggested, most notably the intermingling of the best traits of Yankee, Southerner, and North European immigrant.[26] No one, however, challenged either the image itself or its presumed explanation. Existing ills and abuses in the society—such as business speculation, the rising number of farm tenants, and prejudice against emigrants from southern and eastern Europe—were steadfastly ignored by writers on the regional character.

The systematic avoidance of an obvious inconsistency between the pastoral and the life-cycle themes was perhaps most telling of the strength of the "middle" image. If large cities and manufacturing greatness were imminent for the region and indeed were necessary components of a mature society, what would happen to pastoral bliss? Writers used cities and other nonfarming activities only sparingly in their arguments: "But what of mining, logging, and manufacturing, all told? Islets of exception in an ocean of rule. Corn is king. The hog, a corn-field on legs, made Chicago. Scratch a Middle-Westerner, and you find a farmer. Either he lives on a farm or in a farming village or in a city that was a farming village only yesterday."[27] Interpreters of the Middle West thus confronted the classic problem of the pastoral dream and reacted to it in a familiar manner—denial. When the "machine" threatens the "garden," ignore the machine. Whistling in the dark, Middle-western writers even claimed that isolation would keep the region in its harmonious middle state.[28]

The flattering image of the Middle West as a mature rural

paradise filled with wholesome, progressive people was virtually unchallenged between 1898 and 1915, regardless of what geographical boundaries were used to delimit the region. The few writers who hinted at criticism spent the bulk of their words on praise. In retrospect, however, one can see the beginnings of change even as the dominant image was becoming firmly established. A visiting New York journalist in 1904, for example, differentiated between the prairies east and west of Chicago. He lavished the familiar praise on the western section but reported that to the east, the land was "level, flat and dismal, and its people are as correspondingly commonplace."[29] Were Indiana and Ohio communities becoming "fished-out," like some New England towns?[30] Another writer reported increased conservatism and lessened intensity in Middle-western politics as early as 1903 and 1907, respectively, as business affairs came to dominate community interests.[31] The word progressive as a cultural descriptor in the popular literature declined in frequency after reaching a peak in about 1906. Finally, one writer suggested that Middle Westerners, who put the emphasis on agriculture, home economics, and business management at their developing state universities, might have become a bit too "practical minded."[32]

Deviation from the pastoral-maturity norm had become a significant minority view by 1915. The war in Europe served as catalyst for discussion, particularly the issue of whether the United States should enter the conflict. This debate assumed a sectional guise: Easterners were more inclined to fight, Middle Westerners to demur. German raids on neutral vessels off the Atlantic seaboard in 1916, for example, received widely differing levels of attention in the newspapers of the two regions.[33] Observers granted that the insular position of the Middle West could explain much of the difference, but increasingly the Eastern press came to doubt the idealism of the Middle West. Agricultural profits had soared with high wartime prices, and critics thought they saw smug satisfaction "in the faces of Middle-western entrepreneurs, a people as remote mentally from the European conflict in all its phases . . . as the tropics are from the North Pole."[34] The Middle West's German population was accused of mixed

loyalties, and its people as a whole were accused of selfishness
in the abdication of their role as the center of American national-
ism. A New York correspondent saw things thus in 1916:

> One thing is clear to me from the investigation of this center
> of old-time American democracy. The movement toward Na-
> tional discipline and preparation . . . is not this time com-
> ing from the grass roots. . . . The laboring class in the
> Middle West [has] never received such high wages and was
> never so prosperous. It is reflecting not so much upon the
> country as upon creature comfort.[35]

It should be emphasized that criticism of the region in the 1915–
17 period was far outweighed by the familiar praise. Defenders
of Middle-western honor pointed out that the United States traditionally had been isolationist. There was nothing immoral about
making money or about staying out of conflict on another continent. "Call the Middle-West smug, materialistic, local-minded,
it retorts that the East is romantic when it is not designing."[36]

Still, any criticism, where before there had been none, is significant. Catcalls continued until the United States entered the war in
April, 1917. With this action came vindication for Middle-western
virtue. Editorials bearing titles such as "The Maligned Middle
West" and "Patriotism, East and West" trumpeted high rates of enlistment and large amounts of money given to the war effort. Indiana and Illinois, for example, had produced two-thirds and
one-half, respectively, of their enlistment quotas by May, whereas
the highest rate among Eastern states was Pennsylvania's one-third.
Kansas' William Allen White observed that "we who are really doing our part in furnishing soldiers and sailors might well consider
the puzzle of the East and the flabbiness of New England."[37]

THE MIDDLE WEST IN 1920

The criticism and reassessment of the traditional Middle-western
character were suspended during the war years and immediately

thereafter. The pastoral-maturity dyad seemed once more to be entrenched. Doubts had been raised, however, and as wartime nationalistic fervor declined, these doubts began to surface again, slowly at first and then with increasing frequency. Was the region becoming fat, lazy, and materialistic? Was progressive liberalism being replaced by stolid conservatism? Old age might not be far in the future.

As the 1920s began, popular literature reflected such doubts only indirectly. Everyone seemed to sense that if the traditional Middle-western character was in danger, so was the United States as a whole. As I will explain in the next chapter, a few humanists, including Sherwood Anderson, Willa Cather, and Sinclair Lewis, voiced concern; but most commentators fell back on cliches. Declining political activism was explained away, with the rationalization that previous ardor had already accomplished the needed reforms. Activism had given way to a middle position, neither liberal nor conservative, which was widely portrayed as the best of all possible worlds. Similar apologies were issued for materialistic tendencies. Yes, the people now possessed some luxuries; but no, they had not sacrificed their pastoral virtues in order to obtain them.

The year 1920 marks a clear apogee for the Middle West. The region reached its maximum territorial extent and its greatest credibility at about this time. The year also represents the capstone for the set of images dominated by the concepts of pastoralism, maturity, and the embodiment of the national spirit. Criticism existed, but it had not yet seriously eroded the feeling of self-confidence within the region.

4
Rural Imagery in an Urbanizing Nation

The reign of the Middle West as the self-confident symbol of the United States was remarkably short-lived. Flaws in the heroic framework, initially exposed in the years just prior to World War I, were expressed at an increasing rate throughout the 1920s. Criticism abated during the depression of the 1930s and the early war years of the 1940s, but soon it resumed in more intense and varied forms. The nadir came about 1950. Many positive things still could be and were said, but the previous strong sense of local pride was gone. At best it was a region with mixed feelings about itself; at worst the nation's heartland had become a backwater.

It is not always easy to document a shift in cultural values, but for the Middle West, the initiation of a change from ebullient self-assurance to doubt and defensiveness can be dated rather precisely at 1920. Two events mark the time: an agricultural recession and a book called *Main Street*.[1] That such things could initiate a major negative change in regional image and alter basic national myths as well seems unlikely at first appearance, for similar events at an earlier time certainly had no such impact. In fact, an agricultural crisis in the 1890s actually had helped to create feelings of self-confidence and even the original cultural identity for the Middle West. As far as novels were concerned, previous attempts at realism in regional literature, notably *Main-Travelled Roads* and other works by Hamlin Garland beginning in the 1890s, had little perceivable effect on the region's image, at least as it was reflected in the popular press.

The shift in image after 1920 seems even more improbable given the overwhelmingly positive attributes of the previous Middle West stereotype and its centrality to American identity as a whole. Consider, once again, the accepted wisdom of 1919. The Middle West was the most vital, the most vigorous, section of the country. Its small towns produced national leaders and moral guidance; its cities, wealth for all. Everyone repeated and apparently believed the old saws about the East's being alien-infested and economically by-passed and about the West's being still a frontier. National trends would hereafter be dictated from the heartland: "The civilization that the Middle West creates within the next fifty years will be the American civilization."[2]

Can the collapse of an elaborate belief system really be explained by a novel and an otherwise rather minor agricultural recession? It can be in a sense. The two events were catalysts, triggering mechanisms, for a powerful, growing, but heretofore amorphous national mood. Attitudes toward pastoralism and the idea of technological-industrial progress, perhaps the two cornerstones of American identity, were changing.

Some background on these two ideas is necessary. Pastoralism and new technology have never coexisted easily in the United States or elsewhere; industrial progress necessarily involves change, and change often threatens the natural harmonies of rural life. This conflict was theoretical, however, as long as America was largely rural and industry relatively unsophisticated. The nation could believe in both ideals and even could conceive that they might operate simultaneously in a particular place.[3] In fact, the Middle West of the 1910s represented the apex for this cultural fusion.

The alliance between pastoral and industrial ideals in the Middle West was doomed by an increasing national concern for technological progress. Enthusiasm for such growth expanded throughout the nineteenth century, and World War I heightened the passion further. New urban industry and its accompanying life style looked increasingly alluring, and by contrast, village and farm life looked increasingly dull. Sinclair Lewis's *Main Street* and the agricultural depression of the early 1920s provided vehicles for finally breaking through pastoral rhetoric, creating a more open dialogue on rural life, and ultimately altering a regional image.

The Middle West, as a focus for both an ascendant and a descendant cultural value in 1920, presented a dilemma for Americans. Could it concurrently be a land of "traditional" agriculture and one of "modern" industry? The question was never debated openly, of course, but popular literature clearly reveals that the answer was no. People seem to have avoided conflict between the two visions by subconsciously modifying regional definitions. I will argue here that pastoralism and industry were segregated mentally: the former was assigned to a regional "box" called Middle West; the latter, to one called East.

The segregation process gradually unfolded during the 1920s. Discussions employing the term Middle West came to focus almost exclusively on rural issues. The realm of technological achievement was either delegated to the East or, in such cases as the Detroit automobile industry, was analyzed without reference to the label Middle West. The results were a progressive loss of esteem and an increasing frustration for heartland people. Rural residents attempted to perfect the dream of a pastoral society, but they received mixed reviews for their efforts. Urban Middle Westerners had steel and other industry worthy of status in the new value system, but they found that Easterners and others still judged them to be provincial farmers.

The degeneration and simplification of the regional image occurred in two stages. The first, during the 1920s, was characterized by mixed judgments from outsiders and by an air of smug self-righteousness within the region. People in the Middle West still had faith in the pastoral-technological fusion and were working to perfect the traditional pastoral vision of a moral society. The goal was noble in a way, but it was out of touch with prevailing national interests in materialism and sophistication. The economic depression after 1929 temporarily aided the moralists by removing the glamour from Eastern urban life and even fostering a "back-to-the-land" movement. However, hard times also eroded cherished rural ideas, particularly claims for self-sufficiency and natural nobility. "Okies," farmers who had failed, competed with the yeoman interpretation of life.

When the time of national crisis ended after 1945 and Americans again had the leisure for self-assessment, it became clear that pastoral values had reached a new low point; the Middle-western image was vastly different from what it had been in 1920. The United States had just demonstrated world leadership in technology. Applications of this power to new and largely urban concerns, not a return to isolated country living, were paramount for the people. The hope that small towns could participate in the industrialization process was dashed by part of the process itself. New automobiles and better roads drew people to the cities, slowly strangling the economy of thousands of smaller towns.

MAIN STREET AND A LOSS OF CONFIDENCE

Accusations that the Middle West had lost its idealism, that it was becoming smug and self-satisfied, were voiced occasionally during the early 1910s, as we sampled in the previous chapter. World War I brought concerns that temporarily glossed over this issue, but in 1920, Sinclair Lewis published *Main Street* and thereby put the debate in a form that no one could ignore. According to one authority, readers accepted Lewis's fiction as a sociological survey.[4] The book immediately became a best seller and had profound impact on the Middle-western psyche. Lewis exposed cultural flaws that the public knew were there but had not wanted to admit. He struck at the heart of traditional values, brought these issues into the open, and thereby set the agenda for a decade of discussion. In popular literature the phrases Main Street and Gopher Prairie (Lewis's fictional Minnesota town) quickly became synonyms for Middle-western America, and writers on the region felt an obligation to address the indictments made in the book. The best way to understand the charges and counter-charges found in the literature is to begin with the critique of traditional Middle-western values provided in *Main Street* itself.

Modern readers of *Main Street* often expect an unrelenting attack on all things Middle Western, but Lewis was a selective critic. He praised the natural landscape, seeing in it "dignity and greatness" and the potential for expanding the human spirit.[5]

Farmers, especially first-generation farmers, also were virtuous. Lewis's claim that progressive politics and other ideas "requiring knowledge, courage, and imagination" were inspired by farmers echoed traditional pastoral rhetoric.[6]

Middle-western literature before *Main Street* seldom differentiated between farm life and village life. Villages invariably had been portrayed as happy places with "hollyhocks and lanes and apple-cheeked cottagers."[7] A few writers had poked fun at old-fashioned speech patterns and similar rustic accoutrements, but this had been the extent of criticism. *Main Street* challenged this view strongly, asserting that a major difference existed between farm and town and taking aim squarely at the values of the town aristocracy. Its method was to contrast the views of Gopher Prairie's own residents with those of an educated, idealistic, but initially naïve outsider. The insider look comes principally from Will Kennicott, the town's doctor; the outsider is his wife, Carol.

Residents of Gopher Prairie saw their town in positive terms that derived from traditional pastoral and stage-of-life arguments. The society was open and honest; everyone had an important role to play. The people called themselves pragmatic. They did the "real" work of building new schools and cement walks, enjoyed the prosperity of the period, and boosted local businesses toward an even more prosperous future. The business orientation was defended as being appropriate for a growing country, but people admitted that it was time to get more involved with poetry, plays, and other "artistic" things.[8]

Young Carol, upon entering Gopher Prairie for the first time, found that her perceptions generally matched those of her husband and other townspeople. The biggest discrepancy was in the physical appearance of the place. Will focused on the improvements; Carol, on the "unsparing unapologetic ugliness" of town architecture.[9] Carol soon converted her disappointment into a challenge. Given the professed interest of residents in cultural improvement, she attempted to lead Gopher Prairie into greatness by introducing ideas about classical design, literature, and other arts. In the process, the views of resident and outsider would be meshed, and both ultimately would conform to the established

view of the Middle West as a blend of pastoral bliss, technological might, and increasingly sophisticated culture. The region
would come into adulthood as planned.

Had Lewis concluded his story at this point, it would have
angered no one. Like the works of Wisconsin's Zona Gale or Indiana's Gene Stratton Porter, it would have been a popular but
soon forgotten tale about village life. Lewis chose to probe deeper
into town culture, however, and found, through Carol, values
that were throttling the development of this new utopian civilization that had been promised by Middle-western ideology. One
was a debilitating conformity within the town, an ostracizing of
independent thought. The mature Carol called it "a rigid ruling
of the spirit by the desire to appear respectable."[10] Negative repercussions from this trait were made worse by a second characteristic, a sense of moral superiority whereby the people saw their
town as nearly without fault, "the climax of civilization."[11] Finally, and again interrelated, was a lack of enterprise toward
anything that was not directly related to money. In sum, Gopher
Prairie was "merely safe," a place in which people lacked noble
goals and even the capacity to play.[12]

Much of *Main Street* is devoted to an elaboration of these
three tendencies, particularly various rules for conformity and
their consequences. An extreme bias toward business and material progress is stressed, for example, as symbolized by the adula-
tion that the townspeople accorded to Percy Bresnahan, an Eastern industrialist with local roots, and James Blausser, a business
consultant. Carol slowly has come to realize that she is uneasy
with the booster mentality not because of an antipathy toward
material success as such but because Gopher Prairie valued this
success above all else.[13]

Ideas that were not directly related to boosterism were discouraged. No one read, no one thought, and discussions were
about personalities, never abstractions.[14] Making a god of materialism meant that schools were evaluated for efficiency rather
than for quality. Anything hinting of socialism was rejected out
of hand because it conflicted with established business philosophy; envy of the material success in Eastern cities became ram-

pant. In this way, Gopher Prairie's businessmen denied their own heritage in many ways, including turning their backs on the local farming community. Swedes, because they were recent immigrants, were judged to be second-class citizens; and cooperative ventures such as the Non-Partisan League were opposed as presenting threats to local mortgage holders.[15]

Lewis ultimately pictured Gopher Prairie, and thus the Middle West, as a tragedy. The potential for a great civilization existed in the fertile land, and a vision of this greatness had been glimpsed by the first generation of settlers. The second generation had lost sight of the dream. Corrupted by an obsession with the material side of success, they broke the pastoral tie. Will Kennicott and other leaders were still speaking about agrarian virtues such as honesty and a broad-minded, unstratified society, but their behavior denied the claim. Lewis described the collective attitude as an intolerance embedded "under a hundred guises and pompous names, such as Polite Society, the Family, the Church, Sound Business, the Party, the Country, [and] the Superior White Race."[16] The society embraced inwardly corrupt but outwardly conforming individuals such as Cy Bogart and rejected those of the opposite mix: the artistic Eric Valborg, the idealistic Fern Mullins, and the intellectual/agnostic Miles Bjornstam.

In attempting to merge the pastoral and the technological, Middle-western society had sacrificed its ideals. Lewis likened the situation to a disease, the "village virus," and saw older Ohio as being more infected than Minnesota.[17] Future greatness was possible, but action toward its achievement would be inhibited by the misguided faith that "the future is already here in the present."[18] Was there a cure? Lewis's later writings provided a mixed answer. On the one hand, a new Middle-western blending of Will's practicality and science with Carol's idealism was possible. Babbitt, in his next novel, was the antithesis of such a person, but Arrowsmith and, especially, Dodsworth each possessed the needed mix. The problem was how to transform the general society. Both Arrowsmith and Dodsworth were loners. Like Lewis, they were frustrated, unsure of how to change others and thus how to achieve a more ideal civilization.[19]

AGRICULTURAL DEPRESSION AND A
LOSS OF CONFIDENCE

Main Street's revelations shook the twin pillars of Middle-western cultural identity. Was pastoral idealism dead? Was the young region only a pale imitation of the East in things urban, cultural, and technological? As these issues began to be debated in the popular literature, agricultural depression descended upon the nation's midsection. This depression, I think, affected the outcome of the Main Street debates and hastened the change in the region's image.

The years during World War I were highly profitable ones for Middle-western farmers. European markets were good, and vast areas of the Great Plains were opened to the plow. This boom collapsed in August, 1920, as overproduction from the new lands coincided with the inability of a devastated Europe to buy. Major losses continued in 1921 and 1922, and it was not until 1925 that the agricultural economy began to make a slow recovery.

In the popular literature, reaction to the depression began in 1921 and peaked in 1923 and 1924. Some things were predictable: the disenchantment of voters with President Warren G. Harding and the Republican establishment in general, as well as the rise of agrarian protest movements of various sorts (see cartoons). Robert M. La Follette of Wisconsin emerged as a spokesman for regional discontent with his Progressive party. Other sympathetic third-party movements gained power in Minnesota (Farmer-Labor) and the Dakotas (Non-Partisan). Some commentators, trying to gauge the extent of the unrest, thought that a good year for agriculture would return things to harmony.[20] Others saw the protests as dangerously radical and as being caused by forces deeper than the depression alone.[21]

In retrospect, one can see that neither contemporary view of this unrest was entirely correct. The Middle West did not remain in financial crisis for long, but neither did it return to normal. The cultural repercussions of the unrest are best understood by noting its intense regional nature. An agricultural depression was

THE EMBATTLED FARMER
—Fitzpatrick in the New York *World*.

THE GOBLIN
—Talburt in the Cincinnati *Post*.

NO REST FOR BOLIVAR

"No Rest for Bolivar," from "The Wheat-Belt Rebellion," *Literary Digest* 78 (Aug. 4, 1923): 18.

a major issue in the Middle West (especially the plains states), where farming dominated the economy, but it was only a modest concern for the industrial East.[22] When appeals for understanding and relief were made, Middle Westerners found out things that were unsettling to their collective psyche.

The depression was a clear demonstration that commercial farmers in the modern world were losing control over their own destiny. To the eternal climatic vagaries were now added the flux of international markets. If one took the view that governmental policy could not stabilize such flux, a sense of hopelessness invaded the yeoman's self-confidence. Alternately, if one held the majority view that governmental policy could be influential, the Middle West was still forfeiting an important measure of its independence to Eastern power brokers. Farmers were forced to question major sections of the pastoral litany in either scenario. Independence was in jeopardy; hard work and thrift might not yield success.

Middle-western farmers quickly perceived that the East was, at best, indifferent to their plight. The immediate effect was to harden

"Cause and Effect," from "The Wheat-Belt Rebellion," *Literary Digest* 78 (Aug. 4, 1923): 19.

regional resolve, but this rebuff, in conjunction with Sinclair Lewis's indictment, also initiated feelings of inadequacy and inferiority. Newspaper comments on the election of Magnus Johnson of Minnesota to the United States Senate provided an important early sign of the mood. Johnson was the Farmer-Labor party's candidate; he was a somewhat rough-hewn farmer himself. Washington reporters, in the words of an Iowa-born observer, "made a holiday of him. They described his roar of a bull. They reproduced his Scandinavian accent. They told the world that he demands a home in the capital which shall have a garden, chickens and a cowbarn."[23]

Middle Westerners were indignant at the treatment accorded to Johnson; they saw it as symptomatic of how the East judged their concerns and problems. Their indignation had no clear outlet, however. If the region trumpeted agriculture, it risked supporting the hayseed image that had already been ridiculed in the attacks on Johnson. If it chose instead to tout its industrial accomplishments like the merchants of Gopher Prairie, it courted unfavorable comparisons with an even more accomplished East.

The result was a crisis of regional identity. Outsiders and insiders held differing views of the place; old images and assumptions of both groups no longer seemed applicable.

Several changes that were set in motion at this time produced, over the next decade or so, a radical reform of the Middle-western image. Three interrelated themes stand out, one initiated outside the region and two within. Much of the Middle West, particularly its more rural sections, stuck firmly to the traditional pastoral view of their society and considered Eastern laughter as a sign of a decadent Atlantic civilization. The Middle-western business community, in contrast, turned away from any rural identification, as deftly described in *Main Street*, and tried to imitate the material and technological success they associated with Eastern cities. Easterners held a third perspective. They gradually came to ignore the urban side of the Middle West and also reinterpreted its rural world. The Middle West was synonymous with agriculture in this view, but it was occupied more by yokels than by noble yeomen.

RURAL SELF-RIGHTEOUSNESS

Of the three themes modifying regional imagery during the 1920s, a retrenchment of pastoralism in the rural areas was perhaps most apparent. In a way, this was nothing new, of course, but it differed from the past in being quite self-conscious and increasingly petty. Middle Westerners now knew that the national mood was increasingly materialistic and hedonistic. Nevertheless, through a combination of good intentions, self-delusion, and a lack of alternatives, they continued to strive toward a moral rural society. Proponents saw this group as having achieved the Jeffersonian ideal, while others perceived an increasingly narrow and reactionary culture.

With the advantage of hindsight, it is easy to see that the Middle West, aside from the new states in the northern plains, changed from a liberal to a conservative society during the late

1910s and 1920s. The mainstream of the group took firm positive positions on Prohibition and the church, and equally firm negative ones on aliens and socialism; debate on most intellectual issues lessened. In short, Sinclair Lewis was correct in his overall indictment, but contemporary observers were understandably slow to see this new reality. Some mindlessly championed the traditional idealism, repeating ideas that people liked to hear. Others, the majority, opted for a middle ground of some praise, some condemnation. Such mixed reviews, where previously all had been positive, indicate that a major change in cultural attitude was under way.

Twenty years of prosperous aging explain much of the shift from liberal to conservative philosophy. Iowa and the central plains generally had moved from youthful exuberance to settled complacency. Reflecting on this change, one long-time observer noted that whereas the plainsman of 1890 had "everything to gain and little to lose" by supporting experimental legislation, his 1920s counterpart

has all the accretion of the years since; land has increased in value 200 to 300 percent; he has made improvements on it and has equipped it with modern machinery. . . . The bank deposits have grown vastly — all of which is an inducement to the Westerner, farmer and townsman alike, to think twice before upsetting the stability of property rights or bringing about a situation that would militate against the interests of his community.[24]

Narrow moralism, a second important component of the emergent culture of the 1920s, has more complex origins. A basic moral stance permeates pastoralism, of course. Some commentators assumed that the aging process, with its conservative and materialistic accoutrements, was enough to distort this moralism, but historian Carl L. Becker argued persuasively that Middle-western ideas toward World War I were the most important factor. He began by contrasting initial Middle-western opposition to the war with the high levels of effort and sacrifice made in the region once the United States had formally entered the conflict. Becker explained this change in moral terms. The region, reacting in part to charges of crass materialism that were made in the Eastern press and perhaps beginning to sense the elusiveness of pastoral idealism, envisioned the war as an altruistic crusade. Despite the sacrifices, fighting "the war to end war" made people feel noble and thereby "satisfied a profound psychological need."[25]

Dropping from the exalted war mood suddenly in 1918 was difficult and not without important consequences in the heartland. In Becker's words:

> . . . many of our official and self-constituted leaders, deprived of the German menace upon which to expend an accumulation of heroic and self-righteous emotion, have been busily engaged in turning up lesser menaces at home. These they find everywhere in the guise of aliens who preach the proletarian revolution, Socialist deputies who hold opinions "inimical to the best interests of the country," college professors who dispassionately discuss the institution of private property, school teachers who are said to read the *Nation*, the *New Republic*, and the *Dial*. They tell us that the world must be made safe for democracy at home as well as abroad. And they find a measure of support because we resent that anyone, especially aliens, should criticise our beloved institutions at the moment when they have, as it seems to us, stood the supreme test, or question the motives and enthusiasms which during the war won us the admiration of humanity, and which still enable us to feel complacent in a disillusioned world. We do not wish to be disillusioned; and so our exalted mood is giving place to irritation, to spasmodic outbursts of petulance, and puerile talk, and purposeless persecution.[26]

Carl Becker, like Sinclair Lewis, was able to see the Middlewestern scene through clear eyes. His insights into a changed culture were confirmed by other thoughtful natives, including

Sherwood Anderson, Willa Cather, and Glenway Wescott, but not immediately by the public as a whole.[27] Old conceptions would take time to alter, particularly when the old idea — pastoralism — was so hallowed a part of national lore. Widespread attention given by the press to left-wing political actions such as the Non-Partisan League and the Farmer-Labor party created another impediment to recognizing this overall change toward conservative thought. Although these political groups did propose radical change, the press overstated their power. Only small portions of the Middle West ever came under their control, and even in these places, the support during the 1920s was generally weak. Robert La Follette of Wisconsin, the central figure in this liberal movement, is usually seen as a champion of new ideas. This was true for the 1900–14 period, but by the 1920s he could be characterized better as the last great embodiment of the old rural idealism. As the voice for a coalition of socialist-inclined farmers of Scandinavian descent, university intellectuals, and traditionalists, he was loved by many. His hurrah was brief, however; it was doomed by an emerging majority of business-minded, narrowly conservative people.[28]

Acknowledgment of the changed Middle-western character varied considerably by region. One extreme existed in the most rural parts of the heartland, where pastoral ideas might be expected to be ingrained most deeply and where opportunities for participation in the new urban society were few. A siege mentality, similar to that found throughout the South, developed there, whereby people blindly protected the old traditions against corrupting influences that were perceived to be coming in from outside.[29] The cultural significance of this mentality is not so much in the rejection of new values as in the degeneration of the old values by increasing allegiance to the letter of their existence rather than to their spirit.

Evidence for the new rural situation can be seen in articles that were intended as rebuttals to the accusations of *Main Street*.[30] Typically they praised the tranquillity of Middle-western life but admitted that it was "immensely conventional, both morally and mentally."[31] Community standards, instead of being subject to ongoing debate, were accepted as "something settled a long time since."[32] Being conventional gradually changed into being reactionary. Movements by the Non-Partisan League to create state-owned grain elevators, banks, and other socialistic reforms were regularly opposed by the mainstream of society with little or no debate. Church attendance became a requisite for social acceptance instead of an individual option, and similar allegiance was required for Prohibition and other moral issues of the time. Middle-western true believers even felt that American civilization was being "gravely imperiled" by jazz, cigarette smoking, dancing, and comparable degradations. They were thankful that their "citadel of Americanism and righteousness" had not been greatly affected by these things, and they feared that the East's overindulgence could lead it to "the bottomless pit of impotent and inferior races."[33]

Kansas and Indiana were generally regarded as foci for the new moralism. As largely rural states, their leadership might have been predicted. In addition, writers saw Kansas as special because of its history of moral concern, beginning with the abolitionist crusade of the 1850s and 1860s (see illustration).[34] Indiana's notoriety derived from the Ku Klux Klan, whose candidates briefly gained control of the state in 1924. Analysts tied the success of the Klan there, not to religious or racial strife, but to the organization's image of "super-Americanism and super-righteousness."[35] The Klan was able to symbolize various moral concerns and to provide the voice for a vague rural discontent with urban prosperity.

A NARROWED DEFINITION
OF MIDDLE-WESTERN CULTURE

As people in the rural Middle West pursued their quest for a moral society during the 1920s, Eastern and other outside observers were initially of several minds about how to interpret the changes. Early in the decade the traditional argument that the Middle West was the nation's core remained common.[36] A competing image, that of a radical agitator, surfaced briefly in the

"Virtuous Kansas," from Charles W. Wood, "Where Tomorrow's Ideas Are Born," *Collier's: The National Weekly* 71 (May 12, 1923): 9.

middle of the decade during the agricultural crisis.[37] Charges of materialism, isolationism, and insensitivity, the core of Sinclair Lewis's indictment, formed a third image.[38] Lewis's view of the Middle West as soulless and materialist might have been expected to become dominant during the decade. It would appeal not only to introspective Middle Westerners such as Lewis himself, who believed that the great potential for their region had been squandered, but also to Easterners in general as a way to express disparagement over the rise of Middle-western economic power. Writers only rarely employed this seemingly potent and obvious argument; the avoidance of it is culturally significant.

Eastern scribes most certainly knew the scenario of the heartless businessman. They had employed it frequently in 1915 and 1916, before the war, and with *Babbitt,* Lewis's new novel, the nation had been given a vivid symbol for the idea.[39] The avoidance, I think, lies in a major new conception that Easterners developed about themselves and about the Middle West. Over the course of the 1920s the East stopped viewing the Middle West as a competitor for the leadership of the nation. The process was complex, but essentially it involved a recognition that urban, not rural, forces would set the dominant tone in twentieth-century life. Easterners began to perceive their cities as vital, glittering places instead of concentrations of poverty-stricken immigrants.

Self-confidence revived, and with it came a perhaps inevitable decline in the honor accorded to farmers and to farming regions.[40]

The revived sense of national leadership and self-confidence in the East was hastened and, in part, even caused by a series of largely rural and negatively perceived events in the Middle West. Respect for pastoral concepts in Boston, for example, had to have been lessened by the reports of radicalism in the Dakotas. Esteem for the heartland was diminished further in Eastern eyes by the moral crusades against dancing, drinking, and the like. *Main Street* was probably the biggest factor of all. By drawing attention to critical flaws in the Middle-western character, it clearly boosted the self-image of the East as much as it subverted that of Minnesota.

The emergent images during the 1920s were of the East as urban, liberal, and sophisticated and of the Middle West as rural, conservative, and overly moralistic. One glaring issue stood in the way of this clear demarcation: What was to be done with the highly visible and successful urban Middle West as represented by Chicago, Cleveland, and Detroit? These cities had long been an essential part not only of regional reality but of regional image as well. They provided the youthful vitality that supposedly blended well with settled farm life and that was said to be the envy of the crumbling industrial complexes in the East. This belief held firm as late as 1921.[41]

Certainly one can detect no decline in the prosperity and vitality that were attributed to these cities by the commentators of the 1920s, regardless of the writer's regional background. Instead, these cities and the Middle West label were cleanly severed one from the other. I find no acknowledgment of this remarkable occurrence among any writers of the time, but the situation is clear in retrospect. Among the thirty-eight articles I located in the popular literature of the 1920s which attempted to assess general conditions and prospects in the place called the Middle West, only three contain more than a passing reference to the urban-industrial sphere.[42] When contrasted with the nearly universal inclusion of such references during the previous two decades, the change is telling.

How can one account for the rural-only view of the Middle West? A natural tendency for an Eastern-dominated popular press to report about Middle-western events that differed from life in the East underlies the situation. Carl Becker, for example, a well-traveled, intellectual man who certainly knew about the urban power of the Middle West, nevertheless defined the place as "that great agricultural inland region" and stressed the differing perspectives of the rural Middle West and the urban East on international affairs.[43] The largely rural nature of the two major generators of Middle-western news during the decade — agricultural depression and debate over *Main Street* — augmented this tendency. Still, a contrast between the East and the Middle West had always existed and had not before prompted a change in regional image.

A key difference between the 1920s and earlier decades seems to be the growing difficulty people had in imagining a single, encompassing definition for Middle West. Whereas Chicago could be linked with the rural areas as long as both were young and vital, the still-frenetic cities did not fit into a 1920s discussion of small-town conservatism or rural despair. One alternative — to consider Chicago and Detroit as Eastern — would have required a considerable amount of cognitive gymnastics. For journalists, the easiest solution was simply to consider those cities as outside the context of regional labels. This left the term Middle West free to be employed in Becker's manner, as a synonym for rural America.

The simplification and narrowing of the image of the Middle West might have been countered, or at least delayed, had the business communities of Chicago and similar cities fought the process; but they raised no objection. In fact, the popular literature strongly suggests that these cities were embarrassed by any association with the 1920s farming world. City folk wanted to see themselves as sophisticated, like their cohorts in the East. Thinly disguised envy of New York appears in many articles, sometimes accompanied by disdain for the local farming community. Farmers had become backward, wrong-thinking peasants in their minds, with the radical rural politics in the mid 1920s causing special discomfiture. If Eastern writers wished to restrict the definition of Middle West to rural regions, so much the better from the perspective of *Main Street.* No regional name was better than one that was perceived negatively by New Yorkers and by others whom you were emulating.[44]

THE GREAT DEPRESSION, WORLD WAR II, AND REGIONAL IMAGES

Any attentive observer of American regionalism in 1929 would have concluded that the Middle West had declined dramatically from the pinnacle of national leadership and self-confidence it had held only ten years before. In rural areas, moral pettiness still seemed to be on the rise. People in small cities, aware through *Main Street* and its entourage that Easterners thought them bucolic, dissociated themselves culturally from their embarrassing farming heritage; they took up cigarette smoking and other habits in a vain attempt to imitate Eastern sophistication. The result was a loss of much that was genuine in the region and, with this, a loss of self-respect.[45] Things were so changed, in fact, that a literary critic noted the difficulty of celebrating any aspect of Middle-western life in the 1920s "without a certain air of bravado or apology."[46]

Given the general agreement on the new state of regional affairs in 1929, it would have been easy to predict changes in image for the next decade. Easterners would continue to speak with condescension about farming hicks beyond the Appalachians, and in the rural Middle West, people would gradually abandon the futile moralist crusade and come to accept their fallen status in an urban America. World events, particularly the Great Depression, which began in late 1929, and World War II, which started a decade later, disrupted this simple scenario. The net result was to delay the general acceptance of the 1929 wisdom, cited above, for approximately two decades.

Because the worldwide depression of the 1930s was general

across the nation, regional rivalries were not as big a concern as they had been in the early 1920s. From the perspective of Middle-western imagery, the initial effects of hard times were mostly positive. Many early commentators thought that moderate economic hardships might create a useful "winnowing" action. Farmers without adequate financing and knowledge, who had hung on only because of rising land values, would be forced out. This would help to usher in a new wave of scientific agriculture, based on the same technological expertise that had made American industry the envy of the world. Middle-western agriculture thus would not only be able to bask in part of the technological glow theretofore largely denied to the realm of farming, but it simultaneously would rid itself of the "peasants" who had been responsible for the damnable hick image.[47]

A claim that the depression would rid the region of complacency was a second positive theme that emanated from the literature of the early 1930s. This argument accepted the earlier charge of conservatism-materialism as truth but said that the act of fighting economic problems would cure cultural as well as economic ills. Action would revive the old spirit of optimism, liberalism, and experimentation. Imbued with this spirit, Middle Westerners thus could not tolerate a "do-nothing policy" even from native son Herbert C. Hoover.[48] They preferred energy, even though it came from an Easterner named Franklin D. Roosevelt.[49] Similarly, a grass-roots action in Iowa to withhold crops from market drew general approval from the region for its initiative, even though the action collapsed without raising prices, as it was intended to do.[50] Fighting the depression was often compared with heroic acts from the regional past: the pioneer's conquest of the land and the passage of progressive political reforms in the face of Eastern complacency. Former governor Theodore Christianson of Minnesota captured the mood well:

> Unlike the New Yorker, who still spells depression with a big D and dates it from October, 1929, the mid-Westerner is no recent shell-shocked recruit. After twelve years of "double drill and no canteen" he is a veteran inured to the

hardships of a long siege. . . . The men who built an empire on the prairies had to devise expedients to meet conditions. . . . It is natural, therefore, for their sons to assume
when conditions change that policies must change also, and
that when something goes wrong something must be done
about it.[51]

Both cultural themes that had defined the Middle West during
its halcyon days of the 1910s were revived to some extent in the
1930s. The tone of the winnowing and adversity arguments, noted
above, suggest the idea of a life cycle. Metaphorically, at least,
a middle-aged Middle West was getting itself back into youthful
shape and once again was feeling good about itself. A "back-to-
the-land" movement, stemming from the disillusionment of working people with their relatively new urban life, simultaneously
restored pastoralist rhetoric to respectability.

No one has carefully studied the number of people who emigrated from urban to rural locations during the 1930s, but contemporary writers estimated the numbers to be in the millions
and could see no abatement to the movement. The federal government encouraged the process by sponsoring some one hundred
resettlement colonies.[52] Roosevelt argued that money spent in this
way would reduce relief payments in urban areas considerably.[53]
Symbolically, the whole process was immensely beneficial to the
Middle West, a justification of the region's traditional way of life.
Many commentators grew misty-eyed in their analyses. "As progress slowed," concluded one, "many men turned their eyes back
to the land, to the old homestead, to security, to a memory."[54]

By 1933, popular literature again tentatively began to celebrate rustic virtues. Most articles still started by addressing Lewis's criticism, but then the writers began to grow confident. The
Nebraska novelist Bess Streeter Aldrich provided a typical example
when she claimed to "grow weary of hearing the sordid spoken
of as real life, the wholesome as Pollyanna stuff."[55] The pastoral
literature from the 1930s stressed hospitality and warmth. Middle-
western towns were seen as havens for body and soul, places
where people "still believe in old moralities, such as simplicity in

thought and action, justice in the relations between men, and good sportsmanship and fair play in our relations with our neighbors overseas."[56]

One can sense momentum growing from 1933 to 1935 both for the renewed pastoralist stance and for a general self-confidence. Eastern writers joined Middle-western ones in the praise. Bolder souls even began to make the case that Chicago had an "instinctively small-town spirit" and that Middle-western literature was the "richest, most indigenous" to be found in the country.[57] The supporting arguments for all this praise were familiar: a pure and genuine part of America unsullied by speculator, tourist, or other special-interest groups; a mature region self-assured and sophisticated enough to assume the role of national leadership; a place hardened by adversity yet blessed with common sense. Repetitions of this liturgy seemed first to soothe but then to inspire even bolder claims. One writer went so far as to claim that President Roosevelt's recovery policies were "essentially Midwestern," inspired by the progressive ideas of Robert La Follette's Wisconsin.[58]

The revival of regional pride peaked about 1936. A cartoon in Collier's that year showed a Middle-western farmer controlling the reins of the nation (see cartoon), and articles appeared with such titles as "The Middle West Takes up the Torch" and "The Middle West Rules America."[59] Parallel sentiments occurred in the movies, radio, novels, and other expressions of popular culture.[60] Perhaps the clearest expression of mood, however, was the national respect accorded a trio of Middle-western painters: Thomas Hart Benton, John Steuart Curry, and Grant Wood. These three broke sharply from the European traditions that had theretofore dominated art. They praised local scenes and used a realistic mode in the belief that good art ought to reflect the places and cultures that individual artists knew best. The nation, in accepting this credo and the authority of the three, gave tacit support to the ideas of regional pride and renewed Middle-western leadership among American regions.[61]

The series of forces that created an increasingly positive image for the Middle West faltered soon after mid decade. Economic recovery drew much of the energy away from pastoralism, and

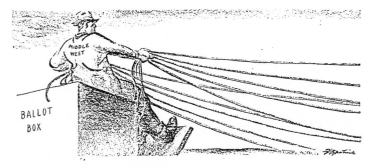

"Out Where the Vote Begins," from "Out Where the Vote Begins," *Collier's* 98 (July 16, 1936): 66.

the rural-to-urban stream of migration reestablished itself. The winnowing argument disappeared, too, as cities began to attract more and more of the brightest rural children. Before the arguments of decline had been fully marshaled, however, let alone accepted by the citizenry, a new war rendered them impotent again.

The regional literature between 1940 and 1943 echoes every sentiment and argument that had been put forth during the previous world war. Early in this period, Eastern and Middle-western writers debated the extent to which the Middle West was complacent and isolationist, its people growing rich by selling goods to a desperate Europe. Then, after Pearl Harbor, regional bickering was overwhelmed by a tremendous surge of action. Isolationist tendencies gave way to confidence, vigor, and idealism, and again the Middle West was seen as a national leader. In the words of a *Life* correspondent, it constituted "the steady heart of a nation at war."[62]

Economic prosperity for rural America continued for several years after the war and, with prosperity, the general euphoria that a combination of money and a decisive military victory might be expected to generate. Not until about 1950 did political and business affairs attain some sense of normalcy and allow time for the reassessment of regional roles in the new national order. The emergent perception was not positive for the Middle West.

The decades of the 1930s and 1940s are difficult to assess in terms of regional imagery, for the period clearly was a transitional one, and the arguments are often contradictory. Moreover, the two major national emergencies of the time created rhetoric that, although interesting, is more complicated to analyze than is the normal run of popular literature. Thus far, I have stressed the arguments that contributed to a revival of pride in the Middle West. Other arguments, ones that were to dominate by 1950, were all coexistent throughout this transitional period.

Although the initial effects of the Great Depression and World War II were to improve Middle-western idealism and self-esteem, the longer-term impact of each on the region's image was negative. Both crises led to increased portrayals of the Middle West as a rural place—the depression through "back-to-the-land" and "Dust Bowl" rhetoric, and the war through praise for the "breadbasket of the world." Twenty years of such emphasis effectively killed any chance for the region to reacquire the urban aspect of its image that had initially disappeared in the 1920s. A totally rural image need not be necessarily negative, of course, as one can see in the wave of pastoral articles written in the early 1930s, but negativism gradually increased later in the decade. By 1950, even Middle Westerners had largely accepted the earlier Eastern view of their region not only as rural but also as a place that was somewhat backward culturally and was functioning largely as a "colony" of the East.

The central element of Middle-western negativism—what might be called the colony argument—involved an initial resentment toward the East and then a resignation to inferior status. A typical statement would begin with a recitation of how the ratio of farm prices to the cost of other items had fallen. Assuming the price structure of 1914–19 to be a standard, one writer reported that the ratio stood at 92 in 1925, 89 in 1929, 63 in 1931, and 50 in 1933.[63] This crisis had its beginning with increases in land prices during the boom years of World War I. The changes had been accompanied by an influx of investors, many of whom were Easterners. As prices fell, foreclosures occurred, with the rate achieving "tidal wave" proportions by 1931 and 1932.[64] Farmers blamed themselves for this crisis to a degree, but as they were joined in financial ruin by local banks and merchants, it became easy to identify the enemy as the East. The attitude was typified by these words from an Iowa farmer: "We just don't know what we are going to do, but I'll tell you this, we want the Eastern bankers to stay over in their country and leave us alone in the West. They can have their gold if they can keep it, but we are going to hold on to our farms."[65]

Resentment toward the East was nothing new for Middle Westerners, but unlike earlier situations in which this had spurred action, the mood of the 1930s quickly changed to resignation. Hard times had existed on the farm for a decade, and the resources apparently were no longer there to fight. As foreclosures led to absentee ownership, liquidated farmers found that although rents might be less than taxes and interest had been, pride was gone. Similar things happened to townspeople, and the results were said to be devastating psychologically. The words of the economist and political scientist Alvin S. Johnson in 1935 have proved to be prophetic: "Prosperity may return, but no conceivable prosperity will restore the failed bank nor vest title to the farm in the foreclosed farmer. . . . The depression casualty continues vocal for a time, but eventually his voice, too, is stilled or ignored. One can't listen forever to a man who has failed."[66]

The first explicit statement of the new status of the Middle West came in 1933, when J. M. Nolte boldly labeled it "the fief of futility." He asserted that Sinclair Lewis's points were devastatingly accurate. When massive loss of control over local resources was coupled with Lewis's truths, the result was colonial status for the region both in a commercial and in a psychological sense. The Middle West had developed "a malignant and destructive inferiority complex."[67]

Nolte's claim was by no means universally accepted in the mid 1930s. His assertions rang true for many people but were temporarily balanced by claims of a restored pastoral civilization. Journalists were unsure as to which image represented the real Middle West. This balance is illustrated nicely by the treatment accorded the major drought suffered by the plains states. A straightforward depiction of the human tragedy there—word and camera portraits of farmers who were clearly no longer in control of their own destiny—would strengthen Nolte's argument. On the other hand, acknowledgment of wholesale crop failures in a section of the historically fertile Middle West would perhaps be hard for most Americans to accept. Two strategies may be observed: some writers went ahead, described the failures, and linked them to the Middle West label; others attempted to engage in some geographical sleight of hand. For this second group, the tragedy was just as real, but it did not occur in the Middle West. That region was shifted a bit to the East, leaving the Dust Bowl either in the West or in a newly popularized area labeled the Great Plains.[68] This attempt to excise the plains from the Middle West is interesting, but it was never widespread, even at the height of the drought. Apparently the view of Middle West as a rural backwater was sufficiently well established by 1935 or so that Dust Bowl imagery was not seen as distinct enough to necessitate a new regionalization.

Throughout the 1930s, negative arguments multiplied. The Middle West was conservative; it lacked vitality; old age was at hand. Even the regional literature, once a source of pride, began to be denigrated. One critic characterized it as "stylized farm-background dullness" and noted that the region's most talented writers—Sherwood Anderson, Willa Cather, Ernest Hemingway, and Sinclair Lewis—had all emigrated. He wondered whether Cather and her fellow writers had sensed that the Middle West had become "a geographical blunder, an intellectual dead spot, a spiritual swamp."[69]

Calling the Middle West an intellectual dead spot was an extreme position, but the consensus of observers throughout the late 1930s and the 1940s was that there had been a loss of regional vitality. The bubble of rejuvenation that accompanied World War II was shorter-lived than that for the previous war, and even the most positive of accounts argued only that "in the Middle West today, progress and reaction seem to be in balance, with a tendency toward the latter."[70]

Most of the regional literature from the 1940s is superficially positive in tone. It celebrates the war effort and then the economic boom of the immediate postwar years. Between the lines, however, the idea that the Middle West was being by-passed both economically and culturally always seems to lurk. Even as authors extolled the heavy industry and the complexity of the region, for example, it was still being summarized as "basically" agricultural, and its goals and needs were being compared to those of the "industrial" East.[71] Isolation as a regional trait, which had been a popular assessment before the war, returned again as early as 1943, along with a distrust of labor unions and other urban affairs.[72] The war had hastened the evolution of the United States into an urban-industrial power, and the Middle West, now having convinced even itself of its essentially rural nature, began to recognize the consequences of this role. A 1944 editorial in *Life* stated directly what many others had hinted: "At its worst [the Middle West] . . . is suspicious of foreigners, of the East, of big cities (including its own), of Wall Street, and of Big Business."[73]

THE MIDDLE WEST IN 1950

As 1950 approached, the Middle West was at a low point of self-esteem. The farming image was entrenched more firmly than ever, but farming did not carry the national respect that it had enjoyed thirty years earlier. A combination of agriculture plus a solid industrial base (which was still never discussed in conjunction with the regional label) produced prosperity and congeniality but only a superficial sense of pride. Local destiny and even local image were controlled by others. An Iowa editor summarized the bittersweet situation well in 1949:

Washington has assumed the role of spokesman for our affairs, both public and private. The nation's gossip is dispensed out of New York, giving prominence to people of little use or importance. Our manners — God save the mark — are portrayed by Hollywood. The quoted opinions regarding the state of business come from Eastern Seaboard economists, and the dicta as to what we shall wear, read and think issue from the same area. The interior of the country is strictly a bench-warmer in the national line-up. Yet it is the most stable, normal and happy part of the United States.[74]

5

A Need for Pastoral Values

Regional issues were not prominent among American concerns in the 1950s and early 1960s. The years of the Eisenhower presidency were generally prosperous for farmers and manufacturers alike, and no social problems loomed large on the scene. One who is seeking to learn how Middle-western culture was perceived in this period finds many statements but no consensus. Little was written that had not been said before, and probably as a consequence, few of the writers seem impassioned. The period is best seen as a transitional one. The dominant viewpoint reflected the continuing attraction of Americans toward urban places and an associated constellation of materialism, obsession with new technology, and change for the sake of change. The eastern and western seaboards profited from this mind set; the Middle West, still firmly identified with rural themes, suffered.

Almost hidden among the assertions of Middle-western backwardness and other assorted viewpoints, a new perspective on the region emerged. This was nostalgia. Slowly and uncertainly during the 1950s a vague sense of loss seems to have developed among many city dwellers. One can infer this from a careful reading of the popular literature. Instead of generating wholesale condemnation by writers, small towns and traditional farms, indeed the entire Middle-western culture, began to be labeled quaint. Support for this viewpoint quickened in the mid 1960s, and by the early 1970s it was perhaps the dominant image that outsiders held about the region. From this perspective, the Middle West had become a museum of sorts. No up-and-coming citizen wanted to live there, but it had importance as a repository for traditional values. The Middle West was a nice place to visit occasionally and to reflect upon one's heritage. It was America's collective "hometown," a place with good air, picturesque farm buildings, and unpretentious "simple" people.

Portraying the Middle West as a museum perhaps could serve a useful psychological purpose for Americans, but in order to do so, the old pretext of seeing only the rural side of Ohio and Michigan had to be maintained. This pretext became increasingly awkward after the late 1960s as racial conflict and industrial collapse in Detroit, Cleveland, and elsewhere became major national news stories. Surveys show that the public's response was to rework its collective cognitive map of Middle-western location. Ohio and Michigan now were partially excluded, and the regional core shifted to the Great Plains states. The region thus ironically returned to its birthplace and, in so doing, brought its continuing rural definition closer in line with reality.

THE GROWTH OF NOSTALGIA

The extended period of general prosperity for the United States during the 1950s obscured many regional traits. It tended to mask negative cultural feelings, and it encouraged rosy outlooks. At the height of the period, during the mid 1950s, several writers created visions of the Middle West so glorious that they rivaled the statements of the 1910s. For them the region was once again the "balance-wheel of the nation," home to responsible people with their pioneer virtues still intact. These writers went so far as to reclaim Chicago as the core, thus suggesting the old fusion of industrial and agricultural might.[1] This optimistic interpretation of the region was at least as accurate as the view that equated the Middle West with rural America, but it never gained widespread acceptance, and it disappeared from the popular literature completely after about 1956. It was a hard vision to maintain in the face of the rapid migration of people away from heartland villages.[2]

The more general but negative view of Middle-western culture during this period was stated subtly in the popular literature. It frequently is evident in the phrasing of ostensibly positive statements. An article in *Life* praised the arts in the region but also noted that such achievement would surprise those who "are inclined to patronize" the region. Another telling example in an otherwise sympathetic article was the assertion that backwardness and bigotry "are not the vices" of Middle-western culture.[3] These would seem to be arguments that were trying to change majority opinion. Direct statements of this more negative assessment of Middle-western life exist, but principally in novels and other outlets somewhat outside the popular mainstream. The Wisconsin writer Glenway Wescott had set the tone earlier with his tart definition of the Middle West as "a state of mind of people born where they do not like to live."[4] Wescott's statement, I think, refers to perceived opportunities, especially for the mind. This idea has been elucidated in the memoirs of the contemporary Middle-western-born intellectual Eric Sevareid. Sevareid wrote that his generation of North Dakotans was "the first to grow up without the American West shining before the eye of the mind as a vision of the future. Instinctively we knew that the last of the frontiers had disappeared. From the time when the Indian tales lost their spell and we began to think, we wanted to go east. It was the East that was golden."[5]

Sevareid's move away from the prairies occurred before the time that is under consideration here, but his words capture the essence of the regional image circa 1960. Middle-western towns had lost so many of their young people and so much of their vigor by that time that they had little left to give. Lingering pastoralist sentiment was strong enough in America to prevent many blunt statements of the new status of Middle-western rural life, but the cartoonist Jack Ziegler caught its essence in the *Saturday Review* (see cartoon), and so did several novelists, including William H. Gass. Gass, another Middle Westerner, studied "the heart" (small towns) "of the heart" (Middle West) "of the country," but ironically he found little except decay and bleakness in his Indiana sample. The towns were "rural slums"; the people were lonely and without ambition or resolve.[6] That Gass was close to the truth and that people silently acknowledged this fact is indicated

By Jack Ziegler, reprinted by permission from *Saturday Review* 2 (Jan. 11, 1975): 5. © 1975 Jack Ziegler and *Saturday Review.*

by a complete lack of popular challenge to his assessment. The contrast in the receptions given to *In the Heart of the Heart of the Country* and to *Main Street* forty-eight years earlier says volumes about the decline of the Middle-western image.

The discrepancy between the knowledge of Middle-western decay and its admission in popular literature is a puzzling phenomenon that is not fully explained by the good spirits engendered by economic prosperity. No answer is readily apparent in the literature of the 1950s, but looking back at that period from the 1980s, one can see that alienation, a trait frequently said to be characteristic of modern urban society in this country, was beginning to affect evaluations of the Middle West. Alienation involves a vague sense of loss, a feeling that although urban life fosters many obvious advantages, these advantages have not been attained without a cost. A sense of community and family is seen to have declined, and so have connections to the rhythms of the seasons and other phenomena of the natural world. A society increasingly complex, mobile, and avaricious was beginning to yearn occasionally for simplicity, virtue, and rootedness.[7]

Alienation has ramifications across the spectrum of American life, including the evaluation of regions and environments. Wilderness areas, for example, came to be almost sacred spaces, extolled for their quietness and spirituality; and rural sections of the country, notably the Middle West, began to be romanticized. A gauzy nostalgia competed with the more objective assessments of place.[8]

It is impossible to pinpoint the beginnings of American yearnings for traditional Middle-western values, because through the concept of pastoralism, Middle-western identity has always been linked to nostalgia. One useful indicator of the trend is the popularity of novels about farm life. Few were written in the nineteenth century when the nation was largely rural. The heyday of the genre, from 1920 through 1945, coincided with major rural-to-urban migration. Apparently the audience for these books were nonfarmers, who were sentimental about a passing way of life.[9] Similar studies exist in the periodical literature as well, usually by writers visiting their old hometowns.[10]

By the 1950s this nostalgia for the Middle West had come to assume a different guise. Articles now began to emphasize how aspects of the physical environment had shaped human affairs. Awe, spirituality, and other esthetic qualities were the bywords, not soil fertility and rainfall patterns. Saul Bellow's tone was typical when he wrote that "miles and miles of [Illinois] prairie, slowly rising and falling, sometimes give you a sense that something is in the process of becoming, or that the liberation of a great force is imminent, some power, like Michelangelo's slave only half released from the block of stone."[11] Although these articles ostensibly emphasized nature, their real purpose was to celebrate the rural society living in the midst of the prairie. After coming to know the "limitless, serene, indifferent" land, wrote the novelist Jack

Schaefer, "you begin to understand the quiet unhurried manner that marks so many Dakotans. . . . Dakota as a whole still has an uncluttered, unsoiled air, a simple freshness, untainted by the stale weariness of most older overrun regions. The land, not what man has done with it, still predominates."[12]

Urban society during the 1950s still had many more supporters than detractors, but Schaefer's lines set the tone for arguments that became increasingly common after the mid 1960s. Simplicity, patriotism, and wholesomeness were among the recurrent words—the yeoman traits reborn. Admiring references were made to "pioneer virtues," such as family unity and a lack of pretentiousness, which somehow had been maintained in the prairie towns. Being behind the times was gradually transformed from a negative into a somewhat positive regional trait.[13] The unexpected success of the Broadway play *The Music Man* was the most obvious sign of this movement around 1960. Author Meredith Willson drew inspiration from what he called the "innocent Iowa" of his youth, and this quality was seen as the key to the play's success by most reviewers. *Time* magazine, for example, made the contrast with modern society clearly: "In a fat Broadway season whose successes deal so clinically with such subjects as marital frustration, alcoholism, dope addiction, juvenile delinquency and abortion, *The Music Man* is a monument to golden unpretentiousness and wholesome fun."[14]

Nostalgia has become a more pervasive aspect of Middlewestern identity since 1960. In the early years of that decade, *Holiday* magazine published a series of "Shunpike" tours, showcasing places out of the mainstream where one could find old-fashioned hotels, home-style cooking, and friendly folk. The Middle West was the favorite locale.[15] A spate of articles on the cultural heritage of Harry S. Truman and Dwight D. Eisenhower, in rural Missouri and Kansas, respectively, was another expression of the mood. As with Abraham Lincoln before them, it was argued, the essential decentness of these men could be traced to their upbringing on the prairie. Other writers extended the motif of the Middle Westerner as gentle folk hero even farther. Superman and Dorothy Gale, fictional innocents who epitomized "truth, justice, and the American way," both received their basic values in the Kansas countryside.

The nostalgia movement for the Middle West intensified during the late 1960s and the 1970s. Whereas the tone of the *Holiday* "Shunpike" tours had been pleasant remembrances of older and simpler times, later articles expressed more urgent and complex reasons for escapes to the country. With a series of riots during the mid 1960s, urban America abruptly took on darker tones for its citizens. References to "troubled cities" begin to appear regularly in 1967, and the Middle West more frequently was seen as a haven.[16] Some writers simply championed its low taxes and uncrowded conditions, but usually references were also made to an increasingly "vulgar" urban society, marked by drugs, racial violence, and liberal permissiveness. The escape idea was heightened further in the years immediately after the Vietnam War by a national tendency to move away from international affairs and back to a more isolationist stance.[17]

Most of the gains in image by the Middle West in the 1960s can be attributed, not to changes within its boundaries, but to increasingly negative perceptions of urban America. A more positive reason for viewing rural regions in favorable terms was ecological awareness, which symbolically began with Earth Day in 1970. Although tendencies toward a monoculture, the heavy use of chemical fertilizers, and other aspects of Middle-western rural life came under severe criticism as part of this movement, the general view was that farms, small towns, and the Middle West as a whole had retained the "old-fashioned" ideas of family, community, and sensitivity to nature more than had other places. These were the settings in which to begin a new, more environmentally responsible version of America.[18]

The popular literature from the 1970s depicts Middle-western life in the most positive light it had enjoyed since the 1910s. Although one can still find abundant evidence for an inferiority complex on the part of its residents or a yearning for the perceived sophistication of New York City or California, this is balanced to some extent by a reciprocal envy of a frenzied coastal America for the perceived simpler life in the interior.[19] The change in perception is ironic for, as historian Laurence Lafore noted in 1971: "Main Street has not really changed very much since Sinclair Lewis wrote. A culture universally disdained at a time when Montparnasse was the refuge for sensitive Americans fleeing from the barbaric Midwest, has, merely by remaining the same, become a place that sensitive Americans may well be fleeing *to.*"[20]

THE REGIONAL IMAGE IN 1980

The name Middle West by 1980 bore an increasingly complex and contradictory identity. A tension existed among its images of aging cultural backwater, idyllic innocent, and ecological avantegarde, and the popular literature is unclear as to the relative strengths of the three conceptions. Of potentially greater concern was the long-suppressed recognition of Chicago, Detroit, and other major "Middle-western" cities. The steady growth of these places made the question of their regional allegiance harder to ignore with each passing decade. Racial strife in these cities, the riots at the 1968 Democratic National Convention in Chicago, and the collapse of steel and other heavy industry in these same locations during the 1970s added even more public scrutiny. Would the definition of Middle West finally be changed in the public mind to incorporate this urban melange of images that are so far removed from the familiar farmer stereotype?

Two examples suggest the extent of the problem of defining the region. In the early 1980s the telecasts of the N.C.A.A. basketball tournaments delivered a message to millions of Americans that the country had four regions: East, West, Midwest, and — a new creation of theirs — the Mideast. The N.C.A.A. scheme of regional divisions restricted the Midwest to a Great Plains location; the Mideast included most of the Great Lakes states. The Middle West took an even more extreme buffeting in the popular book *The Nine Nations of North America.* After inviting readers to consider the way North America "really works," the author flatly asserted that "there is no such thing as the 'Midwest.'"[21] Instead, he allotted one portion of the moribund place to a plains "breadbasket" region and another portion to a "foundry" district, focused on the upper Ohio Valley.

The changes in the regional perception that are suggested by these popular examples and the popular literature in general deserve detailed attention. Does the public still recognize the traditional boundaries and cultural characteristics of this region? Is the place perceived differently in various sections of the country and within the traditional twelve-state Middle West?

In an effort to get beyond the information available in the popular literature, I explored the popular image of the Middle West through a survey of university students in January, 1980. Colleagues teaching in thirty-two states administered one-page questionnaires to approximately one hundred undergraduates each.[22] The questionnaire elicited background information on the student's residential history, the state he or she regarded as "home," and the size of the "home" community. Two questions then were asked:

What characteristics do you associate with the Middle West (Midwest) and its people?

On the map on the opposite side of this page, please draw a line around the Middle West (Midwest) as you perceive it.

The outline map, at 1:18,000,000, contained only state boundaries and state names.

From a completed total of 2,767 questionnaires, 1,941 were selected for analysis. I focused on respondents who were most likely to represent the views of their regions — those who were attending college in the same state that they called home. Respondents from foreign countries were excluded, as were American students who had lived in several different states. Information derived from this open-ended survey was grouped with the aid of *Webster's New Dictionary of Synonyms* and other references. The average respondent, whether from a traditional Middle-western state or not, volunteered about four descriptive words or phrases for the region (see table 5.1).

Table 5.1. Per Capita Responses for Descriptive Terms

Type of Term	All Respondents	Insiders (12 States)[a]	Outsiders (20 States)[b]
Physical	1.13	.95	1.24
Economic	1.09	.91	1.20
Cultural	.99	1.44	.70
General population	.49	.51	.48
Other associations	.20	.19	.21
Totals	3.90	4.00	3.83

[a] Insiders are defined here and elsewhere in this study as respondents from Illinois, Indiana, Iowa, Kansas, Michigan, Minnesota, Missouri, Nebraska, North Dakota, Ohio, South Dakota, and Wisconsin.
[b] Outsiders are defined here and elsewhere in this study as respondents from Alabama, Arkansas, California, Colorado, Connecticut, Florida, Kentucky, Louisiana, Montana, New Hampshire, New York, Oklahoma, Pennsylvania, South Carolina, Tennessee, Texas, Utah, Washington, West Virginia, and Wyoming.

In general, the physical terms that were listed were accurate descriptions of the perceived region: a flat plains environment, characterized by cold winters and hot summers (see table 5.2). Insiders tended to see their home region in more positive terms than did outsiders, and some differences also existed among the outsiders. Within the twelve traditional Middle West states, however, discrepancies were minor, suggesting that the conventional regional delimitation is a reasonable one with regard to physical traits.

Rural images were by far the most dominant in the survey (see tables 5.3 and 5.4). General references to farming, agriculture, and farmers were mentioned by 63 percent of the respondents, about four times the frequency of any other economic trait and between two and three times more often than traits of any other type. Farming dominated the images of insiders and outsiders, city residents and small-town residents alike. Moreover, the other economic, population, and cultural characteristics that were volunteered generally served to strengthen and extend this theme.

In contrast with the consistent perception of physical characteristics among respondents from the twelve traditional Middle West

Table 5.2. Perceived Physical Characteristics (as percentages of respondents)[a]

Number and Characteristic	All Respondents	Middle West Respondents (Insiders)			Other Respondents (Outsiders)			
		Great Plains[b]	Old Northwest[c]	All Insiders	Far West[d]	South[e]	Northeast[f]	All Outsiders
N	1,941	256	300	763	172	236	190	1,178
Topography								
Flat (plains)	23.8	16.8[g]	19.0	16.8[g]	30.0	22.9	33.2[g]	28.3[g]
Open	6.1	7.4	3.7	4.7	4.7	4.2	10.0	7.0
Mountains	5.9	1.1[g]	3.0	1.7[g]	6.5	14.8[g]	6.8	8.7[g]
Climate								
Arid (dry)	7.4	2.0[g]	1.3[g]	1.6[g]	6.4	19.5[g]	13.7[g]	11.2[g]
Cold winter	7.0	11.3[g]	8.0	8.6	9.3	5.1	4.7	5.9
Hot summer	5.6	9.4	5.7	6.6	8.1	4.7	3.7	5.0
Snow	3.0	2.0	2.3	2.1	6.4[g]	4.7	3.2	3.6
Hot weather	2.8	—[g]	1.0	0.5[g]	2.9	6.4[g]	6.3[g]	4.3[g]
Cold weather	2.8	3.1	1.3	2.1	3.5	7.6[g]	1.1	3.3
Seasonal weather	2.6	3.5	7.3[g]	5.6[g]	0.6	0.4	1.1	0.7[g]
Vegetation								
Grassland (prairie)	3.2	3.5	1.7	2.9	4.1	2.5	6.3	3.5
Desert	2.1	—	0.3	0.1[g]	2.3	7.2[g]	3.7	3.4[g]
Evaluation								
Vast	4.0	3.1	1.7	1.8[g]	4.7	8.1[g]	6.3	5.4

[a] The figures, other than N, are percentages of respondents who listed the particular characteristic. The minimum requirement for entry in any row was 5 percent.
[b] Kansas, Nebraska, North Dakota, and South Dakota.
[c] Illinois, Indiana, Michigan, Ohio, and Wisconsin.
[d] California, Utah, and Washington.
[e] Alabama, Florida, Louisiana, and South Carolina.
[f] Connecticut, New Hampshire, and New York.
[g] This percentage differs from the average row percentage by an amount that is significant at the 0.01 level.

Table 5.3. Perceived Economic and General Population Characteristics (as percentages of respondents)[a]

Number and Characteristic	All Respondents	"Home" Town of Respondents		Middle West Respondents (Insiders)			Other Respondents (Outsiders)			
		Large Places (>50,000)	Small Places (<50,000)	Great Plains[b]	Old Northwest[c]	All Insiders	Far West[d]	South[e]	Northeast[f]	All Outsiders
N	1,941	820	1,121	256	300	763	172	236	190	1,178
Rural economy										
Agriculture (farming)	62.2	59.5	64.8	51.2[g]	63.0	58.7	63.4	60.2	71.6	65.1
Corn	9.0	9.3	8.8	3.5[g]	11.0	7.2	12.2	5.9	7.4	10.2
Wheat	8.9	9.4	8.6	4.3	5.0	3.9[g]	15.7[g]	11.4	11.0	12.2[g]
Ranching	5.0	3.8	6.1	6.2	0.7[g]	2.8[g]	5.2	7.6	6.3	6.7[g]
Cattle	4.7	4.9	4.6	2.0	1.7	2.2[g]	7.6	5.9	5.8	5.9
Grain	2.9	2.4	3.1	0.4	0.3[g]	0.3[g]	5.2	2.5	4.2	4.8[g]
Urban economy										
Industry	5.1	6.1	4.5	2.0	12.7[g]	6.6	4.1	4.2	2.6	3.6
Population traits										
Rural	14.7	12.9	16.6	11.3	17.0	13.9	14.0	14.4	16.8	15.3
Small town	9.2	9.6	8.9	10.6	10.0	10.4	12.2	5.9	4.7	8.5
Some cities	6.5	6.7	6.3	3.9	7.7	6.2	8.1	6.4	9.0	6.7
Sparsely populated	6.1	4.8	7.1	6.2	2.7	4.5	8.1	6.4	7.9	7.5

[a] The figures, other than N, are percentages of respondents who listed the particular characteristic. The minimum requirement for entry in any row was 5 percent.
[b] Kansas, Nebraska, North Dakota, and South Dakota.
[c] Illinois, Indiana, Michigan, Ohio, and Wisconsin.
[d] California, Utah, and Washington.
[e] Alabama, Florida, Louisiana, and South Carolina.
[f] Connecticut, New Hampshire, and New York.
[g] This percentage differs from the average row percentage by an amount that is significant at the 0.01 level.

Table 3.4. Perceived Cultural Characteristics (as percentages of respondents)

Number and Characteristic	All Respondents	"Home" Town of Respondents		Middle West Respondents (Insiders)			Other Respondents (Outsiders)			
		Large Places (>50,000)	Small Places (<50,000)	Great Plains[b]	Old Northwest[c]	All Insiders	Far West[d]	South[e]	Northeast[f]	All Outsiders
N	1,941	820	1,121	256	300	763	172	236	190	1,178
Friendly	22.0	18.8	24.4	49.2[g]	24.7	35.0[g]	10.5[g]	8.0[g]	13.7[g]	13.7[g]
Traditional	13.0	13.8	12.5	16.0	23.7[g]	18.6[g]	13.4	4.2[g]	7.4	9.4[g]
Easygoing	10.7	9.8	11.4	14.1	11.7	12.7	7.0	4.7[g]	11.6	9.8
Hard-working	9.2	7.4	10.4	18.4[g]	17.3[g]	15.7[g]	7.0	3.0[g]	4.2	4.9[g]
Naïve	5.7	6.2	5.4	7.4	8.0	7.2	7.0	2.5	5.3	4.8
Thoughtful	3.6	1.8[g]	4.9	11.7[g]	3.7	6.8[g]	0.6	0.4[g]	0.5	1.5[g]
Honest	3.4	3.3	3.5	7.8[g]	4.0	5.4[g]	3.5	0.4[g]	2.1	2.1[g]
Practical	3.4	2.7	3.8	3.9	5.7	4.3	4.1	1.3	3.2	2.7
Outdoors oriented	2.6	2.6	2.7	2.3	5.3[g]	3.8	1.7	2.5	0.5	1.9
Intolerant	2.3	2.8	2.0	0.8	3.0	2.1	3.5	1.7	5.8[g]	2.5
All yeoman-related traits[h]	47.8	42.5[g]	51.9[g]	92.5[g]	55.4[g]	70.1[g]	30.3[g]	18.1[g]	34.3[g]	33.9[g]
All young-adult-related traits[i]	3.9	4.0	3.7	4.7	5.3	5.6	—[g]	4.7	0.5	2.7
All old-age-related traits[j]	20.3	20.3	20.4	24.6	35.7[g]	28.1[g]	21.6	7.6[g]	16.4	15.2[g]

[a] The figures, other than N, are percentages of respondents who listed the particular characteristic. The minimum requirement for row entry was 5 percent. Common responses grouped into the various categories include: friendly—neighborly and warm; traditional—backward, conservative, and old-fashioned; easygoing—quiet, relaxed, and slow-paced; hard-working—busy, industrious, and work ethic; naïve—down-home, homey, natural, plain, and simple; thoughtful—considerate, helpful, and kind; honest—frank, genuine, open, and straightforward; practical—common-sensical, down-to-earth, and materialistic; outdoors oriented—close to the land and love of nature; and intolerant—biased, bigoted, hick, narrow-minded, and ethnocentric.
[b] Kansas, Nebraska, North Dakota, and South Dakota.
[c] Illinois, Indiana, Michigan, Ohio, and Wisconsin.
[d] California, Utah, and Washington.
[e] Alabama, Florida, Louisiana, and South Carolina.
[f] Connecticut, New Hampshire, and New York.
[g] This percentage differs from the average row percentage by an amount that is significant at the 0.01 level.
[h] These include friendly, easygoing, naïve, thoughtful, and honest, listed above, plus moral, modest, and their synonyms.
[i] These include vigorous, progressive, tolerant, and their synonyms.
[j] These include traditional, practical, and intolerant, listed above, plus serious, stoic, and their synonyms.

states, several important distinctions within the general rural
framework existed for economic and cultural images. Great Plains
people saw ranching and sparse populations as important parts
of their Middle West. Respondents from the Old Northwest (i.e.,
Illinois, Indiana, Michigan, Ohio, and Wisconsin), although they
still stressed agriculture, saw a somewhat different kind of farming. They were the only ones to give even a modest mention to
dairying, hogs, and soybeans as Middle-western agricultural phenomena. Moreover, these students from the Old Northwest were
the only ones to accord industry an important place in their Middle-
western vision, but even they did not provide details, and they
thought that "rural" was a much better descriptor than "urban"
for their region.

These results from the survey confirm that the Middle West
of 1980 was perceptually little different, in an economic and
population sense, from the region of 1900. The tendency to ignore the place's urban reality and industrial strength, which has
been apparent in the popular literature since the 1920s, had not
lessened at all by 1980. This is a paradox of grand proportions,
because not only has the Middle West become a more urban society with each passing decade but also regional urban concerns
were major news makers in the years immediately preceding this
survey. Why would Americans in general, and especially people
from the eastern Middle West, retain such a rural view? The question probes to the heart of the Middle West's regional character;
it is, I think, essentially a cultural issue. It can be approached by
comparing 1980 images with traits traditionally associated with
the region.

Although the perceived modern cultural characteristics vary
widely, most of them can be grouped under the two general head-
ings that have always prevailed in Middle-western imagery: pastoralism and the life-cycle analogy. Pastoral ideals dominate,
although it is unclear whether these traits are direct survivors
from the turn of the century or are products of recent nostalgia
(see table 5.4). More than 70 percent of the sample from the
twelve traditional Middle-western states saw themselves as citi-

zens in the mold of Jeffersonian idealism; these same traits were also the ones that outsiders offered most frequently.

Commentators on the Middle West during the 1910s invariably coupled the yeoman-farmer pastoral images with the analogy of the region as a young adult. These writers, it will be recalled, noted that the Middle West had outgrown the undesirable traits of youth — thriftlessness, impatience, radicalism, and boomer philosophy. At the same time, problems of old age were far in the future — self-satisfaction, conservatism, the loss of idealism, corruption, and a classed society. This analogy with the life cycle continued to be used for characterizing the region during subsequent decades, but because of the "rejuvenation" forces that accompanied the depression of the 1930s and World War II, the overall public perception is difficult to determine. The nostalgia movement has created additional perceptual complexity. Is the modern-day vision of Middle-western Arcadia more likely to include a still vigorous yeoman or a somewhat decrepit one?

The 1980 survey suggests that old age is now the most prevalent analogy for the Middle West. "Hard working" may be a surviving trait from young adulthood, but this characteristic might equally be attributed to pastoralism. "Traditionalism" was the most commonly volunteered of the old-age characteristics, its synonyms being employed ten times more frequently than antonymous words such as "progressive," "liberal," or "modern." Even Great Plains people and small-town people generally agreed with this assessment. "Practicality" and analogous terms appeared on about 3.9 percent of the questionnaires; "idealism" on virtually none. Synonyms for "intolerance" were volunteered about five times more frequently than labels such as "open-minded" or "broad-minded." Outsiders, especially Northeasterners, stressed this issue. Nevertheless, despite all of these suggestions of old age, not all of the associations that early-twentieth-century commentators had feared had materialized. No respondent characterized the Middle West as smug or self-satisfied. Neither were the people seen as dilettantes, corrupt, or nonegalitarian. The continuance of pastoralism presumably guarded against such things.

Within the dominant framework of pastoral traits and those of an aging society, the 1980 sampling also reveals that significant differences in the perception of cultural traits exist between sections of the traditional Middle West. Plains people expressed friendliness, honesty, and other pastoral traits more frequently than did residents of the Old Northwest; Northwesterners saw the Middle West as an older society than did others.[23] These differences, it will be recalled, parallel discrepancies in how people from the two sections viewed their economies; together the patterns suggest that the two peoples may possess different cognitive maps of the Middle West's location. Both groups may see the region as centered on themselves, plains people thus using venerable yeoman terms and respondents from the Old Northwest volunteering somewhat more mature and urban characteristics. The cognitive maps collected from each group, which I discuss below, substantiate this dichotomy.

COGNITIVE MAPS

The regional images that were elicited from the 1980 survey reinforce the incongruous situation sampled in the popular literature. For some reason, a complex and increasingly diverse region of the country is still being characterized in simplistic and almost totally rural terms. This distortion from reality exists in the minds of people not only outside the traditional twelve-state region but within it as well. It is time to reflect again on this puzzling phenomenon.

We should recall that the original divorce of urban aspects of Middle-western life from popular conceptions of the region occurred during the 1920s. At that time, mixed feelings toward the urbanization of the country produced a stereotyping of regions: the Middle West represented the traditional, pastoral conception of America; the East symbolized the new urban world. This dichotomy was maintained throughout the 1920s and 1930s largely through highly distorted views of Ohio, Michigan, and Illinois, the most industrialized of the traditional Middle-western states.

Writers who employed the label Middle West routinely included these states under this heading, but they declined to discuss non-rural topics. Articles on Chicago, Cleveland, and Detroit rarely mentioned a regional affiliation.

The denial of regional affiliation to a block of major American cities can be understood in the social and regional context of the 1920s and 1930s, but at least two other solutions seem to offer a more straightforward and permanent approach to cultural regionalization. The cultural definition of Middle West could be modified to incorporate urban-industrial imagery, thus reclaiming Detroit and Cleveland. Alternately, the boundary between the East and Middle West could be relocated westward, making these cities part of the East. The cultural images that were found in the 1980 survey provide strong evidence that the former solution has not occurred. Hints of shifts in boundary exist in the literature, however, and the second question on my 1980 survey was designed to determine the form and extent of this phenomenon.

The only formal attempt to determine the extent of allegiance to the label Middle West prior to 1980 was a survey of 480 postmasters, which was conducted in the late 1950s. Joseph W. Brownell simply asked these people whether or not their communities were located in the Midwest region. The map he produced largely confirmed the traditional twelve-state definition of the region, but it also suggested that some relocation toward the west had taken place (see map 5.1).[24] Popular literature from this period supports this partial transplacement, both for Ohio and for the plains border. As early as 1945, for example, a Cleveland writer noted that although people from his city were not disenchanted with the label Middle West, they nevertheless found it difficult "to get the feeling of Middlewesternism." The sentiment came through somewhat more strongly in a series of interviews in 1958. A Cincinnati salesman said that "the East has swallowed Ohio," and an Indianapolis newspaper editor thought that his city was "about on the border" of the region.[25] Most writers continued to define the Middle West as consisting of twelve states, but occasionally the term was used to refer to the trans-Mississippi plains alone or to that region plus Illinois.[26]

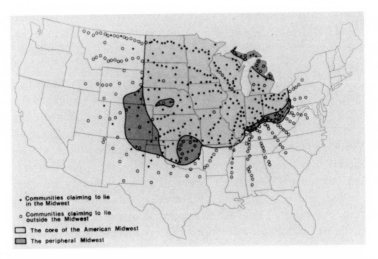

Map 5.1. The Cultural Middle West, Circa 1958. Redrawn from Joseph Brownell, "The Cultural Midwest," *Journal of Geography* 59 (1960): 82–83. The redrawn version is reprinted by permission from John F. Rooney, Jr., Wilbur Zelinsky, and Dean R. Louder, eds., *This Remarkable Continent: An Atlas of United States and Canadian Society and Cultures* (College Station: Texas A & M University Press, 1982), p. 20.

In the 1980 survey of college students, in order to provide an update on regional perception, I collected 1,933 cognitive maps of the Middle West that were suitable for analysis. As was the case with the image question, I focused on respondents who were most likely to represent the views of their regions—those who were attending college in the same state they called home. Respondents from foreign countries were excluded, as were American students who had lived in several different states. With the aid of a transparent overlay of dots that were regularly spaced at centimeter intervals (approximately 100 miles at the map's scale), I counted dots inside a respondent's boundary and, from the totals, created composite isoline maps for each state that I sampled and for the thirty-two-state total (see map 5.2). Shading denotes areas that were marked as part of the Middle West region by more than 70 percent of the respondents. A second summary map was cre-

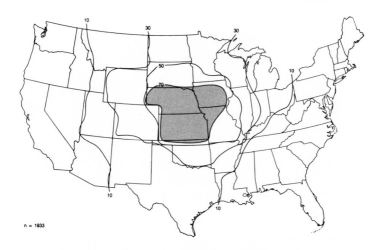

Map 5.2. A Composite View of the Middle West, 1980. The view is compiled from cognitive maps drawn by college students from thirty-two states. Isolines here and on maps 5.4 through 5.10 indicate percentages of respondents who marked an area as part of the Middle West region.

ated by calculating for each state that I sampled the percentage of local respondents who included various sections of their state within their Middle West boundary (see map 5.3).

The summary maps clearly suggest that a major change has occurred in the popular delimitation of Middle West since the late 1950s. If these maps can be considered to reflect general opinion, the vernacular Middle West of 1980 was not coincident with the accepted twelve-state version of scholars and journalists. Chicago, the often-hailed "capital" of the region during the 1910s, is outside the 50 percent isoline. The vernacular region has indeed shifted westward, it seems, with Wyoming and Arkansas having as many "Middle West" adherents as Ohio. Omaha and Lincoln, Nebraska, lie near the heart of the region.

An examination of state-level maps reveals three generalizations about the popular view of the Middle West. Respondents from eight states (Illinois, Iowa, Kansas, Missouri, Nebraska,

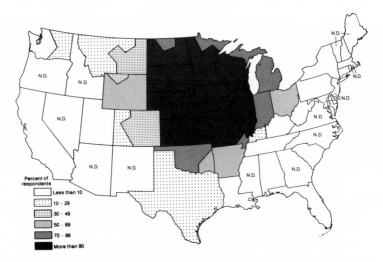

Map 5.3. Each State's View of Itself as Part of the Middle West, 1980. The shadings for each state indicate the percentage of local respondents who included various sections of their state within their Middle West boundary.

North Dakota, South Dakota, and Wisconsin) saw themselves at the center of the Middle West (see maps 5.3, 5.4, and 5.5). Minnesotans had a similar pattern, with their regional core located just outside the state in northwestern Iowa. People from the periphery of the country shared a second view of the region. For Northeasterners, Southerners, and Westerners alike, the Middle West was focused on the central plains, usually in south-central Nebraska (see maps 5.6, 5.7, and 5.8). Maps generated in the nine states adjacent to the traditional Middle West follow the same pattern.

Because the views of the Middle West from the nation's periphery reinforce those from residents of the Great Plains, the two groups together create the dominant image represented on the composite map (see map 5.2). One group deviates markedly from this norm: residents of the five states of the Old Northwest, especially Indiana, Michigan, and Ohio. People from these states appear to be ambivalent about the label Middle West. A majority

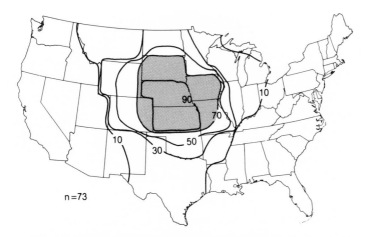

Map 5.4. The Middle West as Seen from Nebraska

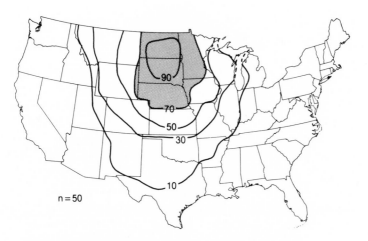

Map 5.5. The Middle West as Seen from North Dakota

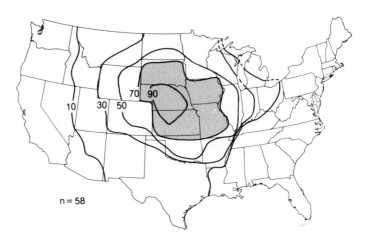

Map 5.6. The Middle West as Seen from New York

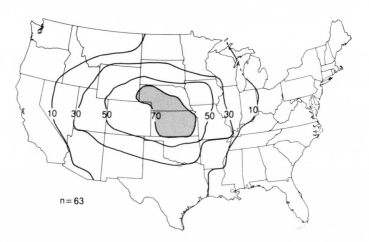

Map 5.7. The Middle West as Seen from Alabama

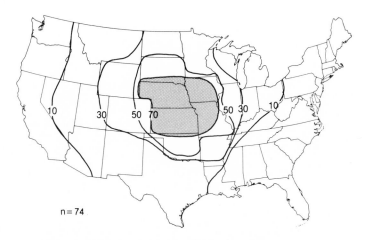

Map 5.8. The Middle West as Seen from California

of respondents there included their states within the Middle West region, but they accorded equal or greater Middle West status to states farther west. Residents of Indiana and Michigan indicated that the core of the region lay several hundred miles beyond their western borders; Ohioans displaced the core about five hundred miles (see maps 5.9 and 5.10).

Uncertainty about the label Middle West in the Old Northwest is indicated also by the extent of the tract that is agreed upon as Middle Western. Whereas the isoline of 90 percent agreement encompassed an area equivalent to two or more states for peoples from the plains and upper Mississippi Valley, this zone shrank to about one state for Michigan residents and to a small section of western Illinois for the Indianans who were questioned. Uncertainty reached a peak for Ohioans, as the 90 percent isoline disappeared. One might expect that increasingly ambiguous identifications of the location of the Middle West would continue eastward beyond Ohio, but this is not the case. Pennsylvanians and West Virginians who were sampled never saw themselves as even marginally Middle Westerners. For them, that region clearly lay beyond the Mississippi.

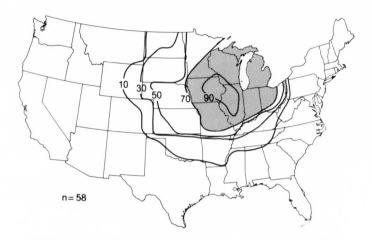

Map 5.9. The Middle West as Seen from Michigan

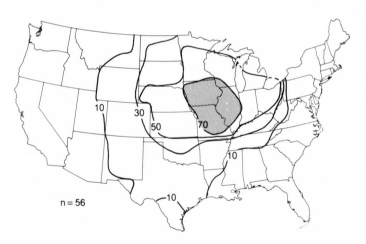

Map 5.10. The Middle West as Seen from Ohio

RECONCILING IMAGE WITH REALITY

My survey of locations and images that are associated with the label Middle West has produced two major questions for regional scholars. Why are Nebraska and Kansas seen as the region's core, a westward displacement from the traditional delimitation made by academicians and journalists? Why do rural, especially pastoral, descriptions continue to dominate the perceived characteristics of this increasingly urbanized part of the country? If the first question were asked in isolation, one might attribute at least part of the focus on the central plains to a tendency for respondents to questionnaires to place any region that contains the word "middle" in its name near the central portion of the map. Doubtless this situation has occurred to some extent, despite the higher-than-average level of education for the population that was sampled. In a historical context, however, the regional images that I found provide the most satisfactory interpretation of the patterns of the cognitive maps, while, in turn, the map patterns help to explain the heretofore puzzling contrast between rural image and the more complex reality of life in the twelve traditional Middle-western states.

Much of this book has been a documentation of the close tie between Middle-western identity and pastoralism. In order to understand the modern Middle West, however, one must recognize that pastoralism is also central to the self-image of the United States as a whole.[27] Many of the country's most cherished values, including self-reliance, democracy, and moral decency, have been said to have derived largely from rural, egalitarian society. The twelve-state Middle West served as the focus of this belief system at least up to 1950, a point that is clearly illustrated by the region's dominance of locales for novels about farm life.[28]

Given the power and persistence of pastoralism, it would seem difficult for any group of Americans — be they Westerners, Southerners, or whatever — now to deny its continued existence. Even residents of the industrialized Old Northwest might be expected to retain the idea about their home. Pastoralism, in the words of many observers, was what had made the region the "most American part of America."[29]

I have argued that pastoral imagery has been associated with the label Middle West since it was coined in the 1880s. When the regional term expanded from its original association with the central plains states to include the Old Northwest Territory in about 1910, pastoral associations became an integral part of the cultural definition of the Middle West. Middle Westerners and other Americans soon faced a major dilemma about image, however, as urbanization and industrialization brought profound changes to the economic and social life of the Great Lakes and Ohio Valley areas. As I indicated earlier, there were two choices: either modify the rural image of the Middle West to conform to the new reality of the area, or shift the regional core westward to the Great Plains, where rural society still prevailed. Cognitive maps and economic, population, and cultural associations for the Middle West suggest that Americans elected the latter course. An independent measure of regional location — a map of businesses and organizations that use variations of Middle West as part of their names — adds credence to this conviction (see map 5.11).

Data for studying the details of the westward movement of the label Middle West are not abundant, but an outline of the general process is possible. The 1950s is a pivotal period. Articles glorifying the industrial prosperity of the Great Lakes and Ohio Valley region were commonplace at that time; many of them were written in anticipation of the completion of the St. Lawrence Seaway.[30] Ostensibly, events would seem to encourage new labeling, but a westward shift of the term Middle West was inhibited by a series of dry years in the Great Plains. Pastoral America could not be focused there so long as "a new Dust Bowl" was feared.[31] A major drought persisted in the plains from 1953 through 1957 and returned again to its northern portion in 1961, so it was probably not until the mid 1960s that the situation was right for relocating the Middle West perceptually.[32]

Americans undoubtedly vary in the rate and degree of acceptance they accord a Middle West centered on the Great Plains. The concept is natural for plains residents for historical reasons. Northeasterners, Southerners, and Westerners, who lack direct contact

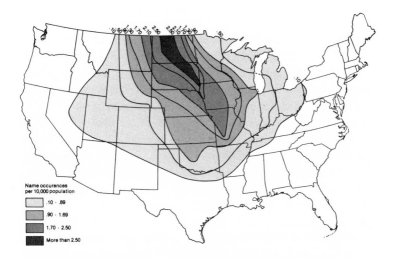

Map 5.11. The Use of "Midwest(ern)" and "Middle West(ern)" in the Names of Businesses and Organizations, 1977–79. Isolines indicate the ratio of white-page entries in telephone directories to estimated SMSA populations for 1976. All SMSAs were included, plus selected other cities between 10,000 and 50,000 in population.

with the region, arguably have a vague and flexible conception of it. They are the ones who are most likely to shuffle locations mentally so as to avoid a juxtaposition of pastoral image with urban-industrial reality. The convenient vagueness of the very words Middle West probably have aided in the mental transition. In contrast, people from the Old Northwest have faced a wrenching dilemma. They have been Middle Westerners for three-quarters of a century; they have taken pride in and have derived strength from the region's vigorous yeoman image. The image is an important part of their self-identity. Still, Middle West could not have been a totally comfortable label, especially after World War II. Not only was the image increasingly removed from reality, its yeoman-farmer focus was becoming less heroic as characteristics of old age replaced those of young adults. Evidence from my sur-

vey suggests that residents of the Old Northwest had not come
to any clear-cut decision by 1980. They shifted the center of the
Middle West region westward from themselves and gave some attention to the industrial face of "their" Middle West, but the old
association and image apparently remained powerful for them.
They still generally called themselves Middle Westerners and saw
that region as being dominated by an agricultural society.

A more precise look at the dynamics of regional affiliation in
the Old Northwest and the nation in general is possible with information collected in 1979 and 1980 by Cobra Communications,
a major manufacturer of citizen-band radios. Among other questions on their warranty cards, Cobra asked its customers to state
their age and to select one of four regional affiliations. Plotted
regional data from 11,689 of these cards generated the familiar
twelve-state Middle West, but with some interesting transition
zones (see map 5.12).[33] A degree of Middle-western affiliation extended beyond the standard borders to the west and the south.
The patterns in Ohio and Michigan, in contrast, indicate an en-
croachment of Eastern affiliation into traditionally Middle-western
territory. This change in Ohio and Michigan should accelerate in
the future, for the people in the transition zone there who labeled
themselves Easterners were significantly younger than those who
selected the label Middle West (see table 5.5).

Much has been written about America's persistent labeling of
the West in terms of youth.[34] Some have argued that this association has impeded the development there of a rational policy for
the use of resources and even that it has retarded the development
of an authentic Western literature.[35]A parallel situation has occurred with the Middle West and its image of an aging yeoman
farmer. It is a positive, yet not totally positive, symbol. Although
it fits many small towns and even works as a generalization for
the plains states, an identity crisis of sorts must be happening in
the Old Northwest. There, image and reality have been out of
synchronization since at least 1910. That place was already industrial when the yeoman-associated label was being adopted.
Yeoman imagery was so complimentary and powerful, however,

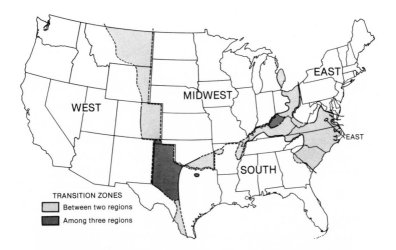

Map 5.12. The East, the West, the South, and the Midwest as Defined by Buyers of Cobra Radios, 1979/80. Shading indicates transitional zones between regions. Dashed lines indicate uncertain boundary locations. Reprinted by permission from James R. Shortridge, "Changing Usage of Four American Regional Labels," *Annals of the Association of American Geographers* 77 (1987): 328.

that industrialization was not widely recognized during the years when it could have been portrayed gloriously.[36] By 1981, when Joel Garreau dubbed the region "the foundry," industrial glamour had disappeared in a wave of unemployment and disillusionment.[37] Perhaps the persistent pastoral imagery was even a factor in delaying adequate responses to these problems.

"Foundry" clearly is an unwanted label for the Old Northwest states today, and "Middle West" is an inadequate one. This is a region in need of a name. The ongoing expansion of the word East into central Michigan and Ohio is one response to this dilemma, but that term may not be appropriate for the mixed industrial and agricultural economies of the remainder of this place. "Mideast," a label that has no historical connections with the term Middle West, may be a candidate, but its viability was hurt

Table 5.5. Association of Regional Allegiance and Age in the
Ohio-Michigan Transitional Zone

Age	East Allegiance		Midwest Allegiance	
	Number	Percentage	Number	Percentage
Under 18	4	1.1	4	0.6
18–24	57	15.6[a]	74	11.5[a]
25–34	89	24.4[a]	115	17.9[a]
35–49	111	30.4	193	30.1
50–64	94	25.8[a]	199	31.0[a]
65 and over	10	2.7[a]	56	8.7[a]
Total	365		641	

[a] Sample proportions are significantly different from one another at the 0.05 level.

in 1985 when it was dropped as a regional label by the highly
visible National Collegiate Athletic Association. Groups in Cleveland are promoting the term "North Coast," but "Great Lakes" is
perhaps the most appealing alternative on the current scene. It
is an accurate description of the region, it is already used as a
state symbol by Michigan, and it is a good advertisement for
what has always been an important natural resource.

6
The Regionalization
of Middle-western Culture

In the previous chapters the Middle West has been examined from a relatively broad perspective. Here I shift the scale and focus to popular literature written at the state level. The idea is to see how local experts depict the relationship between their states and the larger region. Interpretations of Minnesota, for example, should reveal whether or not that state is seen as homogeneous culturally and the extent to which its sections match the general social definitions of the Middle West that are found in other sources. It should also be revealing to see how Minnesota writers choose to use the label Middle West and to analyze whether they place the state at the center or at the periphery of the larger region.

This state-by-state survey of popular literature, in conjunction with the self-identification information reported on map 5.12, reveals three levels of intensity for Middle-western affiliation. The zone of strongest regional feeling is focused on Iowa and, to a lesser extent, neighboring Illinois. These states are the self-proclaimed heart of the Middle West. From them, this heartland extends outward to encompass parts of ten states (see map 6.1). Boundaries for this area come from the state literature, where they are expressed clearly and consistently. South Dakota writers, for example, repeatedly stress the distinction between the farming world east of the Missouri River and the harsher, less forgiving land "West River." Hoosiers speak of a different, a Southern, world south of the old National Road.

Using the terminology of geographer Donald W. Meinig, Iowa and adjacent areas of strong and essentially defining Middle-western traits and feelings may be said to constitute the region's

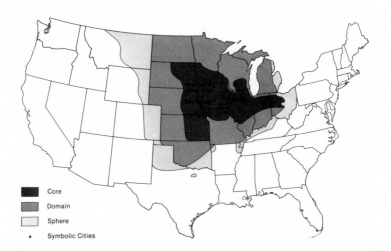

Map 6.1. The Middle West Culture Region in the 1980s. The core boundary is based principally on state-level popular literature; the domain and sphere delimitation is based on self-identification data discussed by me in "Changing Usage of Four American Regional Labels," *Annals of the Association of American Geographers* 77 (1987): 325–36.

culture "core." Surrounding the core are two zones of lesser affiliation with things Middle Western. A "domain," immediately outside the core, identifies places where the culture is "dominant but with markedly less intensity and complexity of development than in the core . . . and where regional peculiarities are clearly evident."[1] The outer boundaries of the domain are defined here by the limit of nearly universal self-identification with the region according to a 1980 survey.[2] Beyond the domain is the "sphere," a zone of transition in which the culture "is represented only by certain of its elements or where its peoples reside as minorities among those of a different culture."[3] The outer boundary here is where Middle-western self-identity in 1980 fell below one-third of the respondents.

I begin this chapter with a brief look at the Iowa-Illinois focus and then concentrate on the nature of the domain and sphere areas surrounding the cultural core. The emphasis is not so much on these borderlands in their own right as on their general relationship to the core. The liberal political tradition of Michigan, Minnesota, and Wisconsin is discussed, for example, as a cultural trait that both helps to define these states and separates them from the Middle West mainstream. This liberal tradition can be traced in large part to clashes between a farming society in the southern parts of these states and lumbering and mining interests in the north. To take a different example, the shared imagery of self-reliance and harmony with nature between yeoman farmers and the ranchers of the western-plains states is discussed from the perspective that this similarity was a factor in the perceptual shift of the label Middle West to the west after 1960.

THE HEART OF THE MIDDLE WEST

Ever since Iowans were first called Middle Westerners around 1900, writers have agreed that the state epitomized the region's values.[4] Iowa's land and climate rank with the best in the world for agriculture, and as is not true in any other Middle-western state, these physical advantages extend over virtually the entire state. The ease with which farmers became prosperous in Iowa quickly became legendary in the nineteenth century, and one authority even claimed that agricultural success created so much competition for labor that manufacturing was being inhibited.[5] Uniformly rich land also helped to foster an egalitarian society, another hallmark of Iowa and the Middle West, but in this achievement a perceived homogeneity of immigrants was thought to be of at least equal importance. The Old Northwest Territory had been occupied by a mix of Northerners and Southerners, or so the argument went, both peoples who were hale but not accustomed to prairie life. Iowa, in contrast, received the fully blended products from this earlier Northwest, so mingled as to produce "not a mosaic but an emulsion."[6]

With the combination of a prosperous agriculture, a relatively homogeneous population, and an absence of major cities, Iowans virtually defined yeoman society. They were a practical people in a practical land — conservative, moral, solid. Political extremism, which emerged in the more arid lands to the west and in the more mixed economies and societies to the north and east, touched Iowa only slightly.[7] One looks nearly in vain to find Iowa portrayed in other than "sensible" terms. Its rural image stays intact right up to the present time, and its popular literature mirrors the changing perceptions of that image, which was discussed in previous chapters.

The only deviations from standard Middle-western interpretations in and about Iowa are ones toward making the state the epitome of this culture: the richest farmers in the world, the nation's highest rate of literacy, a large percentage of native-born residents.[8] Direct claims that Iowa is the heart of the Middle West are frequent too; they have occurred in every decade of this century.[9] Interpretations that the Iowa political caucuses are representative of the entire region are only the most recent example.[10] Finally, if one considers Middle-western symbols, it is striking how many come from Iowa. Grant Wood's painting *Stone City, Iowa*, captures the essence of the verdant but highly disciplined rural landscape of the region. Meredith Willson's rosy recollections of Mason City (i.e., River City) in *The Music Man* have crystallized the national view of the region at the turn of the century. Personal symbols are more varied. "Ding" Darling's political cartoons of big, bluff, friendly farmers originated in Des Moines but represented a region; Wood's figures in *American Gothic* epitomize rural stoicism; and West Branch's Herbert Hoover, even when he was caught in the chaos of economic depression, was a symbol of conservative moral leadership. M*A*S*H's "Radar" O'Reilly, from Ottumwa, brings Middle-western wholesomeness and naïveté down to the present.[11]

Iowa's position as the standard by which Middle-westernness is measured, is challenged in the popular literature only by Illinois. The Illinois claim, however, operates for the most part on another scale. Many writers recognize Illinois as a core, or symbolic place, but the reference is usually to the United States as a whole, not just to the Middle West.[12] The distinction is impor-

Stone City, Iowa (1930), by Grant Wood. Reprinted by permission from the Joslyn Art Museum, Omaha, Nebraska.

tant. Illinois is much less homogeneous than Iowa, whether the quality considered is physical, economic, or cultural. The original flavor of Illinois was strongly Southern; Illinois has traditions in coal and lead mining; and most importantly, it has boisterous, ethnically diverse Chicago. These traits make Illinois more typical of the United States than is Iowa, but less typical of the Middle West, especially the perceived Middle West.

Abraham Lincoln is the most important symbolic asset of Illinois. A continual stream of literature links the man with, in turn, Illinois, the Middle West, and the United States. Each term is presented as a microcosm of the one following it up the scale of size, and Lincoln's Southern origins are quietly ignored.[13] Chicago, unlike Lincoln, has been a mixed blessing for those who have championed Illinois' leadership of the Middle West. Its positive role peaked during the 1910s, when Carl Sandburg was praising the city's vitality and when its links with the surrounding

Three Versions of Uncle John Iowa by "Ding" Darling. Reprinted by permission from David L. Lendt's *Ding: The Life of Jay Norwood Darling* © 1979 by Iowa State University Press, Ames, Iowa 50010 (between pages 54 and 55).

American Gothic (1930), by Grant Wood. Friends of American Art Collection, 1930, 1934. Reprinted by permission from the Art Institute of Chicago © 1988.

countryside were obvious. More recent assessments of Illinois tend to emphasize the differences between the city and "downstate"; there are occasional threats that one of them will secede from the other.[14] Chicago remains a real, working place and, in this sense, matches the overall image of the Middle West, but in most other ways, Des Moines has been seen as a more convincing choice for a modern-day Middle-western "capital." The smaller size of Des Moines is seen as appropriate for a representative of a farming region; and its economy, politics, and ethnic composition all reflect that region.

The consensus in popular literature that claims Iowa as the Middle-western heartland contrasts with the results of the 1980 survey on regional location that I reported in chapter 5 (see map 5.2). To be sure, Iowa was prominent in that survey, but not to the degree that Kansas and Nebraska were. The notion that collegiate perceptions may forecast the future location of the heartland, and that popular literature represents older perceptions is possible but is not supported. It is difficult to explain why a migration of the core of Middle-western images from Iowa to Nebraska would occur, since Iowa continues to epitomize both rural prosperity and other perceived regional traits better than does any state in the Great Plains. I suspect that the plains delimitation may simply represent an overreaction to the perception that Chicago and other major industrial cities were antithetical to definitions of the Middle West. From this perspective, Iowa, although it is thoroughly Middle Western, is nevertheless a relatively small "peninsula" in this culture; the state is being threatened by industrial Illinois to the east and is being restricted by recreational woodlands to the north and by Missouri's "Little Dixie" heritage to the south. Iowa would thus be joined with other rural states to the west to produce a region large enough to merit the name Middle West. The unresolved issue is whether the collegians, if they had been given the choice, would have selected Nebraska or Iowa as the better personification of the label.

THE EASTERN FRINGE

The ongoing dissociation process between Ohio and the label Middle West, as discussed in the preceding chapter, seems straightforward and logical. Eastern associations simply match the reality of life in parts of Ohio better than do Middle-western ones. The dissociation is so logical, in fact, that the more interesting question becomes why people from this borderland place initially accepted and then long sustained an allegiance to a label that was coined to fit conditions in remote Kansas.

In chapter 3, I attempted to explain the expansion of Middle-western allegiance in general terms, principally via the strong national appeal of pastoral and young-adult imagery, coupled with the need for a regional label to replace both the "Old" and the "New" Northwests. This rationale applied in Ohio to be sure, but ostensibly not to the degree that it did in the eleven other traditionally Middle-western states. Ohio was older than the others, for one thing; it achieved statehood in 1803, thirteen years before Indiana, the next state in the group, and about sixty years before Kansas and Nebraska. Ohio was thus a century old when it adopted its new regional label, a middle-aged place, perhaps, trying to recapture some youthful vitality.

In terms of cultural homogeneity, another asserted hallmark of Middle-western identity, Ohio also was an anomaly among the twelve states. Its rural population was sharply divided into Northern and Southern contingents, with each cultural group having immigrated to Ohio directly from its Atlantic hearth and each being highly segregated spatially. New Englanders clustered in Connecticut's Western Reserve north of 41 degrees latitude, whereas Southern migrants focused on the Virginia Military District in the southwest.[15] Although states to the west of Ohio also possessed a north-south mix of settlers, these groups were more acculturated to plains life than they had been in Ohio, and they were less segregated.

By 1899, about when the label Middle West first came to be applied to Ohio, the rural split in the state was still so sharp that one observer "perceived that while, geographically, the Ohio River skirts the southern border of the Buckeye State, it runs, sociologically, historically, and politically, across the middle of Ohio."[16] Moreover, these differences were only part of the heterogeneity. Industrialization had become widespread, attracting to the cities so many new peoples and new ideas that Ohio was again divided. According to one blunt description, urban Ohio was "preponderantly foreign, wet, unionized and pagan, whereas its rural communities are preponderantly Nordic, dry, anti-labor and Fundamentalist."[17]

How could heterogeneous, middle-aged Ohio accept the label of Middle West without a recorded incident of protest? The key to this query is self-perception. Two symbolic themes beyond the obvious pastoral and young-adult ones are relevant; one was stressed before 1900, the other afterward. The first involves the Northwest Ordinance, the 1787 document that established a territorial government for the land north and west of the Ohio River. In the popular literature from the nineteenth century, writers repeatedly stress the nobility of this act and how it for the first time codified and implemented rules for a rural egalitarian society. "This ordinance will justify any extent of panegyric which language can frame," said one commentator, for "so far as we know, it is the first written form of government, in which the three great principles of entire religious freedom, an obligation to encourage schools, and an absolute prohibition of slavery, were ever incorporated together."[18]

The similarities between the cultural traits that have been attributed to the Northwest Ordinance and those that were later associated with the label Middle West are striking. They are, in fact, the two most complete regional embodiments of the pastoral dream to occur in the United States. Whereas the ordinance codified some of the basic beliefs, Middle West provided a regional term nebulous enough to allow the maximum diffusion of the idea. Ohio's ready acceptance of the label Middle West circa 1900 is not mysterious when viewed from this perspective. Middle West was a convenient name whose meaning echoed all that Ohioans had traditionally valued.

The Northwest Ordinance unified Ohio and set the state apart from its neighbors to the south. Despite their common origins in Virginia, for example, southern Ohioans saw themselves as fundamentally different from Kentuckians, sharing instead a special destiny with the Yankees of the Western Reserve. They were a people with the potential for utopia. One outgrowth of this thinking was that heterogeneous Ohio was wrongly, but usefully, assumed to possess "a solid and uniform population."[19] Moreover, since Kentucky and West Virginia were not part of the ordinance, they were largely excluded from the image that eventually would be labeled Middle West. This incipient division was exacerbated in midcentury by self-righteous rhetoric that came from the abolitionist movement, especially because the location of Uncle Tom's Cabin was in Kentucky. Kentucky, even though it had not joined the Confederacy, could never be part of the Middle West; Ohio, even with its numerous factual discrepancies from the image, could not avoid the label.

The symbolic power associated with the Northwest Ordinance lasted until the latter part of the nineteenth century, at which time much of the imagery was subconsciously incorporated into the new concept of Middle West. By this time, the ideal of a unified, hybrid rural society in Ohio had apparently come to fruition, at least in people's minds, for after 1900 one finds few references to the Yankee-Southerner division that had been common before. Writers instead stressed that Ohio was the most "representative" of states, a harmonious mixing ground in which national thinking was able to triumph over narrow regional concerns. Several lines of evidence were commonly advanced to support these assertions: the near balances of rural and urban populations and of Republican and Democratic strength; the dominance of the relatively neutral Methodist church, instead of the Yankee's Congregational or the Southerner's Baptist denominations; and proximity to the nation's center of population.[20] These factors all reinforced Middle-western associations as they existed in about 1910, but some of them became less useful as the urban overtones in the regional definition were gradually pruned away during the 1920s.

After 1920, Ohioans might well have exchanged their label of Middle West for that of the East, had they not noticed and become obsessed with their ability to produce United States presidents. The facts on this matter are astounding, and it is little wonder that the phenomenon became a central part of Ohio's self-image. In 1840, William Henry Harrison was the first president from the state, but beginning in 1868, Ohio's domination over the nation's highest office became nearly complete. Native sons Ulysses S. Grant, Rutherford B. Hayes, and James A. Garfield held the post in consecutive terms and, after Grover Cleveland of New York, Benjamin Harrison and William McKinley continued the trend. Writers began to ponder the significance of all this about 1900, and when William Howard Taft and Warren G. Harding were elected, the pondering became accepted doctrine.

The "presidential" litany asserted that Ohioans incorporated the best of the opposite temperaments of Puritan and Cavalier: morality and concern for education from the former, a "taste for oratory and his liking for the public forum" from the latter.[21] Northerners and Southerners alike could therefore trust a candidate from Ohio, for they could see elements of themselves in him. Kinship between Ohio and the Western states was asserted next. Ohio was the "mother" in this arrangement, having "contributed more of her native-born children to the building of other communities than any other State of the forty-five except New York, and, in proportion to population, her contribution has been far greater than New York's."[22] Ohioans thus had ties with both the East and the West, as well as with the North and the South, and therefore could steer a political course midway between Eastern conservatism and Western radicalness. The state was more truly the nation's keystone at this time than was Pennsylvania; people from Ohio could best speak for the country as a whole.[23]

Through constant repetition of the presidential theme and its attendant imagery after 1900, Ohio assumed a role similar to that of Illinois. Each state was a microcosm of the country. I believe that the allegiance of Ohioans to the label Middle West rested heavily on this role of typicalness, for the state was deficient in other, more rural, regional associations. If Ohio were to represent the country as a whole, it would be natural for it to be part of the most standard of American regions. At the least this logic explains the delayed associations of the state with the East, a place that no one considered typical.

Ohio has maintained its mantle of representativeness down to the present time, as reflected both in the ascendency of urban over rural issues and in the more recent economic crises that involve American heavy industry and the decline in urban health. The increasing self-adoption of an Eastern identification within the state therefore reflects more on the failure of the label Middle West to symbolize American normalcy than on the failure of the label Ohio to do so.

THE NORTHERN FRINGE

A well-defined physical, economic, and cultural line passes about midway through the states of Michigan, Wisconsin, and Minnesota, separating a traditionally agricultural southern sector from a northland of lumber mills, mines, and more recently, tourism. For many writers this line forms the Middle West's northern border. Historian Bruce Catton, for example, has said that his home country in northern Michigan "never grew up," having passed "from lusty adolescence to an uneasy senility" as the lumber boom came and departed. In contrast, southern Michigan was "part of the great middle west, like Ohio and Indiana, gently rolling, with good soil underfoot."[24]

Interaction and conflict between the northern and southern worlds have been important in creating the character of these three states. The product is a modified version of Middle West, the distinctiveness of which its residents recognize. Of the states that have traditionally been grouped as the Middle West, these three (along with Ohio in recent years) find the label most uncomfortable. No real alternative name exists, but Minnesota clung to "Northwest" into the 1930s, and writers elsewhere went to lengths to avoid using any regional term. Since the 1950s, "Upper Middle West" has emerged as a label of choice, a compromise that nicely reflects the region's somewhat hesitant Middle-western status.[25]

The northern parts of Michigan, Wisconsin, and Minnesota share a similar environmental heritage. The ancient rocks and shallow soils of the Canadian Shield extend into each state, and relatively recent glaciation has left many adjacent areas sandy and/or poorly drained. These same lands generally have a growing season that is too short for corn. The earliest nineteenth-century commentators were aware of this environment's special qualities, and after several generations of settlement, its border became widely recognized. Bay City, on Saginaw Bay, marks the eastern terminus. The line passes just north of the Grand River, intercepts Lake Michigan at Muskegon and Manitowoc, and then follows the Fox River southwest to Portage, Wisconsin. Some observers have said that the line continues west from Portage along the Wisconsin River to the Mississippi, but others opt for a northwesterly tack, which is marked by a series of waterfalls at the southern edge of the shield region. Minnesota's extension of this boundary separates timberland from an "agricultural crescent" along a line near the Minnesota River valley and has an arm into the Red River plains.[26]

Although different economies have always existed on each side of this border, the original character of the three states was set in their southern sectors. Early immigrants came largely from New England and New York, and commentators universally praised the "amended and perfected" Yankee rural society that emerged.[27] Soils were good, democratic institutions were in place, and the Great Lakes and the Erie Canal promised good access to markets. The vanguard from New England was soon supplemented by other settlers, particularly Germans and Scandinavians, but these latter peoples were perceived to reinforce the Yankee ideals, rather than to redirect them. The admixture tended "to the maintenance of a stock drawn originally from almost the same sources"; it shared attitudes toward democracy, education, and morality.[28] It was a rural, egalitarian society that was Middle Western in everything but name.

The northern states first began to deviate from the mainstream agrarian society when they became the nation's primary lumber center. This change came to Michigan in the 1840s and to Wisconsin and Minnesota thirty and forty years later, respectively. Society within the states was not wholly transformed, but it was modified in significant ways. Contemporary observers particularly stressed the diversity that lumbering added to the economy. This idea of diversity has come to be a regional hallmark. Even when lumbering declined, diversity and an accompanying optimistic outlook were maintained, first by large-scale iron mining and then by tourism.

Lumbering and mining were highly visible and widely publicized industries during their heydays. In addition to diversifying the economy, they established an image and a reality of industrialization for the three states, an image that set them apart from their neighbors to the south. Because of this identification, when Detroit, Milwaukee, and other cities in the agricultural southern sector later began to develop into major industrial centers, their industrial character was not overwhelmed by rural symbolism as it was elsewhere. Cities, lumbering, and mining reinforced one another. Their presence in the three states provided an air of sophistication and guarded against the "hick" and "victim" stereotypes that were sometimes associated with the Middle West in general.

The northern-fringe states stand apart from the Middle-western core not only in economic structure and image but in politics as well. One student has called the local tradition "issue-oriented," another has called it "moralistic," but the popular term during the first third of this century was "progressive."[29] All three labels refer to a liberal, honest system of government, one in which social reform is considered to be as important as economic regulation. Taxes are high, but so is the level of the government's expenditure for education, health, transportation, and environmental protection. Wisconsin has the deepest association with this system, but it is strong also in the other two states, as well as in North Dakota.

Opinions on the origin of the progressive tradition vary. Contemporary observers usually attributed it simply to the Yankee-German ethnic mix in Wisconsin, together with the magnetic leadership of Robert La Follette. Modern students, however, see its roots as geographic, a clash between the lumber/railroad/mining interests of the north and the rest of the state.[30] Wisconsin was a one-party Republican state throughout the nineteenth century, but beginning in the 1870s, the control of this party passed from farming peoples into the hands of northern businessmen. "One of the United States Senatorships was assigned to the lumber interests, the other to the railroads"; the result was a travesty of New England democratic traditions.[31] Robert La Follette achieved the stature of "a lesser Lincoln" by mobilizing opposition to this hegemony and by creating what came to be known as the "Wisconsin idea" of government and then, more generally, as progressivism.[32] When La Follette was elected governor in 1900, his reforms focused on the big monopolies — the regulation of railroads and utilities — and a primary-election law, so that bosses could not pick candidates. Then came an impressive series of reforms that affected the civil service, business corruption, workman's compensation, child labor, and education. La Follette's allies included both the liberal community within the University of Wisconsin and the "forty-eight Germans" (refugees from a liberal reform movement overseas), but it took a common enemy in the North to mold the new coalition.[33] Iowa, with its professed homogeneity, avoided the abuses of democracy but was never spurred toward liberal reform.

Minnesota, Michigan, and North Dakota came to adopt many of Wisconsin's initiatives in government, but at a slower pace. No La Follette emerged to symbolize the movement, and corruption in their northlands was not so blatant. North Dakota was the second state to become radical. Its Norwegian settlers, accustomed to a more socialistic system than they found in America, responded strongly to feelings of "absentee control and extortion" by the "grain lords" who controlled the transportation, storage, and grading of their wheat crops.[34] Their political vehicle, the Non-Partisan League, assumed power in 1916, after a ten-year period of incubation, and established a state-owned system of grain elevators, banks, and hail insurance, as well as other measures based on the Wisconsin model. Minnesota's large Scandinavian population empathized with the North Dakota movement.

The Scandinavians were initially successful in securing a measure of progressive legislation in their state through the Republican party establishment, but when Minnesota's governor publicly denounced the Non-Partisan League in 1918, a farmer revolt led to the formation of the Farmer-Labor party as a new and more committed vehicle for progressivism.[35]

Michigan, the last of the northern-fringe states to embrace issue-oriented politics, did so in the 1930s. Detroit was the catalyst. The United Auto Workers (UAW) there was the elite among American labor groups; it was also the unchallenged force in Michigan's Democratic party. Under the leadership of Walter P. Reuther, the UAW was able to transcend ordinary wage issues and to champion a better general society. In so doing, it gained the support of liberal professional and business people and created a rare coalition of liberals and labor. Six consecutive gubernatorial terms for G. Mennen Williams, which began in 1948, not only entrenched this coalition but also encouraged the rival Republicans to move toward a similar progressive stance.[36]

Although the northern-fringe states share several important aspects of deviation from the Iowa Middle-western model, each place is also distinctive. Michigan's uniqueness lies in the dominance of its industrial image and, by contrast, in its relatively weak agricultural sector. The image began with lumber and mining, but it really established itself in the 1920s when the Model T Ford and automobiles in general captured the collective imagination of Americans. A loss of political clout by rural counties was noted during the 1930s, and by the early 1950s, writers were candidly admitting that Michigan was "not a leading agricultural state."[37] No one seemed to be even slightly upset at this development, however, for Detroit at this time epitomized the new technological might of the nation. Descriptions exuded pride. According to one author, the city "clamors at you, arrogantly, with all the confidence that comes to men who know they are really in charge of things and who don't mind enjoying the feeling. . . . Here is where we are going, make no mistake about it, and the big financial centers down East can say what they like and be hanged. Detroit sets the pace because this is where the muscle

and knowledge are."[38] Michigan's development through 1960 or
so followed a blueprint that would have made any turn-of-the-
century booster of the Middle West proud. Its diverse economy and
gradual ascendancy toward industrial power were their dreams.
That its development seemed to entail a gradual separation of the
state from the name Middle West presented little cause for concern. Residents occasionally proposed new names for their region, such as the Middle North and the Great Lakes State, but
with a self-confidence born of success, they saw themselves for
the most part as beyond regional concerns.[39]

The kinship of Michigan with other northern-fringe states and
with the Middle West in general has eroded considerably since
the 1960s. Mining operations ceased, and the Detroit empire of
heavy industry saw prosperity change to despair almost over-
night. High taxes and high wages, long a source of pride for
the state, were now perceived as a deterrent to growth. The concentration on wheeled vehicles was suddenly seen as short-sighted;
it had let other regions develop electronics and related aspects of
space-age industry. The empire did not collapse, but self-confidence
did suffer, and social problems were revealed. Poorly educated
workers, both black and white, who had been attracted to Detroit from the South by good jobs, came to be a major social problem in a depressed economy.[40] By the mid 1970s the national press
had tagged Michigan, along with Ohio and the western parts of
New York and Pennsylvania, with the "Rustbelt" label, a place of
antiquated factories and ideas that had been by-passed in a rapidly changing industrial world. This new image was a cause for
much soul-searching in Michigan; it seems also to have initiated
an identification of Michiganders with the East. Boston and other
Atlantic-seaboard cities had undergone industrial crises in other
decades and had survived; they became the appropriate models
for Detroit in the 1980s.[41]

Michigan shares many physical and economic traits with Wisconsin, but the images of the two over the past seventy-five years
have diverged markedly. Despite having a lumber-and-mining
past and a city, Milwaukee, that compares favorably with Detroit
on most urban measures, Wisconsin has never assumed the image

of being a major industrial state. Whereas Michigan's popular literature is dominated by Detroit's successes and failures, articles on Wisconsin discuss Milwaukee's activities (other than brewing) only in passing. The explanation for this centers partly on the diversity of Milwaukee's industry, compared to that of Detroit, which has reduced the former's visibility. More importantly, however, the long-established linkage between Wisconsin and the dairy business has stifled the development of other images.

Wisconsin's dairy claims are legitimate. Milk and cheese were noted as major agricultural endeavors as early as 1891, and they grew to dominate the economy in the decade after 1900, following the local invention of the Babcock milk tester.[42] Babcock's device measured the amount of butterfat in milk, and by helping to eliminate fraud in marketing, it encouraged the breeding of quality dairy stock. As a symbol of state pride, the industry soon came to rival beer and La Follette progressivism. Governor Julius Heil inserted "America's Dairyland" on the state's license plates, where it has remained for half a century, and the state's long history of taxing oleomargarine and preventing its coloration serves as an additional indication of local support for this rural image.[43] Wisconsin does not ignore its paper mills, its machine-tool plants, and other urban industries, but commentators discuss these things as aspects of economic diversity, rather than as central issues. Joel Garreau included Milwaukee in his version of the modern American "Rustbelt," but he made Detroit its capital.[44]

The economies of three Upper Middle West states form a continuum of sorts. All are diversified, but the degree of this diversity and, consequently, of long-term economic health increases from Michigan to Wisconsin to Minnesota. Minnesota, like the other two states, saw lumbering come and go, but it avoided over-reliance on heavy industry, which has recently brought despair to Detroit and parts of Wisconsin. Minnesota's mining activities also prospered to a much greater degree and over a longer time than did those in the other two states. As a result, a spirit of optimism has run continuously throughout the state's history.

The popular literature of Minnesota reads almost exactly like the vision of the future that was sketched by nineteenth-century observers of the general Middle-western scene. If Kansas represents the currently perceived Middle West and if Iowa represents the reality of the region, Minnesota is the closest approximation that we have to the regional dream. The base, as always, is a pastoral society. Traits associated with this ideal persist to the present (witness the popularity and believability of Garrison Keillor's stories about Lake Wobegon), but a host of additions to this base not only have ensured prosperity but have prevented a slide into bucolic isolation, such as eventually enveloped the mainstream of the Middle West.[45]

Agriculture dominated the Minnesota economy until the late 1880s, when the lumbering era began. By the time the virgin stands of pine were exhausted in the 1910s, iron mining in the world-famous Mesabi Range had become a major employer. Iron mining, in turn, remained an economic pillar in the north until tourism had established itself.

Minneapolis–St. Paul forms the final link in the chain of prosperity. The Twin Cities, at the head of navigation on the Mississippi River, initially prospered through aspects of the industry that has already been mentioned: Minneapolis as a milling center for grain and logs, St. Paul as a railroad terminal. Lacking easy access to coal and iron ore, they never developed the heavy industry characteristic of cities on the Great Lakes. This cost them a measure of success around midcentury, when Cleveland was booming. According to one commentator, the state's "coat of prosperity" at that time had sleeves that were "shiny and frayed."[46] The decline proved to be only momentary. Local entrepreneurs, because they were not attempting to compete in heavy industry, thus avoided the crisis that hit Michigan and Ohio during the 1970s. Instead, they began early to develop what in 1955 was called "brain industry," or high tech today. Minneapolis-Honeywell and 3M (Minnesota Mining and Manufacturing Company) epitomized the trend: local companies that were taking advantage of the persistent yeoman work ethic, the corruption-free political system, and the respect for education found in the state.[47] One glowing tribute called the package "the efficient Minnesota atmosphere," and all writers have stressed, with justifiable pride, that the industries were created locally, not attracted from elsewhere with lures of low labor costs or similar incentives.[48]

Why should Minnesota alone have achieved what all Middle-western states had envisioned at the turn of the century? Certainly the yeoman traits were universally in place, but only the three Upper Middle West states possessed the natural resources for an early industrial base and subsequently developed the liberal attitudes to encourage further local innovation. When Michigan and Wisconsin fell victim to an overspecialization around 1970, Minnesota emerged into the limelight.

THE SOUTHERN FRINGE

The Ohio River was established as a southern boundary for the region even before the label Middle West had been coined. The Northwest Ordinance and the Civil War were major factors in this, as I discussed previously, and traditional literature from Kentucky is definitely not Middle Western in flavor. Mountain life in the Cumberland Plateau forms one of the state's poles; the distinctive society of "colonels," blacks, and tobacco, found in the Bluegrass Basin, forms the other one. None of the Kentucky postmasters whom Brownell surveyed in the 1950s called their region the Middle West, and the term never appears in the state's popular literature (see map 5.1). Although future change is possible, as hinted by a few Kentucky residents from the Ohio River fringe who identified with the Middle West in a 1980 survey, the Ohio River remains today as an American cultural boundary of the first order (see map 5.12).

West of the Ohio River the absolute southern limit of Middle-western affiliation is approximated by the northern borders of Arkansas and Texas. Again the Civil War is a cause, but differences between the heritages of these two states and the Middle-western mainstream are profound on many measures. Within these states, vague ties to the Middle West exist only in extreme northwest Arkansas, where recently developed retirement communities and the relatively diverse population at the University of Arkansas are probable explanatory agents; in the cosmopolitan Dallas–Fort Worth area; and in the Texas panhandle, where Middle West, South, and West all meet uncertainly (see maps 5.12 and 6.1).[49]

The real transition zone away from Middle-western values and identification occurs in Oklahoma, in Missouri, and in the southern portions of Illinois, Indiana, and Ohio (see map 6.1). All of these places were settled by peoples from the Upland South, yet for various reasons and to varying degrees, each has fallen under the Middle West's cultural umbrella. Of the five states, Illinois and Ohio are the least "Southern" today. This is not to say that certain sections of these two states do not contain Southern characteristics. "Little Egypt," in southern Illinois, is especially famous for this.[50] Southern attitudes are no longer identified with the overall image of the two states, however. Large numbers of more recent non-Southern settlers are partly responsible for the current pattern of identification, along with the powerful mainstream imagery of Illinois's Lincoln and Ohio's presidential identifications, as I discussed earlier.

Missouri and, to a lesser extent, Indiana are less completely Middle-western. Both may be described even today as Southern cultures in Middle-western latitudes. Missourians and Indianans, together with Oklahomans, possess interesting blends of attitudes and values that resist easy classification. Indiana is now always labeled as a Middle-western state, but never the typical one that its central location and agricultural orientation would suggest. Missouri, despite being nearly surrounded by Middle-western states, continues to resist that regional label. It is literally and figuratively a state in the middle. The state's boosters try to make a virtue of its cultural and other diversity, but there are indications of insecurity as well. Oklahoma shares with Missouri the same uncertainty of regional allegiance. Because of its location and early heritage, Oklahoma has historically been called Southern or Southwestern, but Middle West affiliation exists in its wheat-growing north and west.

Although scholars trace a common origin in southeastern Pennsylvania for people who spread westward into Ohio and southwestward into the Upland South, contemporary observers saw these North Midland and South Midland settlers as distinctive when they met on the Middle-western frontier.[51] Both were rural societies, at least initially, and they shared the pastoral traits of independence and self-reliance. The symbol of a vigorous young adult was never applied to the Southern migrants, however. In place of adjectives such as progressive, enterprising, and forceful, one finds such descriptions of Hoosiers (and Missourians) as this:

> Among our careworn and hurried Americans they are a nonchalant and unhurried race. . . . A Hoosier is unimpressible, incurious and incapable of awe. He lives on an inaccessible height of self-respect, where he neither knows nor cares in what sort of estimation he is held by others. His inherent sense of his own superiority gives him perfect self-possession, with no uneasy self-consciousness, no vulgar anxiety about his manners and appearance. But he is not one to perform high achievements or to pursue an object with unflagging obstinacy. . . . The Hoosier is quite unlike the Buckeye of Ohio, who, being of Puritan strain, is bluff and English-looking, and does everything with such vehement relish that his library, fountain, music, temperance crusade, spelling-bee, wake the nation.[52]

Most of the early descriptions of life in Indiana and Missouri were written by people from the northeastern states and must be evaluated accordingly, but the imagery that was established was consistent and enduring. Missourians, for example, were said in 1839 to "have not exhibited the same degree of public spirit and enterprise that is found in some others of the Western states."[53] The state lagged "far in the rear" in appropriations for railroads, roads, and education, and Missourians were said to have a low appreciation of their own resources.[54] Commentators constantly were frustrated by the contrast between the potential for development in the two states, especially in "the mineral region" of the Missouri Ozarks, and the slow rate of economic progress.

How did Southern culture become so deeply implanted in

these two states? The answer for Missouri is straightforward. Kentucky and Tennessee were occupied considerably earlier than was the Northwest Territory and, consequently, were ready to provide emigrants themselves at a relatively early date. Missouri represented a logical destination for these people. It had similar terrain and climate, and most importantly, the Missouri and Mississippi river systems promised good opportunities for transportation and commerce. The legality of slavery in Missouri also was a factor.[55] A Southern population for Indiana is more anomalous, especially since slavery there was prohibited under the Northwest Ordinance. The explanation is largely a matter of physical geography. Sand dunes discouraged the development of ports along Lake Michigan, and extensive swamplands covered the northern half of the state as well as the area inland from Toledo, the state's gateway from Lake Erie. Historian Richard L. Power has documented how Yankees acquired an image for the state of swamps and fevers and how, subsequently, these people routinely passed over Indiana in favor of Illinois. The most striking single piece of evidence is the distribution pattern of Congregational churches, a marker for New England society. Indiana had only 11 such congregations in 1860, whereas Ohio had 140 and the newer states of Illinois, Michigan, and Wisconsin had 140, 69, and 112 respectively.[56]

Indiana eventually attracted settlers for its northern lands, most of whom came from Yankee and North Midland sources, but the Southern dominance had persisted long enough so that it pervaded the state's overall character. "Hoosier," for example, a word that earlier had been applied only to an uncouth, southern Indianan, became a statewide label for natives. Indiana's novelists and poets have focused on Southern aspects of local life too. Edward Eggleston's *The Hoosier Schoolmaster* was tremendously influential in its time, as was the bucolic writing of James Whitcomb Riley and Gene Stratton Porter.[57] Frank McKinney ("Kin") Hubbard's witty, rustic sayings in the *Indianapolis News* made hilly Brown County and its fictitious town of Bloom Center more of a state symbol early in this century than were either steel mills or lush cornfields.[58] One observer said that local literature still had such a great influence in 1955 that it achieved "a dictatorship of sorts" in Indiana life.[59]

The imagery of Southern life in the works of Riley, Hubbard, George Ade, and others, though it was not what a progressive chamber of commerce might desire, had many positive attributes. A more negative side of Indiana's heritage surfaced in the 1920s when the Ku Klux Klan briefly gained control of the state government. Commentators saw the situation not so much as an anti-black or anti-Jewish statement (though these elements were there) as a regional issue. Southern Indiana had stagnated economically while the north had prospered, first with a natural-gas boom around Muncie and then, somewhat later, with steel mills at Gary. Rural Indiana feared for its future, and the Klan was there to meld this fear together with sentiment against alcohol, the Democratic party, and Catholicism. The results were a narrow, conservative mind set and a temporary halt to the Indiana tradition of speaking one's mind; pastoral ideals were severely distorted.[60]

The Klan's influence faded rapidly after 1930 and, with it, Indiana's open ties with the South. Popular literature from the last fifty years shows that the state gradually has become part of the Middle-western mainstream. It is not so much a matter that Indiana has changed, of course, as it is that the Middle West has assumed more of a rural definition. Boosters championed the state as a happy meeting ground for north, south, east, and west, rather than as a zone of conflict; they drew strength for this argument from the proximity of Indiana to the nation's center of population and from Helen M. and Robert S. Lynd's selection of Muncie for *Middletown,* a sociological study of a city "as representative as possible of contemporary American life."[61] Despite this trend toward Middle-western conformity, writers still do not ignore Indiana's Southern heritage. In fact, traits such as "a half-Southern and yet not Southern way of speaking" are related with pride.[62] Indianans seem to draw a measure of the old "perfect self-possession" from the traditional Hoosier background which serves as a source of special pride and identity.[63] This regional independence likely will be needed, as Indiana increasingly finds itself an "island" of relatively rural society separated by several hundred miles from the current perceptual "main-land" of Middle-western culture in the central plains.

In Missouri, the Klan has never dominated the state govern-ment, but in other respects, Missouri's experience with the inter-twinings of Southern and Middle-western cultural values parallels that of Indiana. More than two-thirds of Missouri's population in 1850 came from the states of Kentucky, North Carolina, Ten-nessee, and Virginia, including some 87,000 slaves.[64] The princi-pal cultural divisions in the state were not between Yankee and Southerner but between different types of Southerners and be-tween Southern and German settlers.[65] This Southern image of the state has been reinforced to the outside world by the writings of Mark Twain and Harold Bell Wright as well as by the near legendary exploits of Jesse and Frank James, the Younger broth-ers, and other "border ruffians."

Missouri has been described as being technically aligned with the North but emotionally Southern, and its popular literature consistently bears out this opinion.[66] Surveys reveal that Mis-sourians select the label of Middle West over that of Southern, but the Democratic party and the Southern Baptist Convention control local political and religious life.[67] Articles stress the state's passion for genealogy, country ham, coon hunts, and mules; they also frequently praise its peoples' easygoing tolerance and the absence of the puritanical fanaticism such as supposedly charac-terizes Kansas and other mainstream Middle-western states.[68]

Perhaps the strongest evidence for Southern allegiance in Mis-souri is the continual denial of a dominant cultural role for its cities. Both Kansas City and St. Louis are pictured as anomalies: Kansas City as in but not of the state because of its connections to Kansas grain and cattle, and St. Louis as unusual for a host of reasons. It was Republican and wet during the 1920s, having been heavily influenced by German immigrants; and it was con-sistently seen as too graceful and urbane to be representative of the "real" Missouri.[69] It is also instructive that the students of Missouri character who always split off St. Louis from the rest of the state rarely have seen the Ozarks as a separate world. Until 1940 or so, rural Missouri was portrayed as relatively homogeneous and as the home of the true Missourian. Its heartland was (and is) Little Dixie, an area just north of the Missouri River whose center is in the vicinity of Columbia and Mexico.[70]

Missourians, like Hoosiers, have been unsure about how to deal with their borderland status. They frequently tout their diversity, as might be expected, and they sometimes take pride in having a saner, slower-paced approach to life than do their neighbors in Illinois or Kansas.[71] Missouri's finest hour came with the presidency of Harry S. Truman. Articles described his Southern ancestry and praised his "Missouran's propensity for being himself."[72] Since 1955 or so, the Southern rural image has become less popular and has receded to the Ozarks and to the "boot heel." Unlike the case in Indiana, however, no new image or fusion of images has emerged to take its place. Middle West is still a term used with hesitation in local descriptions, the cities are still seen as atypical, and the cases for the state as being the crossroads of the nation are strained. A longstanding, very Southern tradition of low taxes and low levels of governmental services hurts the argument.[73]

The third Southern frontier of the Middle West extends southwestward from Missouri into central Oklahoma. Here also one finds a large literature that emphasizes the "pivot of the nation" concept, which is based on the state's location and its mix of settlers. Early articles, for example, stressed the equal ease with which wheat and cotton would grow.[74] Oklahoma has clearly been dominated by Southern interests, however, beginning with the acculturation of its principal Indian groups prior to their removal from Georgia, Alabama, Mississippi, and neighboring states. Democratic party politics have been the rule in the state, and the Klan was a major fact of life during the 1920s.[75] Widespread attention given the exodus of the Okies from the state's most Southern sector during the 1930s contributed to the general image also, as did articles on the local tradition of graft in government.[76]

The Southern dominance has obscured a minority tradition of Middle-western culture that has existed in Oklahoma since the initial land rush in 1889. Kansans and Northern settlers claimed most of the open land north of the Canadian River and implanted not only wheat crops but also Republican politics, a concern for higher education, and other things Middle Western.[77] Middle-western allegiance has expanded in recent decades, accompanying and perhaps caused in part by the prosperity of oil. Although it is still rare to find Oklahoma described as a Middle-western state in popular or academic literature, a survey in 1980 showed that only people in extreme southeastern Oklahoma still preferred South over Middle West as an identification label (see map 5.12). Recent literature stresses a renewed sense of enthusiasm for and pride in Oklahoma, including its hybrid culture. Calling the state a mixture of "Indian dignity, Texas pride, Kansas grit, Arkansas humor, Missouri stubbornness, Southern charm and New England energy," as the *Daily Oklahoman* newspaper did in the 1960s, sounds good.[78] Such a mix contains nothing uniquely Oklahoman, however, and whether or not it will be an adequate long-term, identification remains uncertain. It seems probable that Oklahoma, like Missouri, will be a permanent borderland.

THE WESTERN FRINGE

To consider the Great Plains as the western borderland of the Middle West is correct in some senses but incorrect in others. The confusion is a product of the changing perceptions of both regions. The plains were synonymous with the definition of the Middle West in 1900, on the periphery in 1920, and back in the perceptual heartland by 1980. Moreover, the plains have always formed the extreme position for assessments of the Middle West. When the Middle West has been conceived in positive terms, about 1900 and again (though to a lesser degree) at present, the plains have been seen to epitomize these positive features. In the period when little respect was accorded to the Middle West, however, the plains represented the nadir of such feeling.

The role of cities in definitions of the Middle West explains part of the fluctuating relationship between the plains and the Middle West; assessments of the agricultural potential of the plains also is important. Much of the material concerning these two issues has already been related in earlier chapters, for it underlies the overall evolution of the Middle-western concept. It will be recalled that Kansas and Nebraska were not able to maintain the exclusive use of the label Middle West for more than a decade after 1890 or so. Cities were incorporated into the regional definition to bolster the young-adult analogy, and it was not long before writers were identifying Chicago and its environs as the prototype for a hybrid pastoral-industrial society. As time went by and as contradictions between urban life and pastoral idealizations became too great to contain under the single banner of Middle West, the resultant rural region retreated westward a bit but found its center during the 1920s in the rich corn lands of Iowa, rather than on the plains.

The Great Plains could never compete for Middle-western leadership as long as urban life was a part of the regional definition. With this obstacle removed, about 1920 or so, the plains might have been expected to resume a dominant position in Middle West identity. This expectation eventually came to pass, but only after 1960, a delay of some forty years. A central issue in this delay, as well as in the eventual return of the perceptual core to Kansas and Nebraska, is the harshness of the physical environment on the plains and its effects on human society.

It is important to remember that Middle-western rhetoric has always portrayed harshness as an important regional characteristic. The harshness presented a test of sorts, a way of winnowing out weak, undeserving settlers; it was also a factor in bringing people together in friendly, cooperative ventures. Environmental difficulties had to be limited, however, for another basic tenet of pastoralism held that diligent effort would lead to economic success. Most of the Old Northwest Territory and the upper Mississippi Valley had physical conditions that fit within these limits. Seasonal temperatures were extreme, and considerable acreage had to be drained; but the soils were rich and the rains reliable. Then came the plains.

To the commentators who first used Middle West as a descriptor for Kansas and Nebraska in the 1890s, environmental hardship was still a positive factor for the culture. Their writings, in fact, constitute a classic statement of the winnowing argument.[79] Both before and after that time, however, warnings of culture-destroying potential were sounded. The most detailed and eloquent voice was that of the historian Walter Prescott Webb. Webb argued in 1931 that the border of the semiarid plains was a cultural fault line, in which "practically every institution that was carried across it was either broken and remade or else greatly altered."[80] My reading of the popular literature suggests that the plains environment was generally believed to be hostile toward Middle West culture from the mid 1880s until World War II. This negativism was manifested largely through radical, populist politics from the 1890s until World War I and then through the Dust Bowl imagery of the 1930s. During the late 1890s and the early 1900s the positive feeling that was associated with the coinage of the label Middle West caused an anomalous interlude.

Kansas was the early leader in the Populist movement. It was the most densely settled of the plains states and thus suffered the greatest losses during the prolonged economic depression that began in the late 1880s. Eastern writers were aghast when the new political party carried both the governorship and the state senate in 1892 and then began to propose radical solutions to problems of farm tenancy and low grain prices. The *Nation*, for example, editorialized that "such an unexpected outbreak as this . . . shows at least that it is not only in the cities where the foreign-born swarm, that demagogues may thrive and the doctrine of revolution be preached."[81]

Populist activity in Kansas was short-lived, and it occurred before the name Middle West was widely established. Good weather and good markets during the late 1890s led to the payment of debts and a hasty repairing of relationships between the state and the East. Apologist writers stressed that only a few of the Populist leaders were truly radical and that the behavior was only a temporary response to crisis. William Allen White, among others, assured Eastern readers that with the rapid development of small industries and with the maturing of the Kansas economy in other ways, radicalism would be a thing of the past. The only difference between Kansas and Ohio, he said, was that "Ohio has had fifty years' start of Kansas in increasing the number of creditors,— the savers, the men on the right side of the ledger."[82]

The Populist party died with the new prosperity at the turn of the century, but its sentiments and causes proved to be anything but the ephemeral phenomena that White had hoped they would be. They sprang to life again in 1916, after "brewing for ten years." The state this time was North Dakota, and the name was the Non-Partisan League, but the issue was largely the same: farmers in severe economic stress.[83] General agricultural depression after 1920 enlarged the area of protest, but the plains remained its focus.

Students debate the extent to which the Populist, Non-Partisan, and similar protest movements were environmentally caused, but they agree that the plains farmers of this period were distinct from those farther to the east. Some scholars have branded the farmers as irresponsible, others as radical; but neither image conformed well to the yeoman traits that were used in defining the essence of Middle-western culture.[84] White and his fellow writers from the plains tried to counter these images of extremism, but the often strident tones of their articles suggest that public opinion was against them.[85] These general beliefs, I think, help to account for the rapid shift of the perceptual core of the Middle West from its plains birthplace eastward toward the Mississippi River.

Radicalism ceased to be a regional issue in the United States with the onset of the Great Depression, because the nation as a whole accepted openly socialistic programs to help put an end to the crisis. This change in attitude might have helped the plains states to return to the Middle West's cultural mainstream, but concurrent drought created another image that clashed with yeoman traits. As was the case with populism, students of the Dust Bowl disagree on the actual degree of economic stress that was endured on the western plains and on how local people reacted to it.[86] The national response was clear and unanimous, however: the farmers were courageous but pitiable. Heartbreaking photographs by Dorothea Lange and Arthur Rothstein circulated widely, and the tragic *Grapes of Wrath* became a best seller.[87] The associations,

"The Dust Bowl, Cimarron County, Oklahoma, 1936," from Arthur Rothstein, *The Depression Years as Photographed by Arthur Rothstein* (New York: Dover Publications, 1978), p. 19.

right or wrong, were that the plains were equated with the Dust Bowl and that the Dust Bowl symbolized a failure of rural society. For the country to keep alive its vision of yeoman success as codified in the name Middle West, the focus had to be east of the plains.

Dust Bowl imagery was a vivid demonstration to most Americans that the yeoman farming domain had been extended too far west. Many outside observers generalized this boundary in terms of states, and the Dakotas, Nebraska, Kansas, and Oklahoma became symbols for exceedingly harsh environments. Within these same states, however, the environmental line was more finely drawn and had been an acknowledged fact since the late nineteenth century.

Local commentators divided the plains east and west on the basis of climate, but they were careful to emphasize that the line indicated only differing economies, not differing potentials for prosperity. Western Kansas, according to a typical account from the turn of the century, although it was "deficient in moisture and excessive in sunshine and wind . . . does not present above its gates the legend 'All hope abandon ye who enter here'; nor should it, for it is a Paradise for stockmen."[88] Accounts have occasionally differed on the exact location and meaning of this environmental line, but its presence is universal. Walter Prescott Webb placed the division at the 98th meridian; Mari Sandoz placed it at the 100th for Nebraska. Dakotans agree with novelist Jack Schaefer that "the real, the sensible, the logical division of Dakota . . . was made by the Missouri River."[89]

The importance accorded the "East River/West River" line in the Dakotas and its extensions southward across the central plains has waned since the 1930s. This may have been caused partly by the greater security and the decrease in isolation of life on the High Plains with the development of large-scale irrigation, better seeds, crop insurance, and improved communication and transportation. Another important, but largely overlooked, factor is the growing similarity of life east and west of the river in comparison to the rest of the United States. In a nation that is now almost completely urbanized, the plains states, in both their wetter and dryer halves, are distinguished by their rural nature.

The perceived relationship between farmer and cattleman illustrates the new rural synthesis. Nineteenth-century accounts, as well as the modern pulp "westerns," emphasize differences between the two occupations, but modern accounts of life in the plains states stress their similarities. Yeoman traits — particularly openness, independence, and self-reliance — are central to the case. Both groups are "sincere, generous" people; they increasingly represent nostalgia and ecological harmony for a somewhat disillusioned urban nation.[90]

Americans are now in general agreement that the central-plains region is the perceptual heartland of the Middle West. South Dakota, Nebraska, and Kansas all match the associated imagery fairly well: a rural world in which an immensity of sky and land is said to have produced and maintained a genuine, if aging, yeoman society. People in each of these states see themselves as the focus for the Middle West, but a comparison of states with regional imagery shows Nebraska to be a somewhat better representative than either Kansas or South Dakota.

Nebraskans have always taken pride in their agricultural heritage. Although critics may claim that this pride is a result of having had few other economic endeavors to tout, the single-mindedness of the literature has created a consistent, usually positive image.[91] Early in this century, there were claims that even "the Garden of Eden was not more purely pastoral" than Nebraska, with its people mostly "plain, sensible, honest men, who have never begged any odds in the game of life, and whose strongest wish seems to be to stand square with their fellows." This image was firmly implanted in the public mind through the heroic characters of Alexandra Bergson and Ántonia Cuzak in *My Ántonia*, created by Willa Cather, and through Mari Sandoz's portrait of her father, *Old Jules*.[92]

Admirable pastoral qualities in Nebraska came to national attention again during the 1930s and 1940s. The state's low taxes and its pay-as-you-go policy of government were compared with an increased indebtedness elsewhere. "We have lived within our means and we have a state which is as modern as any other American state," wrote Nebraska's governor. Reporters marveled at the new unicameral legislature, which was designed to save $60,000 per session over the old two-house system, and at how a new $10-million state capitol had been built without a bond issue through the straightforward procedure of building it over a ten-year period and paying for it directly with tax dollars. Nebraska, these articles implied, was a place of common sense in a country that might be going astray.[93]

Nebraska mirrored the rest of the plains states during the post–World War II years in becoming perceived as an American backwater area, but it has led in the more recent resurgence of the image of the plains-focused Middle West as a serene haven. The pure pastoral associations are again the leading factors, this time with a blending of ranching and farming traditions into a single image. The specific focus has been on the Sand Hills, a truly magnificent ranching region that occupies most of the north-central part of the state. Cattlemen have controlled most of this vast area from the period of initial settlement. The holdings are large, the grass is good, and the people are secure and self-confident. Journalists and others, upon discovering the place, often hail it as one of the best modern survivors of the pastoral tradition.[94]

South Dakota possesses agricultural traditions similar to those of Nebraska. It also has the Middle West's most symbolic building, the Corn Palace at Mitchell. Despite these features, two traits have limited the state in its associations with the Middle West: a large Indian population and "Wild West" tourism in the Black Hills. From a Nebraskan's perspective, "South Dakotans figuratively push their big hats back with the dash of old Deadwood" and have a "venturesome" history featuring land booms and gunfights, Sitting Bull and Wild Bill Hickok.[95]

The thirty thousand Indians in South Dakota actually have a low profile within the state; generally they are either ignored or disliked by other residents. They live in quiet poverty, but they constitute an important part of the overall "Western" flavor that most of the popular literature gives to South Dakota.[96] This flavor is rooted in tourism; it has been increasingly visible since 1927, when President Calvin Coolidge summered in the Black Hills and, simultaneously, Gutzon Borglum began to sculpt four presidential faces atop Mount Rushmore.[97] Business was described as "booming" by 1941 and has increased ever since. The attractions are varied: buffalo herds, caves, patriotism, mines, rodeos, mountain scenery, and the Bad Lands, but the uniting theme is "where the West still lives." In 1947 a *National Geographic* article about the state set the tone for the next forty years of popular literature with its title "South Dakota Keeps Its West Wild." Yeoman descriptions of the Middle West are included but are rarely stressed.[98]

The same Nebraskan writers who noted the western flavor of South Dakota also captured the essence of Kansas' distinctiveness among the plains states. One writer, in the 1920s, called it trucu-lence; the other, thirty years later, saw it as "the righteous self-assurance of the Abolitionists who came West."[99] Both phrases refer to an extraordinary sense of special purpose and destiny in Kansas that sprang from its territorial experience on the eve of the Civil War. In the popular literature, Kansas was "colonized," not merely settled, with New England abolitionists in the van-guard.[100] The nobility of that movement was celebrated through-out the North by the leading poets of the age: James Russell Lowell, William Cullen Bryant, Oliver Wendell Holmes, Henry Wadsworth Longfellow, Ralph Waldo Emerson, and John Green-leaf Whittier.[101] Whittier's lines from "The Kansas Emigrant" were perhaps most quoted:

> We cross the prairies as of old
> The Pilgrims crossed the sea,
> To make the West, as they the East,
> The homestead of the free.[102]

The New England influence in Kansas stands up poorly under analysis of census data, but it formed the dominant symbolic force in the state well into the twentieth century. Through at least 1923, the people were said to have been strongly "marked by Puritanism," by which the commentators meant a strong moral quality that had made Kansas a leader in a series of social reform movements. As one observer wrote in retrospect, the state was the "birthplace of the prohibitionist movement in America, seed bed of the Populist party, and embittered agrarian dissent, early and strong adherent of Bull Moose Progressivism."[103] At the time that the label Middle West was first being popularized, Kansans were at a pinnacle of self-confidence. They were well on their way to achieving a rural utopia at a time when America generally regarded this as a national ideal. Historian Carl Becker thus called the Kansas Spirit "the American spirit double distilled" and noted with understanding the local "feeling of superiority."[104]

So long as Prohibition was regarded as a progressive reform and rural life as a utopian existence, Kansas could be the core of the Middle West. The air of puritan self-righteousness in the state contained the potential for a sterile existence, however, and this negative assessment of Kansas behavior gained credence throughout the 1920s. "Out of prohibition grew the mania for passing laws to regulate the personal conduct of the individual," wrote a perceptive observer in 1926, "the policy of trying to legislate morality into morons. . . . The situation has become such that a man must be either a hypocrite or a fanatic if he hopes for any sort of political preferment." Kansas, the rural progressive leader during the 1910s, was quickly transformed into the statewide epitome of Sinclair Lewis's *Main Street*. When a writer complained in 1931 that "like many Americans, I will never recover from my sparse childhood in Kansas," an article of rebuttal could only assert that "Kansas and the people who live there should not be altogether damned as dull and sordid and unhappy."[105]

Kansas moved from national leader to national backwater very quickly, and it has never completely adjusted to the change. Most modern writers note "a smarting memory of past ridicule" in the state. As its leaders continue to champion old ideals to a changed nation, "a bold, creative state pride [has] degenerated into a half-ashamed provincialism."[106] Defensiveness, in turn, has made it difficult for residents to understand and to accept the renewed appreciation that has been accorded to rural America in recent years. While Kansans continue to debate the issue of liquor by the drink and to promote an eccentric image to the rest of the country, less tense Nebraskans seem to be able to accept their own slogan of "Nebraska: the good life."[107]

7
The Middle West as Metaphor

Two generalizations stand out from this study of regional images: the enduring importance of pastoralism to the definition of the Middle West and the widely fluctuating evaluations that the public has made of this representation. The apparent need to maintain a connection between the region and pastoral imagery accounts in large part for the unprecedented series of relocations that the Middle West has undergone, from central plains to the whole upper Mississippi Valley and then back again to the plains (see table 7.1). How, though, can one reconcile this demonstration of attachment to an ideal with assessments of Middle-western character that run the gamut from keeper of fundamental values to rustic simpleton? Beyond the obvious tendency of such contradictory evaluations to make local residents schizophrenic, what conclusions do they imply about the country and its culture?

The context for understanding Middle-western metaphors is national culture, especially the complex, contradictory nature of the United States.[1] Three self-conceptions are important here: pastoral idealism, unfettered youthfulness, and world leadership in technology. As a nation we identify with and draw strength from each of these idealizations; we seem to "need" them all and to know that each one is continuously vital. Obvious contradictions preclude the simultaneous belief in the three traits. A pastoral society demands a certain maturation, for example. Its ecological underpinnings contrast sharply with the exploitive, hedonistic aspects of a youthful society; its cultivated lands imply a realized potential, whereas virgin woodlands and prairies carry only the promise of future greatness. A technologically oriented society is also necessarily opposed to a pastoral one. Progress and innovation carry positive associations in the former world, not cyclic seasonal rhythms; urban sites, not rural ones, are usually the foci for development and praise.

Many scholars have probed the contradictions inherent in the three conceptions of American culture, and some have noted regional shifts in their use, notably a westward retreat of "youthful" wilderness and pastoralism during the nineteenth century.[2] This argument centers on the development of a distinctively American, as opposed to European, culture in the nation's interior, however, not on the reduction of conflict among American self-conceptions. The possibility that such migration and a natural aging process might eventually eliminate these two traits from the American character is ignored.

It is clear from a study of the evolving meaning of Middle West that this regional label owes much of its utility and longevity to its ability to resolve problems of conflict, migration, and succession between the three national images. The label has compartmentalized America's pastoral face and has provided a tangible symbol and a permanent physical location for it. Moreover, the presence of a Middle West has separated the East from the West and thus has freed these places to assume an increased custodial power over the two other national idealizations mentioned above. The East as the embodiment of American technological might and the West as the land of eternal youth are gross oversimplifications to be sure, but the popular associations seem to be as strong as the one between the Middle West and pastoralism.[3]

The role of regional labels as depositories for various national values is largely unrecognized, as far as I can determine, but may in fact be critical to the continued existence of these labels in modern society. Geographer Yi-fu Tuan has noted how unlikely their existence is in theory.[4] Place labels such as neighborhoods are natural, he says, because they are small enough in scope for us to experience them thoroughly and repeatedly; they thus acquire meaning. Entities such as states and nations, on the other hand, are too large for people to "know" in detail, and so loyalty for them must be created through such devices as flags, anthems,

Table 7.1. Summary of Perceived Locations and Images, 1880s–1988

Approximate Dates	Perceived Location	Dominant Cultural Images	Major Reasons for Image and Location
1880s–1902	Kans., Nebr.	pastoralism and a society blended of youth and maturity, both traits viewed as highly desirable	accurate locational and cultural description pastoralism a revered national trait
1903–11	Transition		Transition
1912–19	Ohio, Mich., Ind., Wis., Ill., Minn., Iowa, Mo., N.Dak., S.Dak., Nebr., Kans., with a focus on Ill.	as above, plus a leader in technological achievement the most American part of America	inappropriateness of Old and New Northwest as regional labels desire of other interior states to identify with praised images
1920–29	as above, but excluding Chicago and other major industrial cities	exclusively rural themes a society in middle age mixed positive and negative evaluations	*Main Street* challenges to the pastoral interpretation of rural society regions used to separate conflicting cultural traits (technology leader, pastoralism)

Table 7.1. (continued)

Approximate Dates	Perceived Location	Dominant Cultural Images	Major Reasons for Image and Location
1930–46	same as above	same as above	protraction of status quo via depression and World War II
1947–67	same as above	exclusively rural themes a society in old age negative evaluations	national obsession with technological growth
1968–88	Iowa, northern Mo., S.Dak., Nebr., and Kans. for most Americans; residents of N.Dak., Minn., Wis., Ill., and to a lesser degree Mich., Ind., Ohio, and Okla. see themselves as part of the region	exclusively rural themes mixed positive and negative evaluations	as above, but countered by a revival of pastoralism via urban disenchantment contraction of region to retain separation of pastoral and technological-urban imagery

and the formal study of their history. The American South bene-
fits from some of these same symbolic reinforcements, but the
Middle West, together with the East, the West, and a few other
similar places, seemingly are bereft. Perhaps, however, some of
our patriotic songs may be more specialized than we think.
"America the Beautiful," for example, seems to be firmly tied to
pastoral thought with its celebrations of "spacious skies," "amber
waves of grain," and "brotherhood." Does it contribute to the
maintenance of Middle-western identity?

Once the linkages between regional labels and national culture
traits are recognized, the pulsations of regional imagery are easier
to understand. The Middle West rose mercurially from an ob-
scure to a major place designation between 1890 and 1900 because
it provided a focus for America's pastoral sentiments at a time
when such sentiments were highly regarded. It rose to even loftier
heights, to be seen as the most American part of America, around
1915, when the still-popular pastoralism was merged briefly with
the emergent national fascination with technological might. The
fall from this pinnacle, which was caused by changing national
values, disturbed the regional psyche. The people tried to maintain the noble pastoral stance, but they could not understand
why the familiar praise in the magazines gradually changed to
criticism. They developed a major industrial component to their
economy but could not understand why outsiders continued to
see them as farmers. An ebullient, self-confident regional personality changed into an introspective one, complete with an inferiority complex (see cartoon).

There is evidence to indicate that over the last decade or so,
the image of the Middle West has risen again in the public mind.
Most writers attribute this to a disillusionment with the modern
urban existence of the country, with its emphasis on fast-paced
technological change, ecological irresponsibility, and detachment
from old securities such as family, community, and sense of place.
The East (plus Southern California), as a regional symbol for the
technological age, is thus perhaps past its zenith, and the Middle-
western pastoral life is ready to be rediscovered.

J. B. Jackson, one of the most acute observers of American

The rare and timid prairie people

"The Rare and Timid Prairie People," by Gary Larson. "The Far Side" cartoon is reprinted by permission of Chronicle Features, San Francisco, Calif., from *Beyond the Far Side* (Kansas City and New York: Andrews, McMeel, & Parker, 1983), p. 54.

values, has offered a general argument on the "rediscovery" process that may be involved in the ongoing image of the Middle West. He says that a country such as the United States, which has slowly evolved with a firm attachment to place, celebrates its history not so much by honoring specific historical events as by creating for itself a golden age. This partially real, partially imagined age contains few dates or specific names; it aims instead to recapture "an innocence and a simplicity" that are now lost, a time when the country "was at one with its environment." History is seen, not as a continuity, but as a dramatic discontinuity, with the golden age followed by a period of neglect and then by a time of rediscovery and restoration. The third stage can occur only after the active memory of the golden period has ended, so that the restoration is unhampered by unpleasant or inconsistent facts. The necessary interval is about one hundred years.[5]

The preservation of wilderness areas is one obvious result of the process that Jackson describes; restored New England villages represent another. Veneration of the Middle West may be emerging as a third. Consider the fit between the pastoral rhetoric about the region and the ideas of simplicity and harmony, noted above. Consider that the Middle West's "birth" was approximately a century ago. Perhaps the best evidence for this tie, however, is the symbolic landscape of "Main Street." The small-town Middle West from the Victorian era has achieved the status of an icon. Symbolically, "Main Street is the seat of a business culture of property-minded, law-abiding citizens devoted to 'free enterprise' and 'social morality,' a community of sober, sensible, practical people."[6] Restorations of houses and businesses from this period are celebrated regularly in the new regional magazine *Midwest Living*, and Walt Disney's five-eighths scale versions of Main Street in his two theme parks are phenomenally successful. Disney's creations speak directly to Jackson's theory. The street is loosely modeled after Disney's hometown of Marceline, Missouri, but all the harshness, inconsistencies, and filth of the original have been removed.[7] The recreated Main Street apparently represents the past that America wants to believe existed; it also represents the culture world that the nation increasingly expects to exist even now in the Middle West. Ronald Reagan, for example, seemed to speak to this golden-age/golden-place concept in 1982 when he visited Kansas: "Sometimes living in that big White House in Washington can leave you feeling a little fenced-in and isolated. But there is a tonic: visit a state where tall wheat and prairie grasses reach through a wide open sky; be with people who are keeping our frontier spirit alive — people who work the soil have time to dream beyond the farthest stars. Here in the heartland of America lives the hope of the world."[8]

Discussion of a restoration thesis for the Middle West is necessarily speculative, but New England provides a demonstration that Jackson's three-stage model (i.e., golden age, neglect, restoration) has worked before in this country. Vermont is the best case study. It was a peasant society during its first two centuries of European occupation, an extended community of farming folk unified by a common religion. These Vermonters were necessarily close to the land, and they practiced an architecture, a humor, and a philosophy of life that were blunt, honest, and understated.[9] This society began to enter the second stage of its existence just after the American Revolution, when rich lands to the west lured some of its young people and when factories in southern New England lured others. Vermont became a by-passed state, derided as "fished-out" by writers from the emergent Middle West.[10] Vermonters tried to participate in the new urban-technological world, but the state was poorly situated. Edith Wharton captured the essence of "stage two" life in *Ethan Frome*: gaunt landscapes, suffering, patient endurance, poverty. The situation later in this stage has also been portrayed well in novel format. Wallace Stegner's *Second Growth*, published in 1947, described an embittered, conservative, still-poor village made aware of its inadequacies by a growing colony of prosperous summer residents.[11]

Vermont today still retains traces of stage-two neglect, but it has been almost completely transformed. Waves of new immigrants have arrived, most of them from metropolitan areas to the south. They have money and are educated, and they seek the admirable traits from the Vermont landscape and from the cultural past: beauty, strength of community, individualism, craftsmanship, and the like. They join volunteer fire departments, chop wood, restore old farmhouses, and pay premium prices for food in order to retain an old general store. The result is a Vermont that is analogous to Disney's Main Street, a "restoration" with distortions. Under Laurance S. Rockefeller's influence, in fact, the whole town of Woodstock, Vermont, has been restored in this sense.[12]

The Middle West may never experience a golden-age mania on the level that Vermont has, but there are signs that such a movement has begun. The appearance of the up-scale magazine *Midwest Living* in 1987 is an indicator, as in the growing local popularity of farmers' markets, horse ownership, and the like. The driving force behind the movement is deeper, however, than a desire to have one's own animal. Writers increasingly speak about the Middle West as one of the few "genuine" places left in the country, and they see a growing respect for the region based on this idea.[13]

The West is one big tourist area, according to this argument. New England's genuineness has been overwhelmed by the resort business, while Florida, Arizona, and places in between have become winter havens. Cities, the places where most Americans live, have not experienced the period of neglect that is required for Jackson's restoration process. By elimination, the rural South and the rural Middle West are the sites that are currently eligible for golden-age veneration. The rapid growth of population in North Carolina, Tennessee, and the Ozarks of Missouri and Arkansas can likely be attributed to this process in part, which is an abstraction and an accentuation of the most positive aspects of Southern rural life. The Middle West, however, would seem to be better situated for additional growth of this sort. It may suffer on comparisons of climate, but it offers an image of rural America that largely lacks the stereotypes of racism and poverty still associated with parts of the lower South.

The concept of the Middle West as genuine America is multifaceted. The most important linkage is to pastoralism, of course, but there is more. The geographer Cotton Mather has recently called the place "'standard American'—lacking the presumptions of the East, the traditions of the South, the flamboyance of Texas, the lure of the Golden West."[14] The region is no longer the epitome of all things American, as it was in 1915. Instead, after enduring its time of neglect, the Middle West has reemerged to fill the role of keeper of the nation's values. John Gunther called it "America uncontaminated" in 1947, and that image has become increasingly prominent in recent years.[15] The Middle West is seen today as a producer of wholesome and natural food, a place in which people can still leave their doors unlocked and in which governors will occasionally answer their own telephones.[16] The journalist Joel Garreau found "social calm" to be the most identifiable regional feature, a calm that enabled this place to define America's cultural limits. "In fact," he concluded, "in a time of change in the way we look at the value of work, the desirability of marriage and having a family, how trustworthy our governments are, and what constitutes patriotism, the Breadbasket has come to be the ratifier of what constitutes a truly mainstream continental idea."[17]

One must be careful not to overemphasize the pace of restoration in the Middle West today, for older associations continue to create dilemmas and contradictions for thoughtful residents. The imagery of cowboys and yeoman farmers is flattering in some ways but is hard to reconcile with the largely urban and commercial present realities of the region. The country-rube tag still contains truths about regional defensiveness and parochialism. Still, my reading and experience suggest that the region has gained respect in recent years, not only from outsiders, but from its own residents as well. There is an increased realization that the positive values that grow out of a rootedness in place are needed to give meaning to life and that the Middle West provides the nation with a needed touchstone for such values. The political columnist George F. Will was referring to these things when he claimed that God was "at heart, a Middle Westerner."[18]

It seems appropriate to end a book on symbols and metaphor with two final examples of the Middle West's image. Although one dates from 1930, both illustrate themes that have become increasingly dominant in recent years. Grant Wood's *Stone City*,

Iowa, which was painted during an earlier revival of Middle-western pride, encapsulates the positive aspects of the region better than any other single source I know (see p. 101). The country herein is bright, clean, and straightforward. No mists or jagged tree trunks are present to suggest broodiness or mystery; the Middle West is an honest land. The natural world is vast in *Stone City,* but it is clearly under the dominion of man. Cornfields, haystacks, and pastures dominate, and the geometric shape of the trees suggests that even they are controlled in some fashion. People are dwarfed by the scale of the landscape; they obviously are influenced by this immensity but show no evidence of intimidation. Signs of regularity and of simplicity are everywhere: the stylized trees, the plain architectural lines, the linearity of the crops. One sees nothing to indicate human defensiveness or inferiority. Man and nature have achieved a balance in *Stone City* whereby nature is modified but not overwhelmed. It is American pastoralism at its best.

The second example is the image of the Middle West as a "nice girl." This is a personification of the genuine-place argument and harks back to the character of Dorothy Gale in *The Wizard of Oz.* The best example takes the form of a letter from a glamorous but jaded state, Colorado, to her sister Kansas.[19] Colorado confesses to having become "a scarlet state" but warns Kansas not to try the same tactics, even though "you've been unfairly typecast as a plain Jane." Colorado speaks of Kansas' "quiet purity" and concludes that "those who unwittingly downgraded you may have been your best friends." *Time* magazine ended a cover story on Minnesota with a shorter version of this same idea: "California is the flashy blonde you like to take out once or twice. Minnesota is the girl you want to marry."[20]

Notes

CHAPTER 1. CONTRADICTORY IMAGES

1. Allusions in the Oz stories are discussed at length by Henry M. Littlefield in "The Wizard of Oz: Parable on Populism," *American Quarterly* 16 (1964): 47–58. Littlefield suggests that Emerald City is Washington, D.C., and that the Witches of the East and of the West refer to the evils that exist in those sections of the country.

CHAPTER 2. THE ORIGINS AND EXPANSION OF THE REGIONAL NAME

1. D. W. Meinig, "The Continuous Shaping of America: A Prospectus for Geographers and Historians," *American Historical Review* 83 (1978): 1186–1205, quotation on p. 1205.

2. This survey is discussed at length in chapter 5.

3. Frederick Jackson Turner, "The Problem of the West," in his *The Frontier in American History* (New York: Henry Holt & Co., 1920), pp. 205–21, quotation on p. 205. The essay was originally published in 1896.

4. See, e.g., two essays by John W. Caughey: "Toward an Understanding of the West," *Utah Historical Quarterly* 27 (1959): 7–24; and "The American West: Frontier and Region," *Arizona and the West* 1 (1959): 7–12.

5. Much of this primary literature is analyzed by John A. Jakle in *Images of the Ohio Valley: A Historical Geography of Travel, 1740 to 1860* (New York: Oxford University Press, 1977).

6. Timothy Flint, "Writers of the Western Country," *Western Monthly Review* 2 (1828): 11–21, quotations on p. 21.

7. Mann Butler, "Valley of the Ohio: Its Conquest and Settlement by Americans," *Western Journal and Civilian* 9 (1853): 355; "The Northwest," *DeBow's Review* 15 (1888): 325–41.

8. Henry Nash Smith, *Virgin Land: The American West as Symbol and Myth* (Cambridge, Mass.: Harvard University Press, 1950), p. 133.

9. Charles D. Warner, "Studies of the Great West," *Harper's New Monthly Magazine* 76 (1888): 557.

10. Timothy Flint, "Religious Character of the Western People," *Western Monthly Review* 1 (1827): 268–70, quotation on 270.

11. Charles M. Harger, "New Era in the Middle West," *Harper's New Monthly Magazine* 97 (1898): 276–82; Franklin Matthews, "Bright Skies in the West," *Harper's Weekly* 42 (1898): 113–14, 138–39, 161–63, 186–89, 208–10, 231–32, 256, 278–79, 322–23. Precise statements on the north-south ordering of space are made by Emerson Hough in "The Settlement of the West: A Study in Transportation," *Century Magazine* 63 (1901/2): 359; and by Charles F. Speare in "Business Conditions in the West and Southwest," *American Review of Reviews* 37 (1908): 715–17.

12. Hough, "Settlement of the West," p. 91; "The Spectator," *Outlook* 84 (1906): 1053–54; Charles M. Harger, "The West at Home," ibid., 86 (1907): 32–36, 70–75, 106–10.

13. William R. Lighton, "The Riches of a Rural State," *World's Work* 1 (1900): 93–103, quotations on pp. 93, 96.

14. Harger, "New Era," p. 278.

15. Matthews, "Bright Skies," p. 163.

16. J. K. Miller, "Are the People of the West Fanatics?" *Arena* 13 (1895): 92–97; William V. Allen, "Western Feeling towards the East," *North American Review* 162 (1896): 588–93; John E. Bennett, "Is the West Discontented? Is a Revolution at Hand?" *Arena* 16 (1896): 393–405; Henry L. West, "Two Republics or One?" *North American Review* 162 (1896): 509–11.

17. Allen, "Western Feeling," p. 589; Charles M. Harger, "The New Westerner," *North American Review* 185 (1907): 748–58, quotation on 750.

18. The Lincoln quotation, from his annual message to Congress, is in *The Collected Works of Abraham Lincoln,* ed. Roy P. Basler (New Brunswick, N.J.: Rutgers University Press, 1953), 5:528–29.

19. Harger, "New Era" (1898); "The Prairie Woman: Yesterday and Today," *Outlook* 70 (1902): 1008–12; "An Era of Thrift in the Middle West," *World's Work* 5 (1903): 3091–93, quotation on p. 3093.

20. Booth Tarkington, "The Middle West," *Harper's Monthly Magazine* 106 (1902): 75–83; Henry Loomis Nelson, "In Medias Res," ibid., 109 (1904): 54–59; and "The Spirit of the West," ibid., 109 (1904): 197–203.

21. Nelson, "In Medias Res," p. 54.

22. Donald W. Meinig, "Three American Northwests: Some Perspectives in Historical Geography," paper read at the annual meeting of the Association of American Geographers, Apr. 1, 1957, at Cincinnati, Ohio; abstract published in *Annals of the Association of American Geographers* 47 (1957): 170–71.

23. The four Westerners are Hough, "Settlement of the West," pp. 91-107, 201-16, 355-69; Harger, "Era of Thrift"; idem, "New Westerner," pp. 748-58; idem, "The West at Home;" idem, "The Middle West and Wall Street," *American Monthly Review of Reviews* 36 (1907): 83-86; William R. Lighton, "Where Is the West?" *Outlook* 74 (1903): 702-4; and J. B. Case, "The Future of Western Trade," *North American Review* 188 (1908): 598-608. The Eastern writer who used the plains definition was Speare, "Business Conditions," and the Eastern writers who used the Old Northwest definition are Rezin W. McAdam, "The Peopling of the Plains," *Overland Monthly*, n.s. 42 (1903): 131-40; Stephen M. Dale, "The West through Eastern Eyes," *Independent* 57 (1904): 903-9; and Nelson, "In Medias Res" and "The Spirit of the West." The Tarkington reference is "The Middle West."

24. On the boundary issue see Rollin L. Hartt, "Middle-Westerners and That Sort of People," *Century Magazine* 93 (1916): 169-80. Late users of the Kansas-Nebraska definition include H. J. Haskell, "The U-53 and the Middle West," *Outlook* 114 (1916): 414-15; and Philo M. Buck, Jr., "Pacifism in the Middle West," *Nation* 104 (1917): 595-97.

25. The last incidence of quotation marks I found was in Harger's "New Westerner"; the first occurrence of Midwest is apparently A.P.H., "The Adjournment of Common Sense," *New Republic* 16 (1918): 158-60.

26. Edward A. Ross, "The Middle West: Being Studies of Its People in Comparison with Those of the East," *Century Magazine* 83 (1912): 609-15, 686-92, 874-80, and 84 (1912): 142-48; Meredith Nicholson, "The Valley of Democracy," *Scribner's Magazine* 63 (1918): 1-17, 127-62, 257-76, 385-404, 543-58, 654-65; Sherwood Anderson, *Winesburg, Ohio* (1919; reprint, New York: Viking Press, 1968), p. 240; Sinclair Lewis, *Main Street: The Story of Carol Kennicott* (New York: Harcourt, Brace, 1920), p. 1; Charles M. Harger, "The Middle West's Peace Problems," *Atlantic Monthly* 123 (1919): 555-60.

27. Lincoln, *Collected Works*, 5:528.

CHAPTER 3. AMERICA'S HEARTLAND

1. Edward A. Ross, "The Middle West: Being Studies of Its People in Comparison with Those of the East," *Century Magazine* 83 (1912): 609-15, 686-92, 874-80, and 84 (1912): 142-48, quotation on p. 609.

2. Leo Marx, *The Machine in the Garden: Technology and the Pastoral Ideal in America* (London: Oxford University Press, 1964), p. 3; Henry Nash Smith, *Virgin Land: The American West as Symbol and Myth* (Cambridge, Mass.: Harvard University Press, 1950), pp. 133, 145-54; Walter M. Kollmorgen, "The Woodsman's Assaults on the Domain of the Cattleman," *Annals of the Association of American Geogra-*

phers 59 (1969): 215–39; David M. Emmons, *Garden in the Grasslands: Boomer Literature of the Central Great Plains* (Lincoln: University of Nebraska Press, 1971); Timothy J. Rickard, "The Great Plains as Part of an Irrigated Western Empire, 1890–1914," in *The Great Plains: Environment and Culture,* ed. Brian W. Blouet and Frederick C. Luebke (Lincoln: University of Nebraska Press, 1979), pp. 81–98.

3. Smith, *Virgin Land,* p. 123.

4. Charles M. Harger, "The West at Home," *Outlook* 86 (1907): 32–36, 70–75, 106–10; Ross, "The Middle West"; Meredith Nicholson, "The Valley of Democracy," *Scribner's Magazine* 63 (1918): 1–17, 127–62, 257–76, 385–404, 543–58, 654–65; J. Hector St. John Crèvecoeur, *Letters from an American Farmer* (London: Thomas Davies, 1782); Thomas Jefferson, *Notes on the State of Virginia* (London: John Stockdale, 1785); Albert P. Brigham, "A Geographer's Geography Lesson on the Prairies," *Journal of Geography* 16 (1918): 167–70, quotation on p. 168.

5. T. N. Carver, "Life in the Corn Belt," *World's Work* 7 (1903): 4232–39, quotation on p. 4233. The slavery issue is best discussed by Nicholson in "Valley of Democracy," pp. 14–15.

6. Stephen M. Dale, "The West through Eastern Eyes," *Independent* 57 (1904): 903–9, quotation on p. 908. On the morality issue see Henry Loomis Nelson, "In Medias Res," *Harper's Monthly Magazine* 109 (1904): 54–59, esp. p. 57; Charles M. Harger, "Good Neighbors All," *Outlook* 82 (1906): 367–70; and Louis Howland, "Provincial or National?" *Scribner's Magazine* 43 (1908): 450–55. Alternate conceptions of success are discussed by Sherwood Anderson in *Poor White* (New York: B. W. Huebsch, 1920) and by Rex Burns in *Success in America: The Yeoman Dream and the Industrial Revolution* (Amherst: University of Massachusetts Press, 1976).

7. E. W. Howe, "Provincial Peculiarities of Western Life," *Forum* 14 (1892): 91–93.

8. C. H. Forbes-Lindsay, "The Spirit of the West: How Its Vigor and Resourcefulness Are Affecting the Development of the Whole Country," *Craftsman* 15 (1908): 64–77, quotation on p. 76; see also Ross, "The Middle West," pp. 611–12, and Frederick M. Davenport, "On the Trail of Progress and Reaction in the West," *Outlook* 109 (1915): 886–91, 922–36, and 110 (1915): 94–99, especially pp. 94–95.

9. Emerson Hough, "The Settlement of the West: A Study in Transportation," *Century Magazine* 63 (1901/2): 91–107, 201–16, 355–69, quotation on p. 91; see also Henry Loomis Nelson, "The Spirit of the West," *Harper's Monthly Magazine* 109 (1904): 197–203, esp. p. 199.

10. A good example is Howland, "Provincial," pp. 450–55.

11. Ross, "The Middle West," pp. 609, 613.

12. Ibid., pp. 609–10.

13. Harger, "Good Neighbors," p. 370.

14. Howland, "Provincial," pp. 450–55; Edward Hungerford, "Rediscovering the West," *Harper's Weekly* 55 (Dec. 30, 1911): 11.

15. On literature see Hamlin Garland, "Literary Emancipation of the West," *Forum* 16 (1893): 156–66; on education see Hamilton W. Mabie, "The Intellectual Movement in the West," *Atlantic Monthly* 82 (1898): 592–605, and William R. Lighton, "Where Is the West?" *Outlook* 74 (1903): 702–4; and on manufacturing see Howe, "Provincial Peculiarities," pp. 91–102; "The Manufacturing West," *Independent* 55 (1903): 459–60; Nelson, "In Medias Res"; Harger, "The West at Home"; and J. B. Case, "The Future of Western Trade," *North American Review* 188 (1908): 598–608.

16. Nicholson, "Valley of Democracy," p. 141.

17. Carl Sandburg, *Harvest Poems, 1910–1960* (New York: Harcourt Brace Jovanovich, 1960), pp. 35–36.

18. Carver, "Life in the Corn Belt," p. 4232.

19. Charles M. Harger, "The Prairie Woman: Yesterday and Today," *Outlook* 70 (1902): 1008–12, quotations on pp. 1008, 1012.

20. Booth Tarkington, "The Middle West," *Harper's Monthly Magazine* 106 (1902): 75–83, quotation on p. 75.

21. Charles M. Harger, "The New Westerner," *North American Review* 185 (1907): 748–58, quotation on p. 753.

22. Howland, "Provincial Peculiarities," p. 452.

23. Ross, "The Middle West," p. 613; see also J. K. Miller, "Are the People of the West Fanatics?" *Arena* 13 (1895): 92–97.

24. "West and New East," *Independent* 72 (1912): 322.

25. Harger, "The West at Home," pp. 107, 110.

26. Harger, "New Westerner," p. 756; Rollin L. Hartt, "Middle-Westerners and That Sort of People," *Century Magazine* 93 (1916): 169–80, esp. p. 171; Nicholson, "Valley of Democracy," pp. 260–62.

27. Hartt, "Middle-Westerners," p. 173.

28. Harger, "The West at Home," p. 110; Ross, "The Middle West," pp. 148, 611; "The Attitude of the Middle West," *New Republic* 6 (1916): 119–20; and Philo M. Buck, Jr., "The Middle West and the Peace," *Review* 1 (1919): 34–35. For the larger American context see Smith, *Virgin Land*, pp. 123–260; Marx, *Machine in the Garden*, esp. pp. 115, 127; and Barbara Novak, *Nature and Culture: American Landscape Painting, 1825–1875* (New York: Oxford University Press, 1980), pp. 157–200.

29. Dale, "The West through Eastern Eyes," p. 904.

30. Ross, "The Middle West," p. 613.

31. Charles M. Harger, "An Era of Thrift in the Middle West," *World's Work* 5 (1903): 3091–93; idem, "The Middle West and Wall Street," *American Monthly Review of Reviews* 36 (1907): 83–86, esp. p. 85.

32. Ross, "The Middle West," p. 877.

33. "The Middle West and the Submarine War off Our Coast," *Out-*

look 114 (1916): 362, 371; H. J. Haskell, "The U-53 and the Middle West," *Outlook* 114 (1916): 414–15.

34. James D. Whelpley, "The Middle West and the War," *Outlook* 110 (1915): 870–71; see also Hartt, "Middle-Westerners," pp. 174–75.

35. Frederick M. Davenport, "Political Thinking in the Middle West," *Outlook* 113 (1916): 266–69, quotation on p. 268; see also Nicholson, "Valley of Democracy," p. 656.

36. "Attitude of the Middle West," p. 120; see also Haskell, "U-53 and the Middle West"; "What the Middle West Thinks," *Independent* 86 (1916): 359; and especially Philo M. Buck, Jr., "Pacifism in the Middle West," *Nation* 104 (1917): 595–97.

37. The enlistment figures and the White quotation are in "Patriotism, East and West," *Literary Digest* 54 (1917): 1486; "The Maligned Middle West," *Bellman* 22 (1917): 595.

CHAPTER 4. RURAL IMAGERY IN AN URBANIZING NATION

1. Sinclair Lewis, *Main Street: The Story of Carol Kennicott* (New York: Harcourt, Brace, 1920).

2. W. L. George, "Hail, Columbia! America in the Making," *Harper's Monthly Magazine* 142 (1921): 142–53, quotation on p. 153.

3. Leo Marx, *The Machine in the Garden: Technology and the Pastoral Ideal in America* (London: Oxford University Press, 1964).

4. James D. Hart, *The Popular Book: A History of America's Literary Taste* (London: Oxford University Press, 1950), p. 236.

5. Lewis, *Main Street*, p. 58.

6. Ibid., p. 266.

7. Ibid., p. 32; Hart, *Popular Book*, pp. 202–15; Roy W. Meyer, *The Middle Western Farm Novel in the Twentieth Century* (Lincoln: University of Nebraska Press, 1965), esp. pp. 79–101.

8. Lewis, *Main Street*, pp. 339, 17.

9. Ibid., p. 37.

10. Ibid., p. 265.

11. Ibid., p. ix.

12. Ibid., pp. 75, 155, 157.

13. Ibid., pp. 417–18.

14. Ibid., pp. 20, 48, 51.

15. Ibid., pp. 89, 116, 137–38, 329–30.

16. Ibid., p. 430.

17. Ibid., p. 156.

18. Ibid., p. 340.

19. Glen A. Love, "New Pioneering on the Prairies: Nature, Prog-

ress and the Individual in the Novels of Sinclair Lewis," *American Quarterly* 25 (1973): 558–77.

20. Frederick M. Davenport, "Something Brewing in the Middle West," *Outlook* 132 (1922): 368–70; Bruce Bliven, "A Stroll on Main Street," *New Republic* 37 (1923): 63–66; Charles M. Harger, "The Political Clouds out West," *Independent* 111 (1923): 82–83; William Allen White, "Why All This Rumpus?" *Collier's: The National Weekly* 72 (Aug. 25, 1923): 5, 24.

21. "The Wheat Belt Rebellion," *Literary Digest* 78 (Aug. 4, 1923): 18–19; John Ballard, "The Mouse in the Republican Cheese," *Outlook* 135 (1923): 16–17; Chester H. Rowell, "Why the Middle West Went Radical," *World's Work* 46 (1923): 157–65; idem, "Is Middle West Radicalism Here to Stay?" *World's Work* 46 (1923): 655–58.

22. The case is nicely argued by Arthur Capper in "The Middle West Looks Abroad," *Foreign Affairs* 5 (1927): 529–37.

23. Bruce Bliven, "Why the Farmer Sees Red," *New Republic* 36 (1923): 273–75, quotation on p. 273.

24. Harger, "Political Clouds," p. 83.

25. Carl L. Becker, "Europe through the Eyes of the Middle West," *New Europe* 15 (1920): 98–104, quotation on p. 102.

26. Becker, "Europe," pp. 102–3.

27. May Lamberton Becker, "The Reader's Guide," *Saturday Review of Literature* 8 (1932): 798.

28. The two factions are nicely sketched by Sinclair Lewis in "Main Street's Been Paved," *Nation* 119 (1924): 255–60. The best source for regional political understanding remains John H. Fenton's *Midwest Politics* (New York: Holt, Rinehart & Winston, 1966).

29. The case in the South has been made by John Shelton Reed in *The Enduring South: Subcultural Persistence in Mass Society* (Chapel Hill: University of North Carolina Press, 1974), p. 88.

30. Good examples are Bliven, "A Stroll"; Allen D. Albert, "Where the Prairie Money Goes," *Scribner's Magazine* 82 (1927): 476–80; and Maude Parker, "Our Town," *Saturday Evening Post* 200 (July 30, 1927): 13, 42, 47, 49.

31. Claude C. Washburn, "Zenith," *Freeman* 8 (1924): 518–20, quotation on p. 519.

32. Ibid., p. 519.

33. John R. McMahon, "Our Jazz-Spotted Middle West," *Ladies' Home Journal* 39 (Feb., 1922): 38, 181.

34. Extreme positions on Kansas are taken by Charles W. Wood in "Where Tomorrow's Ideas Are Born," *Collier's: The National Weekly* 71 (May 12, 1923): 9–10; Charles B. Driscoll, "Why Men Leave Kansas," *American Mercury* 3 (1924): 175–78; idem, "Major Prophets of Holy Kansas," ibid., 8 (1926): 18–26.

35. Duncan Aikman, "The Home-town Mind," *Harper's Monthly Magazine* 151 (1925): 663–69, quotation on p. 665; see also Elmer Davis, "Have Faith in Indiana," *Harper's Monthly Magazine* 153 (1926): 615–25; and Samuel W. Tait, Jr., "Indiana," *American Mercury* 7 (1926): 440–47.

36. "What the Middle West Resents," *Literary Digest* 64 (Feb. 21, 1920): 35; George, "Hail, Columbia!" pp. 137–53; Davenport, "Something Brewing," pp. 368–70.

37. See note 21.

38. Two classic statements of this position are Sherwood Anderson's *Poor White* (New York: B. W. Huebsch, 1920) and Willa Cather's *A Lost Lady* (New York: Alfred A. Knopf, 1923).

39. Sinclair Lewis, *Babbitt* (New York: Harcourt, Brace, 1922).

40. Marx, *Machine in the Garden*; Rex Burns, *Success in America: The Yeoman Dream and the Industrial Revolution* (Amherst: University of Massachusetts Press, 1976); Barbara Novak, *Nature and Culture: American Landscape Painting, 1825–1875* (New York: Oxford University Press, 1980).

41. George, "Hail, Columbia!" p. 147.

42. Ibid.; Waldo Frank, "Mid-America Revisited," *American Mercury* 8 (1926): 322–26; Arthur Pound, "Manning the Middle West's Machines," *Atlantic Monthly* 140 (1927): 690–98.

43. Becker, "Europe," p. 98.

44. Sinclair Lewis provides the clearest statements of this position in *Main Street*, *Babbitt* and "Main Street's Been Paved." Much can be inferred too from a statement by the Massachusetts poet Amy Lowell: "I, too, have traveled throughout the Middle West. I have read the novels and poems which come out of Chicago and the flat farms along the Mississippi Valley. I have tried to like that country. And I am forced to declare it hideous. The little towns I saw from the train depressed me terribly, they were so disordered and dull; in one of those meaningless farmhouses I am sure I could never take a breath, let alone compose a line" ("The House on the Prairie," *Nation* 123 [1926]: 287–88, quotation on p. 287); see also Bliven, "A Stroll," and Frank, "Mid-America."

45. A typical example of this view is Bruce Bliven's "Twenty Hours to New York," *New Republic* 64 (1930): 198–201. An extreme statement is Meridel LeSueur's "Corn Village," *Scribner's Magazine* 90 (1931): 133–40.

46. Becker, "Reader's Guide," p. 798.

47. Edith F. Thompson, "Farmers Back to Earth," *World's Work* 60 (1931): 61–64; Josephine Strode, "Kansas Grit," *Survey* 72 (Aug., 1936): 230–31.

48. "Midwest Discontent," *Nation* 132 (1931): 495.

49. "Hope in the Middle-West," *Spectator* 151 (1933): 44–45.

50. Jay N. Darling, "The Farmers' Holiday," *New Outlook* 161 (1932):

18–20, 44; Josephine Herbst, "Feet in the Grass Roots," *Scribner's Magazine* 93 (1933): 46–51.

51. Theodore Christianson, "The Mood of the Mid-West," *Current History* 36 (May, 1932): 137–42, quotation on p. 137.

52. Arthur Pound, "Land Ho! The Trek toward Economic Security," *Atlantic Monthly* 151 (1933): 714–21; Russell Lord and Paul H. Johnstone, eds., *A Place on Earth: A Critical Appraisal of Subsistence Homesteads*, U.S. Department of Agriculture, Bureau of Agricultural Economics (Washington, D.C.: Government Printing Office, 1942).

53. Franklin Roosevelt, "Back to the Land," *Review of Reviews* 84 (Oct., 1931): 63–64.

54. Paul K. Conklin, *Tomorrow a New World: The New Deal Community Program* (Ithaca, N.Y.: Cornell University Press, 1959), p. 11.

55. Bess Streeter Aldrich, "Why I Live in a Small Town," *Ladies' Home Journal* 50 (June, 1933): 21, 61, quotation on p. 21.

56. J. Lionberger Davis, "From Main Street to Wall Street," *Forum* 93 (1935): 365–66, quotation on p. 365.

57. Christopher Morley, "The Bowling Green," *Saturday Review of Literature* 11 (1934): 327; Harriet Monroe, "Comment," *Poetry: A Magazine of Verse* 42 (1933): 272–77, quotation on p. 276.

58. "Out Where the Vote Begins," *Collier's* 98 (July 18, 1936): 66; see also Duncan Aikman, "The Middle West Rules America," *American Mercury* 37 (1936): 439–47; Margaret Culkin Banning, "The Middle-Aged Middle West," *Harper's Monthly Magazine* 173 (1936): 403–11; and A. Washington Pezet, "The Middle West Takes up the Torch," *Forum* 96 (1936): 285–89.

59. Pezet, "Middle West"; Aikman, "Middle West."

60. Michael C. Steiner, "Regionalism in the Great Depression," *Geographical Review* 73 (1983): 430–46.

61. The three painters were featured in the cover story "U.S. Scene" in *Time* 24 (Dec. 24, 1934): 24–26; see also Steiner, "Regionalism," and Joshua C. Taylor, *America as Art* (New York: Harper & Row, 1976), pp. 229–38.

62. "The Middle West," *Life* 13 (Nov. 9, 1942): 103–11, quotation on p. 103. Good examples of the renewed regional vigor are Herbert Agar's "The Middle West Wants Facts," *Atlantic Monthly* 172 (1943): 83–85; Bernard De Voto's "The Easy Chair," *Harper's Magazine* 187 (1943): 93–96; Eliot Janeway's "The Midwest's Mood," *Life* 15 (Sept. 13, 1943): 11–14, and 15 (Sept. 20, 1943): 11–14; and "Will America Follow the Midwest Again?" *Saturday Evening Post* 217 (Sept. 2, 1944): 104.

63. F. B. Nichols, "The Farmer and Free Trade," *North American Review* 237 (1934): 448–52, reference on p. 450.

64. Remley J. Glass, "Gentlemen, the Corn Belt," *Harper's Monthly Magazine* 167 (1933): 199–209, quotation on p. 200.

65. Oswald G. Villard, "Issues and Men: By Bus through the Middle West," *Nation* 136 (1933): 223–24, quotation on p. 223; see also Christianson, "Mood," pp. 137–42; Glass, "Gentlemen," pp. 199–209; Herbst, "Feet," pp. 46–51; and Davis, "From Main Street," pp. 365–66.

66. Alvin Johnson, "The Anniversary Postbag," *Yale Review,* n.s. 25 (1935): 8–10, quotation on pp. 8–9.

67. J. M. Nolte, "The Fief of Futility," *North American Review* 236 (1933): 293–302, quotation on pp. 296–97.

68. Geographer Guy-Harold Smith, e.g., wrote that "the Middle West ends at the twenty-inch mean annual isohyet" ("What Is Middlewestern?" *Saturday Review of Literature* 10 [1934]: 392). *Review of Reviews,* in a two-part analysis of politics in 1936, grouped Indiana, Illinois, Michigan, Minnesota, Wisconsin, and Iowa under the title "Our Debatable Middle West," 93 (Feb., 1936): 41–46, 77, and left Missouri, Oklahoma, Kansas, Nebraska, and Colorado with the nonlabel "Missouri to the Rockies," 93 (Apr., 1936): 53–57.

69. John Abbot Clark, "The Middle West—There It Lies," *Southern Review* 2 (1937): 462–73, quotations on pp. 462–64.

70. Robert Morss Lovett, "The Future of the Middle West," *New Republic* 101 (1939): 54–56, quotation on p. 56; see also Arville Schaleben, "The North Central States," *Nation* 148 (1939): 690–93; and William L. White, "The Middle West Drifts to the Right," *Nation* 148 (1939): 635–38.

71. W. W. Waymack, "The Middle West Looks Abroad," *Foreign Affairs* 18 (1940): 535–45, quotation on p. 535; "Midwest Miffed," *Business Week,* Jan. 25, 1941, pp. 16–17.

72. Janeway, "Midwest's Mood," pp. 12–14.

73. "Advice to the Republicans," *Life* 16 (May 22, 1944): 34.

74. E. H. Taylor, "Middle West Takes No Backchat from Broadway or Hollywood," *Saturday Evening Post* 222 (Oct. 22, 1949): 12. Another excellent summary statement is Kenneth S. Davis's "East Is East and Midwest Is Midwest," *New York Times Magazine,* Nov. 20, 1949, pp. 17, 56–57, 59–60.

CHAPTER 5. A NEED
FOR PASTORAL VALUES

1. Louis Bromfield, "The Midwest," in *Look at the U.S.A.,* ed. the editors of *Look* (Boston: Houghton Mifflin, 1955), pp. 263–70, quotation on p. 270; William S. White, "The 'Midwest Mind' in Congress," *New York Times Magazine,* Mar. 1, 1953, pp. 18, 31; John Garland, ed., *The North American Midwest: A Regional Geography* (New York: John Wi-

ley & Sons, 1955), pp. 12–16; "Higher on the Hog," *Fortune* 54 (Aug., 1956): 77–81, 206, 209–10, 212.

2. "Cities Crowding – Countryside Losing: Latest on the Way People Are Moving," *U.S. News and World Report* 52 (May 7, 1962): 76–80.

3. "The Creative Middle West," *Life* 34 (May 18, 1953): 143–54, quotation on p. 143; Maynard Kniskern, "Clues to the Midwestern Mind," *New York Times Magazine*, Sept. 15, 1963, pp. 33, 110, 112–13, quotation on p. 110.

4. Quoted by Wallace Stegner in "The Trail of the Hawkeye: Literature Where the Tall Corn Grows," *Saturday Review of Literature* 18 (July 30, 1938): 4.

5. Eric Sevareid, *Not So Wild a Dream* (New York: Alfred A. Knopf, 1946), p. 11.

6. William Gass, *In the Heart of the Heart of the Country and Other Stories* (New York: Harper & Row, 1968), esp. pp. 176–201, quotation on p. 181. Other representative novels include Larry McMurtry's *The Last Picture Show* (New York: Dial Press, 1966) and Wright Morris's *Ceremony in Lone Tree* (New York: Atheneum, 1960).

7. Good introductions to this general subject are E. Relph's *Place and Placelessness* (London: Pion, 1976) and Yi-fu Tuan's *Space and Place: The Perspective of Experience* (Minneapolis: University of Minnesota Press, 1977).

8. Linda H. Graber, *Wilderness as Sacred Space*, Association of American Geographers monograph no. 8 (Washington, D.C.: Association of American Geographers, 1976).

9. Roy W. Meyer, *The Middle Western Farm Novel in the Twentieth Century* (Lincoln: University of Nebraska Press, 1965), pp. 3, 13, 79, 93.

10. See, e.g., Leo A. Borah, "Iowa: Abiding Place of Plenty," *National Geographic Magazine* 76 (1939): 143–82; Ivan Dimitri, "Dakota Winter," *Saturday Evening Post* 212 (Jan. 20, 1940): 14–15, 39; Murdock Pemberton, "Town without a Sage," *New Yorker* 23 (July 5, 1947): 58, 61–64.

11. Saul Bellow, "Illinois Journey," *Holiday* 22 (Sept., 1957): 62–63, 102–7, quotation on p. 62.

12. Jack Schaefer, "Dakota," *Holiday* 17 (May, 1955): 34–42, 84–93, quotations on pp. 86, 93; see also "The Prairie: Its Loneliness and Its Awesome Immensity Shape a Distinctive Way of American Life," *Life* 33 (Dec. 15, 1952): 116–25; Kenneth S. Davis, "Under the Enormous, Pitiless Sky," *New York Times Magazine*, July 19, 1953, pp. 8, 16–17; Wallace Stegner, "The Central Northwest," in *Look at the U.S.A.*, pp. 399–406; Wright Morris, "Our Endless Plains," *Holiday* 24 (July, 1958): 69, 138–42; and Frances Gillis, "Winter North of the Mississippi," *Atlantic Monthly* 205 (Mar., 1960): 84–86.

13. Two examples of this mood are Lauren Soth's "Report from the American 'Heartland,'" *New York Times Magazine*, June 3, 1962, pp. 22–23, 66–68; and Hugh Sidey's "At the Heart of the Land Ocean," *Life* 66 (June 13, 1969): 4.

14. "Pied Piper of Broadway," *Time* 72 (July 21, 1958): 42–46, quotations on pp. 44, 46. The continuing popularity of both the sentiment and the musical is suggested in an article sixteen years later: Gordan Lee Burgett, "Land of the Music Man," *Travel* 141 (June, 1974): 46–49.

15. All three were written by J. R. Humphreys: "The Summer Side of Michigan," *Holiday* 31 (June, 1962): 18, 22–26, 28; "The Sleepy South of Illinois," ibid., 34 (Sept., 1963): 18, 20–23, 25; "The Fields and Fairs of Iowa," ibid., 36 (Sept., 1964): 20, 24, 26, 28–29.

16. See, e.g., "At the Grass Roots: Peace and Plenty," *U.S. News and World Report* 63 (Aug. 14, 1967): 57; and Sidey, "At the Heart."

17. See, e.g., "Where There Is No 'Population Explosion,'" *U.S. News and World Report* 69 (Sept. 28, 1970): 82; "Political Trends in a Key Area: Latest Survey of the Midwest," ibid. (Oct. 19, 1970): 37–40; Calvin Trillin, "The Folks at Home," *New Yorker* 46 (May 16, 1970): 108, 110–13; George Melloan, "Midwest Mood: Looking toward Home," *Wall Street Journal*, Nov. 19, 1971, p. 14; "Minnesota: A State That Works," *Time* 102 (Aug. 13, 1973): 24–35; Scott Seegers and Kathleen Seegers, "Bountiful Iowa," *Reader's Digest* 109 (Aug., 1976): 90–95.

18. The most complete case against current agricultural practice has been made by Wendell Berry, *The Unsettling of America: Culture and Agriculture* (San Francisco, Calif.: Sierra Club Books, 1977).

19. The inferiority idea is documented by Wynona H. Wilkins in "The Idea of North Dakota," *North Dakota Quarterly* 39 (Winter, 1971): 5–28; Peter Gould and Rodney White, *Mental Maps* (Baltimore, Md.: Penguin Books, 1974), pp. 93–118; and James R. Shortridge, "Vernacular Regions in Kansas," *American Studies* 21 (Spring, 1980): 73–94.

20. Laurence Lafore, "In the Sticks," *Harper's Magazine* 243 (Oct., 1971): 108–15, quotation on p. 109. Another perceptive study in this vein is Judah Stampfer's "Midwestern Taste and Eastern Critics," *Nation* 219 (1974): 473–76.

21. Joel Garreau, *The Nine Nations of North America* (Boston, Mass.: Houghton Mifflin, 1981), pp. 1, 5.

22. The following people were kind enough to administer questionnaires at the institutions noted: James P. Allen (California State University–Northridge), John Alwin (Montana State University), Byron Augustin (Southwest Texas State University), C. Murray Austin (University of Northern Iowa), Carol Barrett and Ward Barrett (University of Minnesota), Robert W. Bastian (Indiana State University), Klaus Bayr (Keene State College), Robert H. Brown (University of Wyoming), George O. Carney (Oklahoma State University), James R. Carter (University of Tennessee),

Robert Clark (University of Northern Iowa), Charles O. Collins (University of Northern Colorado), Paul V. Crawford (Bowling Green State University), Randall A. Detro (Nicholls State University), Rebecca Ditgen (University of Wisconsin at Madison), John Donahue (University of Montana), Dennis Fitzsimons (University of Utah), Russel Gerlach (Southwest Missouri State University), Thomas Graff (University of Arkansas), Richard Groop (Michigan State University), Vern Harnapp (University of Akron), Floyd Henderson (State University of New York at Albany), James Henry (University of Florida), Edward P. Hogan (South Dakota State University), C. Gregory Knight (Pennsylvania State University), Charles Kovacik (University of South Carolina), George Macinko (Central Washington University), Joseph Manzo (Concord College), Roland D. Mower (University of North Dakota), John O'Loughlin (University of Illinois), Karl B. Raitz (University of Kentucky), Timothy J. Rickard (Central Connecticut State College), Curtis C. Roseman (University of Illinois), Paul Simkins (Pennsylvania State University), Theodore Steinke (University of South Carolina), Marvin Stone (Kearney State College), Roger Stump (University of Kansas), and Eugene M. Wilson (University of South Alabama).

23. Progressivism is an exception to this generalization; it is a youthful trait that is ranked high in the Old Northwest, especially in Michigan and Wisconsin. These responses were probably linked to the historic Progressive political party, which had its base of power in Wisconsin: see Russel B. Nye, *Midwestern Progressive Politics: A Historical Study of Its Origins and Development, 1870–1958* (East Lansing: Michigan State University Press, 1959).

24. Joseph W. Brownell, "The Cultural Midwest," *Journal of Geography* 59 (1960): 81–85.

25. Ted Robinson, "The Buckeye Reader: A Report on the Literary Constituents," *Saturday Review of Literature* 28 (Jan. 6, 1945): 19–20, quotation on p. 19; John B. Martin, "The Changing Midwest," *Saturday Evening Post* 230 (Jan. 25, 1958): 31, 103–4, 106, quotations on pp. 31, 104.

26. See, e.g., "Fill up the Panama Canal?" *Saturday Evening Post* 212 (Aug. 19, 1939): 22; "Will America Follow the Midwest Again?" ibid., 217 (Sept. 2, 1944): 104; "Fat Days in the U.S. Farm Belt," *Life* 45 (July 14, 1958): 90–97; "At the Grass Roots: Good News for the Democrats," *U.S. News and World Report* 44 (Mar. 14, 1958): 66–67; "Recession? Not in This Part of the Country," ibid., 44 (May 16, 1958): 37–39.

27. Henry Nash Smith, *Virgin Land: The American West as Symbol and Myth* (Cambridge, Mass.: Harvard University Press, 1950); Leo Marx, *The Machine in the Garden: Technology and the Pastoral Ideal in America* (London: Oxford University Press, 1964).

28. Meyer, *Middle Western Farm Novel*, p. 5.

29. E.g., Meredith Nicholson, "The Valley of Democracy," *Scribner's Magazine* 63 (1918): 1–17, 127–62, 257–76, 385–404, 543–58, 654–65.

30. See, e.g., Raymond Moley, "Ohio, an Industrial Empire," *Newsweek* 47 (Apr. 30, 1956): 112; Richard Austin Smith, "The Boiling Ohio," *Fortune* 53 (June, 1956): 109–14, 250, 252, 254, 257–58; "The Great Lakes," *Atlantic Monthly* 200 (Nov., 1957): 28–33; Joe McCarthy, "Will the Seaway Be a Boon or a Flop?" *Look* 22 (Sept. 30, 1958): 39–40; Nathaniel T. Kenney, "New Era on the Great Lakes," *National Geographic Magazine* 115 (1959): 439–87.

31. "A New Dust Bowl in the West," *U.S. News and World Report* 38 (Jan. 21, 1955): 71–72.

32. Roscoe Fleming, "The Dust Blows Again," *Nation* 177 (1953), inside front cover; "Fifty Million Acres – Dust Bowl Danger Zone," *Newsweek* 43 (Mar. 8, 1954): 68–69; "Eight Years of Drought: What It Does to People," *U.S. News and World Report* 42 (Feb. 15, 1957): 48–54; George Tames, "Drought Grips the Plains," *New York Times Magazine,* July 23, 1961, pp. 8–9; "Parched Plains: Firsthand Report," *U.S. News and World Report* 51 (Aug. 7, 1961): 71–73.

33. James R. Shortridge, "Changing Usage of Four American Regional Labels," *Annals of the Association of American Geographers* 77 (1987): 325–36.

34. Walter Rundell, Jr., "Concepts of the 'Frontier' and the 'West,'" *Arizona and the West* 1 (1959): 13–41; Wallace Stegner, "Born a Square: The Westerner's Dilemma," *Atlantic Monthly* 213 (Jan., 1964): 46–50.

35. Wallace Stegner, "History, Myth, and the Western Writer," *American West* 4 (May, 1967): 61–62, 76–79; David Lavender, "The Petrified West and the American Writer," in *Western Writing,* ed. Gerald W. Haslam (Albuquerque: University of New Mexico Press, 1974), pp. 143–56.

36. The largely negative images that Americans traditionally associated with cities is documented by Blanche H. Gelfant in *The American City Novel* (Norman: University of Oklahoma Press, 1954).

37. Garreau, *Nine Nations.*

CHAPTER 6. THE REGIONALIZATION
OF MIDDLE-WESTERN CULTURE

1. D. W. Meinig, "The Mormon Culture Region: Strategies and Patterns in the Geography of the American West, 1847–1964," *Annals of the Association of American Geographers* 55 (1965): 191–220, quotation on p. 215.

2. James R. Shortridge, "Changing Usage of Four American Regional Labels," *Annals of the Association of American Geographers* 77 (1987): 325–36.

3. Meinig, "Mormon Culture," p. 216.

4. The earliest writer I have found who specifically linked Iowa with the Middle West was Rollin L. Hartt, "The Iowans," *Atlantic Monthly* 86 (1900): 195–205.

5. Justice Miller, "The State of Iowa," *Harper's New Monthly Magazine* 79 (1889): 164–80, reference on p. 170.

6. Hartt, "The Iowans," p. 202. A few writers acknowledged a Southern component in the early settlement of Iowa. Novelist Herbert Quick, e.g., wrote in 1916 that "South of the 'Q' [i.e., the Chicago, Burlington and Quincy Railroad] one still finds the political and social life profoundly affected by the early settlers of the Boone and Crockett stripe" ("Can Any State Beat Iowa?" *American Magazine* 82 [July, 1916]: 37, 75–76, quotation on p. 37). Another culture line, between Yankee and midland settlers across northern Iowa, is never acknowledged in the popular literature; see John C. Hudson, "Yankeeland in the Middle West," *Journal of Geography* 85 (1986): 195–200.

7. The exceptional nature of the Iowa Farmer's Holiday revolt in 1932 and 1933 was noted by most observers of the time: see, e.g., Bruce Bliven, "The Farmers Go on Strike," *New Republic* 72 (1932): 66–68; "Behind the Iowa Farm Riots," *Literary Digest* 115 (May 13, 1933): 8; and John S. Nollen, "Revolt in the Cornfields," *Review of Reviews and World's Work* 87 (June, 1933): 24–25.

8. All three claims appear regularly after the 1920s. Typical articles include James B. Weaver, "Iowa: The Structure of Her Life," *Review of Reviews* 73 (1926): 259–65; John S. Nollen, "Culture in the Corn Belt," *Review of Reviews and World's Work* 88 (Aug., 1933): 46, 60; "Iowa Centennial," *Life* 21 (Sept. 30, 1946): 99–107; Paul Engle, "Iowa," *Holiday* 20 (Oct., 1956): 43–44, 46, 48, 50–51, 89–90; and Scott Seegers and Kathleen Seegers, "Bountiful Iowa," *Reader's Digest* 109 (Aug., 1976): 90–95.

9. See the sources in note 8 above, plus Rollin L. Hartt, "The Political Lead of Iowa," *World's Work* 3 (1902): 1989–91; Quick, "Can Any State Beat Iowa?"; Ruth Suckow, "Iowa," *American Mercury* 9 (1926): 39–45; and Wallace Stegner, "The Trail of the Hawkeye: Literature Where the Tall Corn Grows," *Saturday Review of Literature* 18 (July 30, 1938): 3–4, 16–17.

10. See, e.g., Adam Clymer, "The Pulse Remains Steady across the Iowa Heartland," *New York Times*, Jan. 20, 1980, p. 2E.

11. On Darling's influence see Henry G. Felsen, "The State of Iowa," *American Mercury* 66 (1948): 454–61, esp. p. 459; and David L. Lendt, *Ding: The Life of Jay Norwood Darling* (Ames: Iowa State University Press, 1979).

12. See, e.g., James P. Munroe, "The Heart of the United States," *Atlantic Monthly* 102 (1908): 334–42; Frank O. Lowden, "Illinois: The

New Keystone of the Union," *American Review of Reviews* 57 (1918): 271–72; Junius B. Wood, "Illinois: Crossroads of the Continent," *National Geographic Magazine* 59 (1931): 523–94; Albert Parry, "Illinois," *American Mercury* 65 (1947): 269–77; Clyde B. Davis, "Illinois," *Holiday* 20 (Sept. 1956): 26, 28–30, 32–33, 35–37, 40, 73–75; and Robert P. Jordan, "Illinois: The City and the Plain," *National Geographic Magazine* 131 (1967): 745–97.

13. See the sources in note 12 above, plus Edna Ferber, "Illinois," *American Magazine* 82 (Dec., 1916): 39; and Leo A. Borah, "Illinois: Healthy Heart of a Nation," *National Geographic Magazine* 104 (1953): 781–820.

14. See, e.g., "Why Chicago Wants to Be a State," *Literary Digest* 86 (July 11, 1925): 14; Ferber, "Illinois"; Donald C. Peattie, "The Best State of the Fifty," *New York Times Magazine,* Apr. 26, 1959, pp. 14–15, 87–88; and Jordan, "Illinois."

15. Hubert G. H. Wilhelm, "The Origin and Distribution of Settlement Groups: Ohio, 1850" (mimeographed ms., Department of Geography, Ohio University, 1982).

16. Rollin L. Hartt, "The Ohioans," *Atlantic Monthly* 84 (1899): 679–90, quotation on p. 684. This article is the earliest reference I know to place Ohio in the Middle West.

17. Don Knowlton, "Ohio," *American Mercury* 7 (1926): 175–81, quotation on p. 175.

18. "View of Ohio," *American Quarterly Review* 13 (Mar., 1833): 94–126, quotations on pp. 96–97; see also "Ohio," *North American Review* 53 (1841): 320–59.

19. Knowlton, "Ohio," p. 175. Good discussions of the special-destiny idea include "Progress of Ohio, Historical and Statistical," *DeBow's Review* 14 (1853): 307–12; Charles F. Thwig, "Ohio," *Harper's New Monthly Magazine* 93 (1896): 286–300; Hartt, "The Ohioans," pp. 679–90; Charles M. Harvey, "A Hundred Years of Ohio," *World's Work* 5 (1903): 3229–39; and Whitelaw Reid, "In an Old Ohio Town," in his *American and English Studies,* vol. 1 (New York: Charles Scribner's Sons, 1913), pp. 289–316.

20. See the sources in note 19 above, plus Murat Halstead, "A Century of the State of Ohio," *American Monthly Review of Reviews* 27 (1903): 426–30; and Frank Carney, "Geographic Influences in the Development of Ohio," *Popular Science Monthly* 75 (1909): 479–89.

21. Brand Whitlock, "Ohio and the Ohio Man," *American Magazine* 82 (Nov., 1916): 31.

22. Harvey, "A Hundred Years," p. 3230.

23. These ideas occur in all the post-1900 Ohio literature cited above. A good summary view is Melville Chater's "Ohio: The Gateway State," *National Geographic Magazine* 61 (1932): 525–91.

24. Bruce Catton, *Waiting for the Morning Train: An American Boyhood* (Garden City, N.Y.: Doubleday, 1972), p. 32.

25. One of the first to label Minnesota as Middle West in the popular periodical literature was Glanville Smith in "Minnesota: Mother of Lakes and Rivers," *National Geographic Magazine* 67 (1935): 273–318. Two early users of the term Upper Middle West are "Rich Land of Lakes," *Newsweek* 45 (Apr. 11, 1955): 102–10; and Clay Blair, Jr., "Minnesota Grows Older," *Saturday Evening Post* 234 (Mar. 18, 1961): 30–31, 85, 87–88. A recent definitive user is John R. Borchert, *America's Northern Heartland* (Minneapolis: University of Minnesota Press, 1987).

26. Some examples of this delimitation appear in Phil Stong, "Holiday in Michigan," *Holiday* 10 (July, 1951): 27–39, 120–21; Andrew H. Brown, "Work-hard, Play-hard Michigan," *National Geographic Magazine* 101 (1952): 281–320; Glanville Smith, "On Goes Wisconsin," ibid., 72 (1937): 1–46; Chet Vonier, "The State of Wisconsin," *American Mercury* 67 (1948): 234–39; and Smith, "Minnesota."

27. E. P. Powell, "New England in Michigan," *New England Magazine* 13 (1895): 419–28, quotation on p. 427; see also Gregory S. Rose, "South Central Michigan Yankees," *Michigan History* 70 (Mar./Apr., 1986): 32–39; and Hudson, "Yankeeland."

28. L. F. Hubbard, "The Progress of Minnesota," *North American Review* 144 (1887): 22–28, quotation on p. 23; see also Ellis B. Usher, "New England in Wisconsin," *New England Magazine* 22 (1900): 446–61; Mary Dopp, "Geographical Influences in the Development of Wisconsin," *Bulletin of the American Geographical Society* 45 (1913): 401–12, 490–99, 585–609, 653–63, 736–49, 831–46, 902–20, reference on pp. 597–98; and "Minnesota: Chief of the Northwestern States," *Harper's Weekly* 46 (1902): 1587–90, 1607.

29. John H. Fenton, *Midwest Politics* (New York: Holt, Rinehart & Winston, 1966), p. 4; Daniel J. Elazar, *American Federalism: A View from the States,* 2d ed. (New York: Thomas Y. Crowell, 1972), pp. 84–126.

30. Elmer Davis, "Wisconsin Is Different," *Harper's Monthly Magazine* 165 (1932): 613–24; Mark Schorer, "Wisconsin," *Holiday* 6 (July, 1949): 35–53; Fenton, *Midwest Politics,* pp. 44–49.

31. Davis, "Wisconsin Is Different," p. 617.

32. Schorer, "Wisconsin," p. 48.

33. Fenton, *Midwest Politics,* pp. 44–49; see also C. P. Ilbert, "The Wisconsin Idea," *Living Age* 281 (1914): 287–93; Ray S. Baker, "Wisconsin," *American Magazine* 83 (Feb., 1917): 37, 59; Arthur Warner, "La-Follette in Wisconsin," *Nation* 119 (1924): 158–61; and Russel B. Nye, *Midwestern Progressive Politics: A Historical Study of Its Origins and Development, 1870–1958* (East Lansing: Michigan State University Press, 1959).

34. Frederick M. Davenport, "The Farmers' Revolution in North Dakota," *Outlook* 114 (1916): 325–27, quotations on p. 325; see also "North Dakota's Farmer-Revolt," *Literary Digest* 54 (Jan. 20, 1917): 115–16; and Arthur Ruhl, "The North Dakota Idea," *Atlantic Monthly* 123 (1919): 686–96.

35. Fenton, *Midwest Politics*, pp. 76–92.

36. Ibid., pp. 9–24.

37. Arthur Pound, "As Goes Michigan," *Atlantic Monthly* 159 (1937): 73–78, reference on p. 74; Brown, "Work-hard," p. 286.

38. Bruce Catton, "The Real Michigan," *Holiday* 22 (Aug., 1957): 26–39, quotation on p. 28.

39. The name Middle North is used by Arnold Mulder in "Authors and Wolverines: The Books and Writers of Michigan," *Saturday Review of Literature* 19 (Mar. 4, 1939): 3–4, 16.

40. An early, insightful view of Michigan in flux is Harold H. Martin, "Michigan: The Problem State," *Saturday Evening Post* 234 (Feb. 25, 1961): 13–15, 86–88.

41. Shortridge, "Changing Usage"; see also Jerry Flint, "Trouble in the Heartland," *Forbes* 127 (Mar. 16, 1981): 120–26.

42. W. F. Vilas, "The State of Wisconsin," *Harper's New Monthly Magazine* 82 (1891): 676–96, reference on p. 687; Clifton Johnson, "Old Times and New in Wisconsin," *Outing Magazine* 49 (1906): 737–42; Dopp, "Geographical Influences," pp. 841–42.

43. Vonier, "State of Wisconsin," pp. 235–36.

44. Joel Garreau, *The Nine Nations of North America* (Boston, Mass.: Houghton Mifflin, 1981).

45. Garrison Keillor, *Lake Wobegon Days* (New York: Viking Press, 1985).

46. Blair, "Minnesota," p. 87.

47. "Rich Land"; Frederick G. Vosburgh, "Minnesota Makes Ideas Pay," *National Geographic Magazine* 96 (1949): 291–316.

48. "Minnesota: A State That Works," *Time* 102 (Aug. 13, 1973): 24–35, quotation on p. 34; Maureen Smith, "Mystique of the Upper Midwest," *Update* (University of Minnesota) 14 (Feb., 1987): 8–10.

49. Shortridge, "Changing Usage."

50. Robert M. Crisler, "The Regional Status of Little Dixie in Missouri and Little Egypt in Illinois," *Journal of Geography* 49 (1950): 337–43; Douglas K. Meyer, "Southern Illinois Migration Fields: The Shawnee Hills in 1850," *Professional Geographer* 28 (1976): 151–60.

51. Wilbur Zelinsky, *The Cultural Geography of the United States* (Englewood Cliffs, N.J.: Prentice-Hall, 1973), pp. 88–94, 110–29.

52. Mary Dean, "The Hoosiers at Home," *Lippincott's Magazine of Popular Literature and Science* 23 (1879): 441–44, quotation on pp. 442–43.

53. Alphonso Wetmore, "Gazetteer of the State of Missouri," *North American Review* 48 (1839): 514–26, quotation on p. 521.

54. "Missouri," *DeBow's Review* 11 (1851): 268–85, quotation on p. 283; "Missouri," *Western Journal* 6 (1851): 71–76.

55. William O. Lynch, "The Influence of Population Movements on Missouri before 1861," *Missouri Historical Review* 16 (1922): 506–16; Russel L. Gerlach, *Settlement Patterns in Missouri: A Study of Population Origins with a Wall Map* (Columbia: University of Missouri Press, 1986), pp. 11–24.

56. Richard L. Power, "Wet Lands and the Hoosier Stereotype," *Mississippi Valley Historical Review* 22 (1935): 33–48, the church data are from p. 47; see also Charles R. Dryer, "Geographic Influences in the Development of Indiana," *Journal of Geography* 9 (1910): 17–22; Gregory S. Rose, "Hoosier Origins: The Nativity of Indiana's United States–Born Population in 1850," *Indiana Magazine of History* 81 (1985): 201–32; and Gregory S. Rose, "Upland Southerners: The County Origins of Southern Migrants to Indiana by 1850," ibid., 82 (1986): 242–63.

57. Robert La Follette, "Interstate Migration and Indiana Culture," *Mississippi Valley Historical Review* 16 (1929): 347–58, reference on p. 349; Richard A. Cordell, "Limestone, Corn, and Literature: The Indiana Scene and Its Interpreters," *Saturday Review of Literature* 19 (Dec. 17, 1938): 3–4, 14–15.

58. William E. Wilson, "Indiana," *Holiday* 8 (Aug., 1950): 27–34, 100–104, reference on pp. 100–101; Pat Colander, "Back Home in Indiana," *New York Times*, June 9, 1985, sec. 10, pp. 16, 32.

59. James Stevens, "Partners in Eden," *American Mercury* 35 (1935): 324–31, quotation on p. 325.

60. Lowell Mellett, "Klan and Church," *Atlantic Monthly* 132 (1923): 586–92; Stanley Frost, "The Klan Shows Its Hand in Indiana," *Outlook* 137 (1924): 187–90; Duncan Aikman, "The Home-town Mind," *Harper's Monthly Magazine* 151 (1925): 663–69; Elmer Davis, "Have Faith in Indiana," ibid., 153 (1926): 615–25; and Samuel W. Tait, Jr., "Indiana," *American Mercury* 7 (1926): 440–47.

61. Robert S. Lynd and Helen M. Lynd, *Middletown: A Study in Modern American Culture* (New York: Harcourt, Brace & World, 1929), p. 7. The impact of this study is suggested by two subsequent books: Robert S. Lynd and Helen M. Lynd, *Middletown in Transition: A Study in Cultural Conflicts* (New York: Harcourt, Brace & World, 1937) and Theodore Caplow, Howard M. Bahr, Bruce A. Chadwick, Reuben Hill, and Margaret H. Williamson, *Middletown Families: Fifty Years of Change and Continuity* (Minneapolis: University of Minnesota Press, 1982).

62. Wilson, "Indiana," p. 28.

63. Dean, "Hoosiers," p. 442. See, e.g., George H. Mosser, "The State of Indiana," *Journal of the National Education Association* 14

(1925): 151–52; Frederick Simplich, "Indiana Journey," *National Geographic Magazine* 70 (1936): 267–320; Elmer Davis, "The Indiana Faith," *Saturday Review of Literature* 23 (Apr. 12, 1941): 3–4, 19; Wilson, "Indiana"; "Indiana: Soft Spots but No Gloom," *Business Week*, May 28, 1960: 81–82; Berton Roueché, "Profiles: To Hear a Rooster Crow," *New Yorker* 54 (Jan. 1, 1979): 35–45; and Neal R. Peirce and Jerry Hagstrom, *The Book of America: Inside Fifty States Today* (New York: W. W. Norton, 1983), pp. 282–96.

64. Perry McCandless, *A History of Missouri*, vol. 2: *1820–1860* (Columbia: University of Missouri Press, 1972), p. 37.

65. Gerlach, *Settlement Patterns*.

66. Eugene R. Page, "I'm from Missouri," *Saturday Review of Literature* 22 (Apr. 27, 1940): 3–4, 19.

67. Shortridge, "Changing Usage"; Russel L. Gerlach, "Geography and Politics in Missouri: A Study of Electoral Patterns," *Missouri Geographer* 18 (1971): 27–36.

68. On the tolerance issue see Charles M. Harvey, "Missouri," *Atlantic Monthly* 86 (1900): 63–73; Samuel W. Tait, Jr., "Missouri," *American Mercury* 8 (1926): 481–88; and Phil Stong, "Missouri," *Holiday* 14 (Nov., 1953): 103–12, 148–52. For "Southern" traits see Julian Street, "In Mizzoura," *Collier's: The National Weekly* 53 (Aug. 29, 1914): 18–19, 31–34; Jonas Viles, "Sections and Sectionalism in a Border State," *Mississippi Valley Historical Review* 21 (1934): 3–22; Frances Tucker, "When Kinfolks Gather in Missouri," *Christian Science Monitor Weekly Magazine*, Nov. 30, 1940, p. 15; and "Harry Truman's Missouri," *Life* 18 (June 25, 1945): 75–78.

69. Frederick Simplich, "Missouri: Mother of the West," *National Geographic Magazine* 43 (1923): 421–60; "The Missouri Democracy Goes Dry," *Literary Digest* 98 (Aug. 25, 1928): 12; MacKinlay Kantor, *Missouri Bittersweet* (Garden City, N.Y.: Doubleday, 1969), p. xi.

70. Robert M. Crisler, "Missouri's Little Dixie," *Missouri Historical Review* 42 (1948): 130–39; Howard W. Marshall, *Folk Architecture in Little Dixie: A Regional Culture in Missouri* (Columbia: University of Missouri Press, 1981).

71. Good examples of the diversity argument are Herbert S. Hadley, "The South's Most Northern State," *Collier's: The National Weekly* 44 (Jan. 22, 1910): 21; "The State of Missouri: Part Northern, Part Southern, Part Eastern, Part Western—and Wholly American," *Fortune* 32 (July, 1945): 113–21, 212, 215–18; L. H. Robbins, "First State, Pro Tem, of the Nation," *New York Times Magazine*, June 29, 1947, pp. 17–19; Stong, "Missouri"; and Roul Tunley, "Missouri: Four States in One," *Saturday Evening Post* 233 (Sept. 3, 1960): 11–13, 71–73.

72. "A Touch of Missouri Will Do No Harm," *Saturday Evening*

Post 218 (July 14, 1945): 104; see also "Harry Truman's Missouri" and "The State of Missouri."

73. Tunley, "Missouri"; see also Fred W. Lindecke, "Poverty's Second Generation," *Nation* 199 (1964): 163–65; Calvin Trillin, "The Folks at Home," *New Yorker* 46 (May 16, 1970): 108, 110–13; and C. W. Gusewelle, "'A Continuity of Place and Blood': The Seasons of Man in the Ozarks," *American Heritage* 29 (Dec., 1977): 96–109.

74. Clarence H. Matson, "Oklahoma: A Vigorous Western Commonwealth," *Review of Reviews* 32 (1905): 310–19, quotation on p. 312; see also Day A. Willey, "A Patchwork Quilt of Humanity," *Lippincott's Monthly Magazine* 84 (1909): 321–28; Bryan Mack, "Oklahoma: Forty Years Young," *Review of Reviews* 80 (1929): 132–44; and Burton Rascoe, "Boomers and Sooners," *Saturday Review of Literature* 25 (Feb. 14, 1942): 16–17.

75. Michael F. Doran, "Population Statistics of Nineteenth Century Indian Territory," *Chronicles of Oklahoma* 53 (1976): 492–515; Grant Foreman, "Statehood for Oklahoma?" *Independent* 63 (1907): 331–35; Stanley Frost, "Behind the White Hoods," *Outlook* 135 (1923): 492–95; George Milburn, "Oklahoma," *Yale Review*, n.s. 35 (1946): 515–26.

76. Arthur W. Baum, "Oklahoma: The State That Struck It Rich," *Saturday Evening Post* 234 (July 1, 1961): 18–19, 69–70; Faubion Bowers, "Oklahoma, OK!" *Holiday* 43 (May, 1968): 72–74, 113–17, 121, 124; Burton Rascoe, "Oklahoma: Low Jacks and the Crooked Game," in *These United States: A Symposium*, ed. Ernest Gruening, 2 vols. (New York: Boni & Liveright, 1923, 1924), 2:154–69; Johnston Murray, "Oklahoma Is in a Mess!" *Saturday Evening Post* 227 (Apr. 30, 1955): 20–21, 92, 96; "Oklahoma's Mess," ibid., 227 (June 4, 1955): 4.

77. Howard W. Morgan and Anne H. Morgan, *Oklahoma: A Bicentennial History* (New York: W. W. Norton, 1977), pp. 55–57.

78. Bowers, "Oklahoma, OK!" p. 124; see also Baum, "Oklahoma"; Eric Allen, "The Best of Oklahoma," *Holiday* 31 (Mar., 1962): 19–25; "Oklahoma 1970: The Dust Bowl of the 1930's Revisited," *Time* 95 (Jan. 26, 1970): 16–17; Robert P. Jordan, "Oklahoma: The Adventurous One," *National Geographic Magazine* 140 (1971): 149–89; and Paul R. Recer, "Where History, Farms, Oil and Industry Blend," *U.S. News and World Report* 88 (Jan. 28, 1980): 50–53.

79. Charles M. Harger, "New Era in the Middle West," *Harper's New Monthly Magazine* 97 (1898): 276–82; Franklin Matthews, "Bright Skies in the West," *Harper's Weekly* 42 (1898): 113–14, 138–39, 161–63, 186–89, 208–10, 231–32, 256, 278–79, 322–23.

80. Walter Prescott Webb, *The Great Plains* (New York: Ginn, 1931), p. 8. The best-known nineteenth-century statement is John Wesley Powell's *Report on the Lands of the Arid Regions*, ed. Wallace Stegner (Cam-

bridge, Mass.: Harvard University Press, 1966), originally published as House Executive Document no. 73, U.S. Congress, House, 45th Cong., 2d sess., 1878 (serial set no. 1805). For recent material see Brian W. Blouet and Frederick C. Luebke, eds., *The Great Plains: Environment and Culture* (Lincoln: University of Nebraska Press, 1979).

81. "The Kansas Situation," *Nation* 56 (1893): 43–44, quotation on p. 44. For general background see O. Gene Clanton, *Kansas Populism: Ideas and Men* (Lawrence: University Press of Kansas, 1969).

82. William Allen White, "Kansas: Its Present and Its Future," *Forum* 23 (1897): 75–83, quotation on p. 76; see also J. W. Gleed, "Is New York More Civilized Than Kansas?" ibid., 17 (1894): 217–34; Edwin Taylor, "In Defence of Kansas," *North American Review* 164 (1897): 349–55; and Frank W. Blackmar, "Kansas after the Drought," *Review of Reviews* 24 (1901): 314–20.

83. Davenport, "The Farmer's Revolution," p. 325; see also "North Dakota's Farmer-Revolt"; Ruhl, "The North Dakota Idea"; and W. G. Roylance, "Americanism in North Dakota," *Nation* 109 (1919): 37–39.

84. Benchmark studies include John D. Barnhart, "Rainfall and the Populist Party in Nebraska," *American Political Science Review* 19 (1925): 527–40; John D. Hicks, *The Populist Revolt* (Minneapolis: University of Minnesota Press, 1931); and Lawrence Goodwyn, *Democratic Promise: The Populist Movement in America* (New York: Oxford University Press, 1976).

85. See, e.g., Robert George Paterson, "North Dakota: A Twentieth Century Valley Forge," in *These United States*, 2:310–21.

86. Contrasting conclusions are drawn by Paul Bonnifield in *The Dust Bowl: Men, Dirt, and Depression* (Albuquerque: University of New Mexico Press, 1979) and by Donald E. Worster in *Dust Bowl: The Southern Plains in the 1930s* (New York: Oxford University Press, 1979).

87. Dorothea Lange and Paul Taylor, *An American Exodus* (New Haven, Conn.: Yale University Press, 1969); Arthur Rothstein, *The Depression Years as Photographed by Arthur Rothstein* (New York: Dover Publications, 1978); John Steinbeck, *The Grapes of Wrath* (New York: Viking Press, 1939). Two other accounts that were important in molding the public view are Lawrence Svobida's *Farming the Dust Bowl: A First-Hand Account from Kansas* (Lawrence: University Press of Kansas, 1986), originally published in 1940 as *An Empire of Dust*; and Frederick Manfred's *The Golden Bowl* (Albuquerque: University of New Mexico Press, 1976), originally published in 1944, with the author using the name Feike Feikema.

88. Taylor, "In Defence," pp. 350, 352. A similar statement for Nebraska is William R. Lighton's "The Riches of a Rural State," *World's Work* 1 (1900): 93–103.

89. Webb, *The Great Plains*, p. 8; Mari Sandoz, "Nebraska," *Holiday* 19 (May, 1956): 103–14, 154–55, reference on p. 114; Jack Schaefer, "Dakota," ibid., 17 (May, 1955): 34–42, 84–93, reference on p. 42.

90. Frederick Simplich, "South Dakota Keeps Its West Wild," *National Geographic Magazine* 91 (1947): 555–88, quotation on p. 571. On the recent farmer-cattleman synthesis see James R. Shortridge, "Cowboy, Yeoman, Pawn, and Hick: Myth and Contradiction in Great Plains Life," *Focus* 35 (Oct., 1985): 22–27, and recent popular literature on the Nebraska Sand Hills: e.g., John Madson, "Land of Long Sunsets," *National Geographic Magazine* 154 (1978): 493–517.

91. Notable exceptions to this positive position are the thoughtful but grim novels of Wright Morris, notably *Ceremony in Lone Tree* (New York: Atheneum, 1960); see Robert D. Harper, "Wright Morris's 'Ceremony in Lone Tree': A Picture of Life in Middle America," *Western American Literature* 11 (1976): 199–213.

92. Lighton, "Riches," pp. 93, 96; Willa Cather, *O Pioneers!* (Boston: Houghton Mifflin, 1913), and *My Ántonia* (Boston: Houghton Mifflin, 1918); Mari Sandoz, *Old Jules* (New York: Hastings House, 1935).

93. Dwight Griswold, "The Nebraska Story," *Saturday Evening Post* 216 (Sept. 4, 1943): 9–11, 73–75, quotation on p. 10; Marc A. Rose, "Grasshopper Thrift," *Reader's Digest* 32 (Apr., 1938): 108–10; Leo A. Borah, "Nebraska: The Cornhusker State," *National Geographic Magazine* 87 (1945): 513–42.

94. Berton Roueché, "Profiles: Stapleton, Nebraska," *New Yorker* 46 (Jan. 2, 1971): 29–40; Madson, "Land of Long Sunsets"; Shortridge, "Cowboy."

95. Sandoz, "Nebraska," p. 112; Gretchen Lee, "Nebraska," *American Mercury* 4 (1926): 102–4, quotation on p. 104.

96. John R. Milton, *South Dakota: A Bicentennial History* (New York: W. W. Norton, 1977), pp. 131–36, 168.

97. Elizabeth Eiselen, "The Tourist Industry of a Modern Highway: U.S. 16 in South Dakota," *Economic Geography* 21 (1945): 221–30; Milton, *South Dakota*, pp. 137–38.

98. "South Dakota: Its Boundless Plains Are the Heart of a Continent," *Life* 11 (Oct. 6, 1941): 98–109, quotation on p. 102; Leslie G. Kennon, "South Dakota Wonderland," *American Forests* 60 (Aug., 1954): 18–19, 52, quotation on p. 18; Simplich, "South Dakota"; Edgar Cheatham and Patricia Cheatham, "The Voices of South Dakota," *Travel* 144 (July, 1975): 24–29, 66–67.

99. Lee, "Nebraska," p. 104; Sandoz, "Nebraska," p. 112.

100. See, e.g., "Colonization of Kansas," *Littell's Living Age* 43 (1854): 113–15; and John James Ingalls, "Kansas: 1541–1891," *Harper's New Monthly Magazine* 86 (1893): 696–713, reference on p. 701.

101. Ingalls, "Kansas," p. 703.

102. Lorrin Leland, ed., *The Kansas Experience in Poetry* (Lawrence: University of Kansas, Division of Continuing Education, 1978), pp. 8–9.

103. James C. Malin, "Kansas: Some Reflections on Culture, Inheritance, and Originality," *Journal of the Central Mississippi Valley American Studies Association* 2 (Fall, 1961): 3–19; William Allen White, "Kansas: A Puritan Survival," in *These United States*, 1:1–12, quotation on p. 1; Neal R. Peirce, *The Great Plains States of America: People, Politics, and Power in the Nine Great Plains States* (New York: W. W. Norton, 1972), p. 221.

104. Becker's essay was written in 1910; it was reprinted in his *Everyman His Own Historian: Essays on History and Politics* (New York: F. S. Crofts, 1935), pp. 1–28, quotations on pp. 27, 26. Typical articles praising the Kansas character are William Allen White's "Fifty Years of Kansas," *World's Work* 8 (1904): 4870–72; John Kimberly Mumford's "This Land of Opportunity: How Kansas Has Enriched Her Farmers," *Harper's Weekly* 52 (Sept. 26, 1908): 24–25; and Charles M. Harger's "Those Kansas Editors," *Independent* 68 (1910): 395–98.

105. W. G. Clugston, "Kansas the Essence of Typical America," *Current History* 25 (Oct., 1926): 14–20, quotations on pp. 16–17; Meridel LeSueur, "Corn Village," *Scribner's Magazine* 90 (1931): 133–40, quotation on p. 133; Maureen McKernan, "In Defense of Kansas," *Scribner's Magazine* 92 (1932): 106–8, quotation on p. 108. Among the sharpest criticisms of Kansas puritanism were Charles W. Wood, "Where Tomorrow's Ideas Are Born," *Collier's: The National Weekly* 71 (May 12, 1923): 9–10; Charles B. Driscoll, "Why Men Leave Kansas," *American Mercury* 3 (1924): 175–78; and idem, "Major Prophets of Holy Kansas," ibid., 8 (1926): 18–26. For a good general perspective on this era see Robert Smith Bader, *Prohibition in Kansas: A History* (Lawrence: University Press of Kansas, 1986).

106. Avis D. Carlson, "The Man from Kansas: A Portrait," *Harper's Monthly Magazine* 172 (1936): 584–91, quotation on p. 584; Kenneth S. Davis, "That Strange State of Mind Called Kansas," *New York Times Magazine*, June 26, 1949, pp. 13, 50–53, quotation on p. 52; see also Debs Myers, "The Exciting Story of Kansas," *Holiday* 9 (June, 1951): 52–63, 166–68; and Kenneth S. Davis, "What's the Matter with Kansas," *New York Times Magazine*, June 27, 1954, pp. 12, 39, 41.

107. See, e.g., Calvin Trillin, "U.S. Journal: Kansas," *New Yorker* 54 (Aug. 7, 1978): 68–73; Robert Paul Jordan, "Nebraska: The Good Life," *National Geographic Magazine* 145 (1974): 378–407.

CHAPTER 7. THE MIDDLE
WEST AS METAPHOR

1. Literature on the American character is voluminous. The works of Henry Nash Smith, *Virgin Land: The American West as Symbol and Myth* (Cambridge, Mass.: Harvard University Press, 1950), and Leo Marx, *The Machine in the Garden: Technology and the Pastoral Idea in America* (London: Oxford University Press, 1964), are fundamental for my regionalist interpretations. Additional geographical perspectives can be found in John B. Jackson, *American Space: The Centennial Years, 1865–1876* (New York: W. W. Norton, 1972), and Wilbur Zelinsky, *The Cultural Geography of the United States* (Englewood Cliffs, N.J.: Prentice-Hall, 1973). A good guide to the literature up to 1970 is Michael McGiffert, ed., *The Character of Americans: A Book of Readings*, rev. ed. (Homewood, Ill.: Dorsey Press, 1970). Annual bibliographic essays on the subject appear in the journal *American Quarterly*.

2. Smith, *Virgin Land*; Marx, *Machine in the Garden*, p. 238; Leslie Fiedler, "Montana: Or the End of Jean-Jacques Rousseau," in *The Collected Essays of Leslie Fiedler*, vol. 1 (New York: Stein & Day, 1971), pp. 131–41.

3. On the East see Marx, *Machine in the Garden*, and Rex Burns, *Success in America: The Yeoman Dream and the Industrial Revolution* (Amherst: University of Massachusetts Press, 1976). On the West see Smith, *Virgin Land*; Henry N. Smith, "The West as an Image of the American Past," *University of Kansas City Review* 18 (1951): 29–40; Richard Slotkin, *Regeneration through Violence: The Mythology of the American Frontier, 1600–1860* (Middletown, Conn.: Wesleyan University Press, 1973); idem, *The Fatal Environment: The Myth of the Frontier in the Age of Industrialization, 1800–1890* (New York: Atheneum, 1985); and Robert G. Athearn, *The Mythic West in Twentieth-Century America* (Lawrence: University Press of Kansas, 1986).

4. Yi-fu Tuan, "Place: An Experiential Perspective," *Geographical Review* 65 (1975): 151–65.

5. John B. Jackson, "The Necessity for Ruins," in *The Necessity for Ruins and Other Topics* (Amherst: University of Massachusetts Press, 1980), pp. 89–102, quotations on pp. 98, 100; see also David E. Shi, *The Simple Life: Plain Living and High Thinking in American Culture* (New York: Oxford University Press, 1985), and David Lowenthal, *The Past Is a Foreign Country* (New York: Cambridge University Press, 1985).

6. D. W. Meinig, "Symbolic Landscapes: Some Idealizations of American Communities," in *The Interpretation of Ordinary Landscapes: Geographical Essays*, ed. D. W. Meinig (New York: Oxford University Press, 1979), pp. 164–92, quotation on p. 167.

7. Richard V. Francaviglia, "Main Street USA: The Creation of a Popular Image," *Landscape* 21 (Spring–Summer, 1977): 18–22.

8. *Lawrence* (Kans.) *Journal-World*, Sept. 9, 1982, p. 1.

9. Dorothy Canfield Fisher, *Vermont Tradition: The Biography of an Outlook on Life* (Boston: Little, Brown, 1953).

10. Edward A. Ross, "The Middle West: Being Studies of Its People in Comparison with Those of the East," *Century Magazine* 83 (1912): 609–15, 682–92, 874–80, and 84 (1912): 142–48, quotation on p. 613. The classic study of depopulation in northern New England is James W. Goldthwaite's "A Town That Has Gone Downhill," *Geographical Review* 17 (1927): 527–57.

11. Edith Wharton, *Ethan Frome* (New York: Charles Scribner's Sons, 1911); Wallace Stegner, *Second Growth* (Boston: Houghton Mifflin, 1947). The specific settings of these two books actually are just outside Vermont's borders, in western Massachusetts and in northern New Hampshire, respectively.

12. The "restored" Vermont is best described in three volumes by Noel Perrin: *First Person Rural: Essays of a Sometime Farmer* (Boston, Mass.: David R. Godine, 1978), *Second Person Rural: More Essays of a Sometime Farmer* (Boston, Mass.: David R. Godine, 1980), *Third Person Rural: Further Essays of a Sometime Farmer* (Boston, Mass.: David R. Godine, 1983), and in two volumes by Don Mitchell: *Moving Upcountry: A Yankee Way of Knowledge* (Dublin, N.H.: Yankee Books, 1984) and *Living Upcountry: A Pilgrim's Progress* (Dublin, N.H.: Yankee Books, 1986); see also Harold A. Meeks, *Time and Change in Vermont: A Human Geography* (Chester, Conn.: Globe Pequot Press, 1986).

13. See E. Relph, *Place and Placelessness* (London: Pion, 1976).

14. Cotton Mather, "The Midwest: Image and Reality," *Journal of Geography* 85 (1986): 190–94, quotation on p. 193.

15. John Gunther, *Inside U.S.A.* (New York: Harper & Brothers, 1947), p. 274.

16. See, e.g., the Associated Press articles on life in Pierre, S.D., and a planned promotion by New York's Bloomingdale's department stores, *Lawrence* (Kans.) *Journal-World*, Feb. 4, 1979, p. 9B, and Oct. 20, 1987, p. 5B.

17. Joel Garreau, *The Nine Nations of North America* (Boston, Mass.: Houghton Mifflin, 1981), pp. 334, 336.

18. *Lawrence* (Kans.) *Journal-World*, Mar. 23, 1980, p. 5A.

19. Jack Kisling, "I Wouldn't Kid My Sister," *Denver Post*, June 25, 1978, p. 1.

20. "Minnesota: A State That Works," *Time* 102 (Aug. 13, 1973): 24–35, quotation on p. 35.

Bibliography

SOURCES FROM
THE POPULAR LITERATURE

"Advice to the Republicans." *Life* 16 (May 22, 1944): 34.

Agar, Herbert. "The Middle West Wants Facts." *Atlantic Monthly* 172 (1943): 83–85.

Aikman, Duncan. "The Home-town Mind." *Harper's Monthly Magazine* 151 (1925): 663–69.

————. "The Middle West Rules America." *American Mercury* 37 (1936): 439–47.

Albert, Allen D. "Where the Prairie Money Goes." *Scribner's Magazine* 82 (1927): 476–80.

Aldrich, Bess Streeter. "Why I Live in a Small Town." *Ladies' Home Journal* 50 (June, 1933): 21, 61.

Allen, Eric. "The Best of Oklahoma." *Holiday* 31 (Mar., 1962): 19–25.

Allen, William V. "Western Feeling towards the East." *North American Review* 162 (1896): 588–93.

Anderson, Sherwood. *Poor White.* New York: B. W. Huebsch, 1920.

————. *Winesburg, Ohio.* New York: B. W. Huebsch, 1919; reprint, New York: Viking Press, 1968.

A.P.H. "The Adjournment of Common Sense." *New Republic* 16 (1918): 158–60.

"At the Grass Roots: Good News for the Democrats." *U.S. News and World Report* 44 (Mar. 14, 1958): 66–67.

"At the Grass Roots: Peace and Plenty." *U.S. News and World Report* 63 (Aug. 14, 1967): 57.

"Attitude of the Middle West, The." *New Republic* 6 (1916): 119–20.

Baker, Ray S. "Wisconsin." *American Magazine* 83 (Feb., 1917): 37, 59.

Ballard, John. "The Mouse in the Republican Cheese." *Outlook* 135 (1923): 16–17.

Banning, Margaret Culkin. "The Middle-Aged Middle West." *Harper's Monthly Magazine* 173 (1936): 403–11.

Bauer, Douglas. *Prairie City, Iowa: Three Seasons at Home*. New York: G. P. Putnam's Sons, 1979.

Baum, Arthur W. "Oklahoma: The State That Struck It Rich." *Saturday Evening Post* 234 (July 1, 1961): 18–19, 69–70.

Becker, Carl L. "Europe through the Eyes of the Middle West." *New Europe* 15 (1920): 98–104.

———. "Kansas." In his *Everyman His Own Historian: Essays on History and Politics*. New York: F. S. Crofts, 1935, pp. 1–28.

Becker, May Lamberton. "The Reader's Guide." *Saturday Review of Literature* 8 (1932): 798.

"Behind the Iowa Farm Riots." *Literary Digest* 115 (May 13, 1933): 8.

Bellow, Saul. "Illinois Journey." *Holiday* 22 (Sept., 1957): 62–63, 102–7.

Bennett, John E. "Is the West Discontented? Is a Revolution at Hand?" *Arena* 16 (1896): 393–405.

Blackmar, Frank W. "Kansas after the Drought." *Review of Reviews* 24 (1901): 314–20.

Blair, Clay, Jr. "Minnesota Grows Older." *Saturday Evening Post* 234 (Mar. 18, 1961): 30–31, 85, 87–88.

Bliven, Bruce. "The Farmers Go on Strike." *New Republic* 72 (1932): 66–68.

———. "A Stroll on Main Street." *New Republic* 37 (1923): 63–66.

———. "Twenty Hours to New York." *New Republic* 64 (1930): 198–201.

———. "Why the Farmer Sees Red." *New Republic* 36 (1923): 273–75.

Borah, Leo A. "Illinois: Healthy Heart of a Nation." *National Geographic Magazine* 104 (1953): 781–820.

———. "Iowa: Abiding Place of Plenty." *National Geographic Magazine* 76 (1939): 143–82.

———. "Nebraska: The Cornhusker State." *National Geographic Magazine* 87 (1945): 513–42.

Bowers, Faubion. "Oklahoma, OK!" *Holiday* 43 (May, 1968): 72–74, 113–17, 121, 124.

Brigham, Albert P. "A Geographer's Geography Lesson on the Prairies." *Journal of Geography* 16 (1918): 167–70.

Bromfield, Louis. "The Midwest." In *Look at the U.S.A.*, edited by the editors of *Look*, pp. 263–70. Boston: Houghton Mifflin, 1955.

Brown, Andrew H. "Work-hard, Play-hard Michigan." *National Geographic Magazine* 101 (1952): 281–320.

Buck, Philo M., Jr. "The Middle West and the Peace." *Review* 1 (1919): 34–35.

———. "Pacifism in the Middle West." *Nation* 104 (1917): 595–97.

Burgett, Gordan L. "Land of the Music Man." *Travel* 141 (June, 1974): 46–49.

Butler, Mann. "Valley of the Ohio: Its Conquest and Settlement by Americans." *Western Journal and Civilian* 9 (1853): 355–61.

Caldwell, Erskine. *Afternoons in Mid-America: Observations and Impressions.* New York: Dodd, Mead, 1976.

Capper, Arthur. "The Middle West Looks Abroad." *Foreign Affairs* 5 (1927): 529–37.

Carlson, Avis D. "The Man from Kansas: A Portrait." *Harper's Monthly Magazine* 172 (1936): 584–91.

Carney, Frank. "Geographic Influences in the Development of Ohio." *Popular Science Monthly* 75 (1909): 479–89.

Carter, William. *Middle West Country.* Boston: Houghton Mifflin, 1975.

Carver, T. N. "Life in the Corn Belt." *World's Work* 7 (1903): 4232–39.

Case, J. B. "The Future of Western Trade." *North American Review* 188 (1908): 598–608.

Cather, Willa. *A Lost Lady.* New York: Alfred A. Knopf, 1923.

———. *My Ántonia.* Boston: Houghton Mifflin, 1918.

———. *O Pioneers!* Boston: Houghton Mifflin, 1913.

Catton, Bruce. "The Real Michigan." *Holiday* 22 (Aug., 1957): 26–39.

———. *Waiting for the Morning Train: An American Boyhood.* Garden City, N.Y.: Doubleday, 1972.

Chater, Melville. "Ohio: The Gateway State." *National Geographic Magazine* 61 (1932): 525–91.

Cheatham, Edgar, and Patricia Cheatham. "The Voices of South Dakota." *Travel* 144 (July, 1975): 24–29, 66–67.

Christianson, Theodore. "The Mood of the Mid-West." *Current History* 36 (May, 1932): 137–42.

"Cities Crowding—Countryside Losing: Latest on the Way People Are Moving." *U.S. News and World Report* 52 (May 7, 1962): 76–80.

Clark, John A. "The Middle West—There it Lies." *Southern Review* 2 (1937): 462–73.

Clugston, W. G. "Kansas the Essence of Typical America." *Current History* 25 (Oct., 1926): 14–20.

Clymer, Adam. "The Pulse Remains Steady across the Iowa Heartland." *New York Times,* Jan. 20, 1980, p. 2E.

Colander, Pat. "Back Home in Indiana." *New York Times,* June 9, 1985, sec. 10, pp. 16, 32.

"Colonization of Kansas." *Littell's Living Age* 43 (1854): 113–15.

Cordell, Richard A. "Limestone, Corn, and Literature: The Indiana Scene and Its Interpreters." *Saturday Review of Literature* 19 (Dec. 17, 1938): 3–4, 14–15.

"Creative Middle West, The." *Life* 34 (May 18, 1953): 143–54.

Crèvecoeur, J. Hector St. John. *Letters from an American Farmer.* London: Thomas Davies, 1782.

Dale, Stephen M. "The West through Eastern Eyes." *Independent* 57 (1904): 903–9.

Darling, Jay N. "The Farmers' Holiday." *New Outlook* 161 (1932): 18–20, 44.

Davenport, Frederick M. "The Farmers' Revolution in North Dakota." *Outlook* 114 (1916): 325–27.

———. "On the Trail of Progress and Reaction in the West." *Outlook* 109 (1915): 886–91, 922–36, and 110 (1915): 94–99.

———. "Political Thinking in the Middle West." *Outlook* 113 (1916): 266–69.

———. "Something Brewing in the Middle West." *Outlook* 132 (1922): 368–70.

Davis, Clyde B. "Illinois." *Holiday* 20 (Sept., 1956): 26, 28–30, 32–33, 35–37, 40, 73–75.

Davis, Elmer. "Have Faith in Indiana." *Harper's Monthly Magazine* 153 (1926): 615–25.

———. "The Indiana Faith." *Saturday Review of Literature* 23 (Apr. 12, 1941): 3–4, 19.

———. "Wisconsin Is Different." *Harper's Monthly Magazine* 165 (1932): 613–24.

Davis, J. Lionberger. "From Main Street to Wall Street." *Forum* 93 (1935): 365–66.

Davis, Kenneth S. "East Is East and Midwest Is Midwest." *New York Times Magazine*, Nov. 20, 1949, pp. 17, 56–57, 59–60.

———. "That Strange State of Mind Called Kansas." *New York Times Magazine*, June 26, 1949, pp. 13, 50–53.

———. "Under the Enormous, Pitiless Sky." *New York Times Magazine*, July 19, 1953, pp. 8, 16–17.

———. "What's the Matter with Kansas." *New York Times Magazine*, June 27, 1954, pp. 12, 39, 41.

Davis, Peter. *Hometown: A Portrait of an American Community*. New York: Simon & Schuster, 1982.

Dean, Mary. "The Hoosiers at Home." *Lippincott's Magazine of Popular Literature and Science* 23 (1879): 441–44.

De Voto, Bernard. "The Easy Chair." *Harper's Magazine* 187 (1943): 93–96.

Dimitri, Ivan. "Dakota Winter." *Saturday Evening Post* 212 (Jan. 20, 1940): 14–15, 39.

Driscoll, Charles B. "Major Prophets of Holy Kansas." *American Mercury* 8 (1926): 18–26.

———. "Why Men Leave Kansas." *American Mercury* 3 (1924): 175–78.

"Eight Years of Drought: What It Does to People." *U.S. News and World Report* 42 (Feb. 15, 1957): 48–54.

Engle, Paul. "Iowa." *Holiday* 20 (Oct., 1956): 43–44, 46, 48, 50–51, 89–90.

"Fat Days in the U.S. Farm Belt." *Life* 45 (July 14, 1958): 90–97.

Felsen, Henry G. "The State of Iowa." *American Mercury* 66 (1948): 454–61.

Ferber, Edna. "Illinois." *American Magazine* 82 (Dec., 1916): 39.

"Fifty Million Acres – Dust Bowl Danger Zone." *Newsweek* 43 (Mar. 8, 1954): 68–69.

"Fill up the Panama Canal?" *Saturday Evening Post* 212 (Aug. 19, 1939): 22.

Fleming, Roscoe. "The Dust Blows Again." *Nation* 177 (1953), inside front cover.

Flint, Jerry. "Trouble in the Heartland." *Forbes* 127 (Mar. 16, 1981): 120–26.

Flint, Timothy. "Religious Character of the Western People." *Western Monthly Review* 1 (1827): 268–70.

———. "Writers of the Western Country." *Western Monthly Review* 2 (1828): 11–21.

Forbes-Lindsay, C. H. "The Spirit of the West: How Its Vigor and Resourcefulness Are Affecting the Development of the Whole Country." *Craftsman* 15 (1908): 64–77.

Foreman, Grant. "Statehood for Oklahoma?" *Independent* 63 (1907): 331–35.

Frank, Waldo. "Mid-America Revisited." *American Mercury* 8 (1926): 322–26.

Frost, Stanley. "Behind the White Hoods." *Outlook* 135 (1923): 492–95.

———. "The Klan Shows Its Hand in Indiana." *Outlook* 137 (1924): 187–90.

Garland, Hamlin. "Literary Emancipation of the West." *Forum* 16 (1893): 156–66.

Garland, John, ed. *The North American Midwest: A Regional Geography.* New York: John Wiley & Sons, 1955.

Garreau, Joel. *The Nine Nations of North America.* Boston, Mass.: Houghton Mifflin, 1981.

Gass, William. *In the Heart of the Heart of the Country and Other Stories.* New York: Harper & Row, 1968.

George, W. L. "Hail Columbia! America in the Making." *Harper's Monthly Magazine* 142 (1921): 142–53.

Gilles, Frances. "Winter North of the Mississippi." *Atlantic Monthly* 205 (Mar., 1960): 84–86.

Glass, Remley J. "Gentlemen, the Corn Belt." *Harper's Monthly Magazine* 167 (1933): 199–209.

Gleed, J. W. "Is New York More Civilized Than Kansas?" *Forum* 17 (1894): 217–34.

"Great Lakes, The." *Atlantic Monthly* 200 (Nov., 1957): 28–33.

Griswold, Dwight. "The Nebraska Story." *Saturday Evening Post* 216 (Sept. 4, 1943): 9–11, 73–75.

Gruening, Ernest, ed. *These United States: A Symposium.* 2 vols. New York: Boni & Liveright, 1923, 1924.

Gunther, John. *Inside U.S.A.* New York: Harper & Brothers, 1947.

Gusewelle, C. W. "'A Continuity of Place and Blood': The Seasons of Man in the Ozarks." *American Heritage* 29 (Dec., 1977): 96–109.

Hadley, Herbert S. "The South's Most Northern State." *Collier's: The National Weekly* 44 (Jan. 22, 1910): 21.

Halstead, Murat. "A Century of the State of Ohio." *American Monthly Review of Reviews* 27 (1903): 426–30.

Harger, Charles M. "An Era of Thrift in the Middle West." *World's Work* 5 (1903): 3091–93.

———. "Good Neighbors All." *Outlook* 82 (1906): 367–70.

———. "The Middle West and Wall Street." *American Monthly Review of Reviews* 36 (1907): 83–86.

———. "The Middle West's Peace Problems." *Atlantic Monthly* 123 (1919): 555–60.

———. "New Era in the Middle West." *Harper's New Monthly Magazine* 97 (1898): 276–82.

———. "The New Westerner." *North American Review* 185 (1907): 748–58.

———. "The Political Clouds out West." *Independent* 111 (1923): 82–83.

———. "The Prairie Woman: Yesterday and Today." *Outlook* 70 (1902): 1008–12.

———. "Those Kansas Editors." *Independent* 68 (1910): 395–98.

———. "The West at Home." *Outlook* 86 (1907): 32–36, 70–75, 106–10.

"Harry Truman's Missouri." *Life* 18 (June 15, 1945): 75–78.

Hartt, Rollin L. "The Iowans." *Atlantic Monthly* 86 (1900): 195–205.

———. "Middle-Westerners and That Sort of People." *Century Magazine* 93 (1916): 169–80.

———. "The Ohioans." *Atlantic Monthly* 84 (1899): 679–90.

———. "The Political Lead of Iowa." *World's Work* 3 (1902): 1989–91.

Harvey, Charles M. "A Hundred Years of Ohio." *World's Work* 5 (1903): 3229–39.

———. "Missouri." *Atlantic Monthly* 86 (1900): 63–73.

Haskell, H. J. "The U-53 and the Middle West." *Outlook* 114 (1916): 414–15.

Herbst, Josephine. "Feet in the Grass Roots." *Scribner's Magazine* 93 (1933): 46–51.

"Higher on the Hog." *Fortune* 54 (Aug., 1956): 77–81, 206, 209–10, 212.

"Hope in the Middle-West." *Spectator* 151 (1933): 44–45.

Hough, Emerson. "The Settlement of the West: A Study in Transportation." *Century Magazine* 63 (1901/2): 91–107, 201–16, 355–69.

"House on the Prairie, The." *Nation* 123 (1926): 287–88.

Howe, E. W. "Provincial Peculiarities of Western Life." *Forum* 14 (1892): 91–93.

Howland, Louis. "Provincial or National?" *Scribner's Magazine* 43 (1908): 450–55.

Hubbard, L. F. "The Progress of Minnesota." *North American Review* 144 (1887): 22–28.

Humphreys, J. R. "The Fields and Fairs of Iowa." *Holiday* 36 (Sept., 1964): 20, 24, 26, 28–29.

———. "The Sleepy South of Illinois." *Holiday* 34 (Sept., 1963): 18, 20–23, 25.

———. "The Summer Side of Michigan." *Holiday* 31 (June, 1962): 18, 22–26, 28.

Hungerford, Edward. "Rediscovering the West." *Harper's Weekly* 55 (Dec. 30, 1911): 11, and 56 (Jan. 20, 1912): 11–12.

Hutton, Graham. *Midwest at Noon.* Chicago: University of Chicago Press, 1946.

Ilbert, C. P. "The Wisconsin Idea." *Living Age* 281 (1914): 287–93.

"Indiana: Soft Spots but No Gloom." *Business Week*, May 28, 1960, pp. 81–82.

Ingalls, John James. "Kansas: 1541–1891." *Harper's New Monthly Magazine* 86 (1893): 696–713.

"Iowa Centennial." *Life* 21 (Sept. 30, 1946): 99–107.

Janeway, Eliot. "The Midwest's Mood." *Life* 15 (Sept. 13, 1943): 11–14, and 15 (Sept. 20, 1943): 11–14.

Jefferson, Thomas. *Notes on the State of Virginia.* London: John Stockdale, 1785.

Johnson, Alvin. "The Anniversary Postbag." *Yale Review,* n.s. 25 (1935): 8–10.

Johnson, Clifton. "Old Times and New in Wisconsin." *Outing Magazine* 49 (1906): 737–42.

Jordan, Robert Paul. "Illinois: The City and the Plain." *National Geographic Magazine* 131 (1967): 745–97.

———. "Nebraska: The Good Life." *National Geographic Magazine* 145 (1974): 378–407.

———. "Oklahoma: The Adventurous One." *National Geographic Magazine* 140 (1971): 149–89.

"Kansas Situation, The." *Nation* 56 (1893): 43–44.

Kantor, MacKinlay. *Missouri Bittersweet.* Garden City, N.Y.: Doubleday, 1969.

Keillor, Garrison. *Lake Wobegon Days.* New York: Viking Press, 1985.

Kennon, Leslie G. "South Dakota Wonderland." *American Forests* 60 (Aug., 1954): 18–19, 52.

Kenny, Nathaniel T. "New Era on the Great Lakes." *National Geographic Magazine* 115 (1959): 439–87.

Kisling, Jack. "I Wouldn't Kid My Sister." *Denver Post,* June 25, 1978, p. 1.

Kniskern, Maynard. "Clues to the Midwestern Mind." *New York Times Magazine,* Sept. 15, 1963, pp. 33, 110, 112–13.

Knowlton, Don. "Ohio." *American Mercury* 7 (1926): 175–81.

Lafore, Laurence. "In the Sticks." *Harper's Magazine* 243 (Oct., 1971): 108–15.

Lange, Dorothea, and Paul Taylor. *An American Exodus.* New Haven, Conn.: Yale University Press, 1969.

Lee, Gretchen. "Nebraska." *American Mercury* 4 (1926): 102–4.

LeSueur, Meridel. "Corn Village." *Scribner's Magazine* 90 (1931): 133–40.

Lewis, Sinclair. *Babbitt.* New York: Harcourt, Brace, 1922.

———. *Main Street: The Story of Carol Kennicott.* New York: Harcourt, Brace, 1920.

———. "Main Street's Been Paved." *Nation* 119 (1924): 255–60.

Lighton, William R. "The Riches of a Rural State." *World's Work* 1 (1900): 93–103.

———. "Where Is the West?" *Outlook* 74 (1903): 702–4.

Lincoln, Abraham. *The Collected Works of Abraham Lincoln,* edited by Roy P. Basler. 9 vols. New Brunswick, N.J.: Rutgers University Press, 1953.

Lindecke, Fred W. "Poverty's Second Generation." *Nation* 199 (1964): 163–65.

Lord, Russell, and Paul H. Johnstone, eds. *A Place on Earth: A Critical Appraisal of Subsistence Homesteads.* U.S. Department of Agriculture, Bureau of Agricultural Economics. Washington, D.C.: Government Printing Office, 1942.

Lovett, Robert Morss. "The Future of the Middle West." *New Republic* 101 (1939): 54–56.

Lowden, Frank O. "Illinois: The New Keystone of the Union." *American Review of Reviews* 57 (1918): 271–72.

Lynd, Robert S., and Helen M. Lynd. *Middletown: A Study in Modern American Culture.* New York: Harcourt, Brace & World, 1929.

———. *Middletown in Transition: A Study in Cultural Conflicts.* New York: Harcourt, Brace & World, 1937.

Mabie, Hamilton W. "The Intellectual Movement in the West." *Atlantic Monthly* 82 (1898): 592–605.

McAdam, Rezin W. "The Peopling of the Plains." *Overland Monthly,* n.s. 42 (1903): 131–40.

McCarthy, Joe. "Will the Seaway Be a Boon or a Flop?" *Look* 22 (Sept. 30, 1958): 39–40.

Mack, Bryan. "Oklahoma: Forty Years Young." *Review of Reviews* 80 (1929): 132–44.

McKernan, Maureen. "In Defense of Kansas." *Scribner's Magazine* 92 (1932): 106–8.

McMahon, John R. "Our Jazz-Spotted Middle West." *Ladies' Home Journal* 39 (Feb., 1922): 38, 181.

McMurtry, Larry. *The Last Picture Show.* New York: Dial Press, 1966.

Madson, John. "Land of Long Sunsets." *National Geographic Magazine* 154 (1978): 493–517.

"Maligned Middle West, The." *Bellman* 22 (1917): 595.

Manfred, Frederick. *The Golden Bowl.* Albuquerque: University of New Mexico Press, 1976 (originally published in 1944, with the author using the name Feike Feikema).

"Manufacturing West, The." *Independent* 55 (1903): 459–60.

Martin, Harold H. "Michigan: The Problem State." *Saturday Evening Post* 234 (Feb. 25, 1961): 13–15, 86–88.

Martin, John B. "The Changing Midwest." *Saturday Evening Post* 230 (Jan. 25, 1958): 31, 103–4, 106.

Matson, Clarence H. "Oklahoma: A Vigorous Western Commonwealth." *Review of Reviews* 32 (1905): 310–19.

Matthews, Franklin. "Bright Skies in the West." *Harper's Weekly* 42 (1898): 113–14, 138–39, 161–63, 186–89, 208–10, 231–32, 256, 278–79, 322–23.

Mellett, Lowell. "Klan and Church." *Atlantic Monthly* 132 (1923): 586–92.

Melloan, George. "Midwest Mood: Looking toward Home." *Wall Street Journal,* Nov. 19, 1971, p. 14.

"Middle West, The." *Life* 13 (Nov. 9, 1942): 103–11.

"Middle West and the Submarine War off Our Coast, The." *Outlook* 114 (1916): 362, 371.

"Midwest Discontent." *Nation* 132 (1931): 495.

"Midwest Miffed." *Business Week,* Jan. 25, 1941, pp. 16–17.

Milburn, George. "Oklahoma." *Yale Review,* n.s. 35 (1946): 515–26.

Miller, J. K. "Are the People of the West Fanatics?" *Arena* 13 (1895): 92–97.

Miller, Justice. "The State of Iowa." *Harper's New Monthly Magazine* 79 (1889): 164–80.

"Minnesota: Chief of the Northwestern States." *Harper's Weekly* 46 (1902): 1587–90, 1607.

"Minnesota: A State That Works." *Time* 102 (Aug. 13, 1973): 24–35.

"Missouri." *DeBow's Review* 11 (1851): 268–85.

"Missouri." *Western Journal* 6 (1851): 71–76.

"Missouri Democracy Goes Dry, The." *Literary Digest* 98 (Aug. 25, 1928): 12.

"Missouri to the Rockies." *Review of Reviews* 93 (Apr., 1936): 53–57.

Mitchell, Don. *Living Upcountry: A Pilgrim's Progress.* Dublin, N.H.: Yankee Books, 1986.

———. *Moving Upcountry: A Yankee Way of Knowledge.* Dublin, N.H.: Yankee Books, 1984.

Moley, Raymond. "Ohio, an Industrial Empire." *Newsweek* 47 (Apr. 30, 1956): 112.

Monroe, Harriet. "Comment." *Poetry: A Magazine of Verse* 42 (1933): 272–77.

Morley, Christopher. "The Bowling Green." *Saturday Review of Literature* 11 (1934): 327.

Morris, Wright. *Ceremony in Lone Tree.* New York: Atheneum, 1960.

———. "Our Endless Plains." *Holiday* 24 (July, 1958): 69, 138–42.

Mosser, George H. "The State of Indiana." *Journal of the National Education Association* 14 (1925): 151–52.

Mulder, Arnold. "Authors and Wolverines: The Books and Writers of Michigan." *Saturday Review of Literature* 19 (Mar. 4, 1939): 3–4, 16.

Mumford, John Kimberly. "This Land of Opportunity: How Kansas Has Enriched Her Farmers." *Harper's Weekly* 52 (Sept. 26, 1908): 24–25.

Munroe, James P. "The Heart of the United States." *Atlantic Monthly* 102 (1908): 334–42.

Murray, Johnston. "Oklahoma Is in a Mess!" *Saturday Evening Post* 227 (Apr. 30, 1955): 20–21, 92, 96.

Myers, Debs. "The Exciting Story of Kansas." *Holiday* 9 (June, 1951): 52–63, 166–68.

Nelson, Henry Loomis. "In Medias Res." *Harper's Monthly Magazine* 109 (1904): 54–59.

———. "The Spirit of the West." *Harper's Monthly Magazine* 109 (1904): 197–203.

"New Dust Bowl in the West, A." *U.S. News and World Report* 38 (Jan. 21, 1955): 71–72.

Nichols, F. B. "The Farmer and Free Trade." *North American Review* 237 (1934): 448–52.

Nicholson, Meredith. "The Valley of Democracy." *Scribner's Magazine* 63 (1918): 1–17, 127–62, 257–76, 385–404, 543–58, 654–65.

Nollen, John S. "Culture in the Corn Belt." *Review of Reviews and World's Work* 88 (Aug., 1933): 46, 60.

———. "Revolt in the Cornfields." *Review of Reviews and World's Work* 87 (June, 1933): 24–25.

Nolte, J. M. "The Fief of Futility." *North American Review* 236 (1933): 293–302.

"North Dakota's Farmer-Revolt." *Literary Digest* 54 (Jan. 20, 1917): 115–16.

"Northwest, The." *DeBow's Review* 15 (1888): 325–41.

"Ohio." *North American Review* 53 (1841): 320–59.

"Oklahoma 1970: The Dust Bowl of the 1930's Revisited." *Time* 95 (Jan. 26, 1970): 16–17.

"Oklahoma's Mess." *Saturday Evening Post* 227 (June 4, 1955): 4.

"Our Debatable Middle West." *Review of Reviews* 93 (Feb., 1936): 41–46, 77.

"Out Where the Vote Begins." *Collier's* 98 (July 18, 1936): 66.

Page, Eugene R. "I'm from Missouri." *Saturday Review of Literature* 22 (Apr. 27, 1940): 3–4, 19.

"Parched Plains: Firsthand Report." *U.S. News and World Report* 51 (Aug. 7, 1961): 71–73.

Parker, Maude. "Our Town." *Saturday Evening Post* 200 (July 30, 1927): 13, 42, 47, 49.

Parry, Albert. "Illinois." *American Mercury* 65 (1947): 269–77.

Paterson, Robert George. "North Dakota: A Twentieth Century Valley Forge." In *These United States: A Symposium,* edited by Ernest Gruening, 2:310–21. 2 vols. New York: Boni & Liveright, 1923, 1924.

"Patriotism, East and West." *Literary Digest* 54 (1917): 1486.

Peattie, Donald C. "The Best State of the Fifty." *New York Times Magazine,* Apr. 26, 1959, pp. 14–15, 87–88.

Peirce, Neal R. *The Great Plains States of America: People, Politics, and Power in the Nine Great Plains States.* New York: W. W. Norton, 1972.

———, and Jerry Hagstrom. *The Book of America: Inside Fifty States Today.* New York: W. W. Norton, 1983.

Pemberton, Murdock. "Town without a Sage." *New Yorker* 23 (July 5, 1947): 58, 61–64.

Perrin, Noel. *First Person Rural: Essays of a Sometime Farmer.* Boston, Mass.: David R. Godine, 1978.

———. *Second Person Rural: More Essays of a Sometime Farmer.* Boston, Mass.: David R. Godine, 1980.

———. *Third Person Rural: Further Essays of a Sometime Farmer.* Boston, Mass.: David R. Godine, 1983.

Pezet, A. Washington. "The Middle West Takes up the Torch." *Forum* 96 (1936): 285–89.

"Pied Piper of Broadway." *Time* 72 (July 21, 1958): 42–46.

"Political Trends in a Key Area: Latest Survey of the Midwest." *U.S. News and World Report* 69 (Oct. 19, 1970): 37–40.

Pound, Arthur. "As Goes Michigan." *Atlantic Monthly* 159 (1937): 73–78.

———. "Land Ho! The Trek toward Economic Security." *Atlantic Monthly* 151 (1933): 714–21.

———. "Manning the Middle West's Machines." *Atlantic Monthly* 140 (1927): 690–98.

Powell, E. P. "New England in Michigan." *New England Magazine* 13 (1895): 419–28.

Powell, John Wesley. *Report on the Lands of the Arid Regions,* edited by Wallace Stegner. Cambridge, Mass.: Harvard University Press, 1966 (originally published as House Executive Document no. 73, U.S. Congress, House, 45th Cong., 2d sess., 1878 [serial set no. 1805]).

"Prairie: Its Loneliness and Its Awesome Immensity Shape a Distinctive Way of American Life, The." *Life* 33 (Dec. 15, 1952): 116–25.

"Progress of Ohio, Historical and Statistical." *DeBow's Review* 14 (1853): 307–12.

Quick, Herbert. "Can Any State Beat Iowa?" *American Magazine* 82 (July, 1916): 37, 75–76.

Rascoe, Burton. "Boomers and Sooners." *Saturday Review of Literature* 25 (Feb. 14, 1942): 16–17.

————. "Oklahoma: Low Jacks and the Crooked Game." In *These United States: A Symposium*, edited by Ernest Gruening, 2:154–69. 2 vols. New York: Boni & Liveright, 1923, 1924.

Recer, Paul R. "Where History, Farms, Oil and Industry Blend." *U.S. News and World Report* 88 (Jan. 28, 1980): 50–53.

"Recession? Not in This Part of the Country." *U.S. News and World Report* 44 (May 16, 1958): 37–39.

Reid, Whitelaw. "In an Old Ohio Town." In his *American and English Studies*, vol. 1, pp. 289–316. New York: Charles Scribner's Sons, 1913.

"Rich Land of Lakes." *Newsweek* 45 (Apr. 11, 1955): 102–10.

Robbins, L. H. "First State, Pro Tem, of the Nation." *New York Times Magazine*, June 29, 1947, pp. 17–19.

Robinson, Ted. "The Buckeye Reader: A Report on the Literary Constituents." *Saturday Review of Literature* 28 (Jan. 6, 1945): 19–20.

Roosevelt, Franklin. "Back to the Land." *Review of Reviews* 84 (Oct., 1931): 63–64.

Rose, Marc A. "Grasshopper Thrift." *Reader's Digest* 32 (Apr., 1938): 108–10.

Ross, Edward A. "The Middle West: Being Studies of Its People in Comparison with Those of the East." *Century Magazine* 83 (1912): 609–15, 686–92, 874–80, and 84 (1912): 142–48.

Rothstein, Arthur. *The Depression Years as Photographed by Arthur Rothstein.* New York: Dover Publications, 1978.

Roueché, Berton. "Profiles: Stapleton, Nebraska." *New Yorker* 46 (Jan. 2, 1971): 29–40.

————. "Profiles: To Hear a Rooster Crow." *New Yorker* 54 (Jan. 1, 1979): 35–45.

Rowell, Chester H. "Is Middle West Radicalism Here to Stay?" *World's Work* 46 (1923): 655–58.

————. "Why the Middle West Went Radical." *World's Work* 46 (1923): 157–65.

Roylance, W. G. "Americanism in North Dakota." *Nation* 109 (1919): 37–39.

Ruhl, Arthur. "The North Dakota Idea." *Atlantic Monthly* 23 (1919): 686–96.

Sandburg, Carl. *Harvest Poems, 1910–1960.* New York: Harcourt Brace Jovanovich, 1960.

Sandoz, Mari. "Nebraska." *Holiday* 19 (May, 1956): 103–14, 154–55.

————. *Old Jules.* New York: Hastings House, 1935.

Schaefer, Jack. "Dakota." *Holiday* 17 (May, 1955): 34–42, 84–93.

Schaleben, Arville. "The North Central States." *Nation* 148 (1939): 690–93.

Schorer, Mark. "Wisconsin." *Holiday* 6 (July, 1949): 35–53.

Seegers, Scott, and Kathleen Seegers. "Bountiful Iowa." *Reader's Digest* 109 (Aug., 1976): 90–95.

Sevareid, Eric. *Not So Wild a Dream.* New York: Alfred A. Knopf, 1946.

Sidey, Hugh. "At the Heart of the Land Ocean." *Life* 66 (June 13, 1969): 4.

Simplich, Frederick. "Indiana Journey." *National Geographic Magazine* 70 (1936): 267–320.

———. "Missouri: Mother of the West." *National Geographic Magazine* 43 (1923): 421–60.

———. "South Dakota Keeps Its West Wild." *National Geographic Magazine* 91 (1947): 555–88.

Smith, Glanville. "Minnesota: Mother of Lakes and Rivers." *National Geographic Magazine* 67 (1935): 273–318.

———. "On Goes Wisconsin." *National Geographic Magazine* 72 (1937): 1–46.

Smith, Guy-Harold. "What Is Middlewestern?" *Saturday Review of Literature* 10 (1934): 392.

Smith, Maureen. "Mystique of the Upper Midwest." *Update* (University of Minnesota) 14 (Feb., 1987): 8–10.

Smith, Richard Austin. "The Boiling Ohio." *Fortune* 53 (June, 1956): 109–14, 250, 252, 254, 257–58.

Soth, Lauren. "Report from the American 'Heartland.'" *New York Times Magazine,* June 3, 1962, pp. 22–23, 66–68.

"South Dakota: Its Boundless Plains Are the Heart of a Continent." *Life* 11 (Oct. 6, 1941): 98–109.

Speare, Charles F. "Business Conditions in the West and Southwest." *American Review of Reviews* 37 (1908): 715–17.

"Spectator, The." *Outlook* 84 (1906): 1053–54.

Stampfer, Judah. "Midwestern Taste and Eastern Critics." *Nation* 219 (1974): 473–76.

"State of Missouri: Part Northern, Part Southern, Part Eastern, Part Western — and Wholly American, The." *Fortune* 32 (July, 1945): 113–21, 212, 215–18.

Stegner, Wallace. "The Central Northwest." In *Look at the U.S.A.,* edited by the editors of *Look,* pp. 399–406. Boston: Houghton Mifflin, 1955.

———. "Down the Upper Mississippi." *Blair and Ketchum's Country Journal* 8 (Sept., 1981): 74–86.

———. *Second Growth.* Boston: Houghton Mifflin, 1947.

———. "Trail of the Hawkeye: Literature Where the Tall Corn Grows, The." *Saturday Review of Literature* 18 (July 30, 1938): 3–4, 16–17.

Steinbeck, John. *The Grapes of Wrath.* New York: Viking Press, 1939.

Stevens, James. "Partners in Eden." *American Mercury* 35 (1935): 324–31.

Stong, Phil. "Holiday in Michigan." *Holiday* 10 (July, 1951): 27–39, 120–21.

————. "Missouri." *Holiday* 14 (Nov., 1953): 103–12, 148–52.

Street, Julian. "In Mizzoura." *Collier's: The National Weekly* 53 (Aug. 29, 1914): 18–19, 31–34.

Strode, Josephine. "Kansas Grit." *Survey* 72 (Aug. 1936): 230–31.

Suckow, Ruth. "Iowa." *American Mercury* 9 (1926): 39–45.

Svobida, Lawrence. *Farming the Dust Bowl: A First-Hand Account from Kansas.* Lawrence: University Press of Kansas, 1986 (originally published in 1940 as *An Empire of Dust*).

Tait, Samuel W., Jr. "Indiana." *American Mercury* 7 (1926): 440–47.

————. "Missouri." *American Mercury* 8 (1926): 481–88.

Tames, George. "Drought Grips the Plains." *New York Times Magazine,* July 23, 1961, pp. 8–9.

Tarkington, Booth. "The Middle West." *Harper's Monthly Magazine* 106 (1902): 75–83.

Taylor, E. H. "Middle West Takes No Backchat from Broadway or Hollywood." *Saturday Evening Post* 222 (Oct. 22, 1949): 12.

Taylor, Edwin. "In Defence of Kansas." *North American Review* 164 (1897): 349–55.

Thompson, Edith F. "Farmers Back to Earth." *World's Work* 60 (1931): 61–64.

Thwig, Charles F. "Ohio." *Harper's New Monthly Magazine* 93 (1896): 286–300.

"Touch of Missouri Will Do No Harm, A." *Saturday Evening Post* 218 (July 14, 1945): 104.

Trillin, Calvin. "The Folks at Home." *New Yorker* 46 (May 16, 1970): 108, 110–13.

————. "U.S. Journal: Kansas." *New Yorker* 54 (Aug. 7, 1978): 68–73.

Tucker, Frances. "When Kinfolks Gather in Missouri." *Christian Science Monitor Weekly Magazine,* Nov. 30, 1940, p. 15.

Tunley, Roul. "Missouri: Four States in One." *Saturday Evening Post* 233 (Sept. 3, 1960): 11–13, 71–73.

"U.S. Scene." *Time* 24 (Dec. 24, 1934): 24–26.

Usher, Ellis B. "New England in Wisconsin." *New England Magazine* 22 (1900): 446–61.

"View of Ohio." *American Quarterly Review* 13 (Mar., 1833): 94–126.

Vilas, W. F. "The State of Wisconsin." *Harper's New Monthly Magazine* 82 (1891): 676–96.

Villard, Oswald G. "Issues and Men: By Bus through the Middle West." *Nation* 136 (1933): 223–24.

Vonier, Chet. "The State of Wisconsin." *American Mercury* 67 (1948): 234–39.

Vosburgh, Frederick G. "Minnesota Makes Ideas Pay." *National Geographic Magazine* 96 (1949): 291–316.

Warner, Arthur. "LaFollette in Wisconsin." *Nation* 119 (1924): 158–61.

Warner, Charles D. "Studies of the Great West." *Harper's New Monthly Magazine* 76 (1888): 556–69, 768–76.

Washburn, Claude C. "Zenith." *Freeman* 8 (1924): 518–20.

Waymack, W. W. "The Middle West Looks Abroad." *Foreign Affairs* 18 (1940): 535–45.

Weaver, James B. "Iowa: The Structure of Her Life." *Review of Reviews* 73 (1926): 259–65.

West, Henry L. "Two Republics or One?" *North American Review* 162 (1896): 509–11.

"West and New East." *Independent* 72 (1912): 322–23.

Wetmore, Alphonso. "Gazetteer of the State of Missouri." *North American Review* 48 (1839): 514–26.

Wharton, Edith. *Ethan Frome*. New York: Charles Scribner's Sons, 1911.

"What the Middle West Resents." *Literary Digest* 64 (Feb. 21, 1920): 35.

"What the Middle West Thinks." *Independent* 86 (1916): 359.

"Wheat Belt Rebellion, The." *Literary Digest* 78 (Aug. 4, 1923): 18–19.

Whelpley, James D. "The Middle West and the War." *Outlook* 110 (1915): 870–71.

"Where There Is No 'Population Explosion.'" *U.S. News and World Report* 69 (Sept. 28, 1970): 82.

White, William Allen. "Fifty Years of Kansas." *World's Work* 8 (1904): 4870–72.

———. "Kansas: A Puritan Survival." In *These United States: A Symposium*, edited by Ernest Gruening, 1:1–12. 2 vols. New York: Boni & Liveright, 1923, 1924.

———. "Kansas: Its Present and Its Future." *Forum* 23 (1897): 75–83.

———. "Why All This Rumpus?" *Collier's: The National Weekly* 72 (Aug. 25, 1923): 5, 24.

White, William L. "The Middle West Drifts To the Right." *Nation* 148 (1939): 635–38.

White, William S. "The 'Midwest Mind' in Congress." *New York Times Magazine*, Mar. 1, 1953, pp. 18, 31.

Whitlock, Brand. "Ohio and the Ohio Man." *American Magazine* 82 (Nov., 1916): 31.

"Why Chicago Wants to Be a State." *Literary Digest* 86 (July 11, 1925): 14.

"Will America Follow the Middle West Again?" *Saturday Evening Post* 217 (Sept. 2, 1944): 104.

Willey, Day A. "A Patchwork Quilt of Humanity." *Lippincott's Monthly Magazine* 84 (1909): 321–28.

Wilson, William E. "Indiana." *Holiday* 8 (Aug., 1950): 27–34, 100–104.

Wood, Charles W. "Where Tomorrow's Ideas Are Born." *Collier's: The National Weekly* 71 (May 12, 1923): 9–10.

Wood, Junius B. "Illinois: Crossroads of the Continent." *National Geographic Magazine* 59 (1931): 523–94.

SCHOLARLY WORKS

Athearn, Robert G. *The Mythic West in Twentieth-Century America.* Lawrence: University Press of Kansas, 1986.

Bader, Robert Smith. *Prohibition in Kansas: A History.* Lawrence: University Press of Kansas, 1986.

Baker, Joseph E. "The Middle West: A Case of Identity." *University of Kansas City Review* 24 (1958): 249–55.

——. "The Midwestern Origins of America." *American Scholar* 17 (1948): 58–68.

Barnhart, John D. "Rainfall and the Populist Party in Nebraska." *American Political Science Review* 19 (1925): 527–40.

Berry, Wendell. *The Unsettling of America: Culture and Agriculture.* San Francisco, Calif.: Sierra Club Books, 1977.

Blouet, Brian W., and Frederick C. Luebke, eds. *The Great Plains: Environment and Culture.* Lincoln: University of Nebraska Press, 1979.

Bonnifield, Paul. *The Dust Bowl: Men, Dirt, and Depression.* Albuquerque: University of New Mexico Press, 1979.

Borchert, John R. *America's Northern Heartland.* Minneapolis: University of Minnesota Press, 1987.

Brownell, Joseph W. "The Cultural Midwest." *Journal of Geography* 59 (1960): 81–85.

Burns, Rex. *Success in America: The Yeoman Dream and the Industrial Revolution.* Amherst: University of Massachusetts Press, 1976.

Caplow, Theodore; Howard M. Bahr; Bruce A. Chadwick; Reuben Hill; and Margaret H. Williamson. *Middletown Families: Fifty Years of Change and Continuity.* Minneapolis: University of Minnesota Press, 1982.

Caughey, John W. "The American West: Frontier and Region." *Arizona and the West* 1 (1959): 7–12.

——. "Toward an Understanding of the West." *Utah Historical Quarterly* 27 (1959): 7–24.

Clanton, O. Gene. *Kansas Populism: Ideas and Men.* Lawrence: University Press of Kansas, 1969.

Conklin, Paul K. *Tomorrow a New World: The New Deal Community Program.* Ithaca, N.Y.: Cornell University Press, 1959.

Crisler, Robert M. "Missouri's Little Dixie." *Missouri Historical Review* 42 (1948): 130–39.

——. "The Regional Status of Little Dixie in Missouri and Little Egypt in Illinois." *Journal of Geography* 49 (1950): 337–43.

Dopp, Mary. "Geographical Influences in the Development of Wisconsin." *Bulletin of the American Geographical Society* 45 (1913): 401–12, 490–99, 585–609, 653–63, 736–49, 831–46, 902–20.

Doran, Michael F. "Population Statistics of Nineteenth Century Indian Territory." *Chronicles of Oklahoma* 53 (1976): 492–515.

Dryer, Charles R. "Geographical Influences in the Development of Indiana." *Journal of Geography* 9 (1910): 17–22.

Eiselen, Elizabeth. "The Tourist Industry of a Modern Highway: U.S. 16 in South Dakota." *Economic Geography* 21 (1945): 221–30.

Elazar, Daniel J. *American Federalism: A View from the States.* 2d ed. New York: Thomas Y. Crowell, 1972.

Emmons, David M. *Garden in the Grasslands: Boomer Literature of the Central Great Plains.* Lincoln: University of Nebraska Press, 1971.

Fenton, John H. *Midwest Politics.* New York: Holt, Rinehart & Winston, 1966.

Fiedler, Leslie. "Montana: Or the End of Jean-Jacques Rousseau." In *The Collected Essays of Leslie Fiedler,* vol. 1, pp. 131–41. New York: Stein & Day, 1971.

Fisher, Dorothy Canfield. *Vermont Tradition: The Biography of an Outlook on Life.* Boston: Little, Brown, 1953.

Francaviglia, Richard V. "Main Street USA: The Creation of a Popular Image." *Landscape* 21 (Spring–Summer, 1977): 18–22.

Gelfant, Blanche H. *The American City Novel.* Norman: University of Oklahoma Press, 1954.

Gerlach, Russel L. "Geography and Politics in Missouri: A Study of Electoral Patterns." *Missouri Geographer* 18 (1971): 27–36.

———. *Settlement Patterns in Missouri: A Study of Population Origins with a Wall Map.* Columbia: University of Missouri Press, 1986.

Goldthwaite, James W. "A Town That Has Gone Downhill." *Geographical Review* 17 (1927): 527–57.

Goodwyn, Lawrence. *Democratic Promise: The Populist Movement in America.* New York: Oxford University Press, 1976.

Gould, Peter, and Rodney White. *Mental Maps.* Baltimore, Md.: Penguin Books, 1974.

Graber, Linda. *Wilderness as Sacred Space.* Association of American Geographers monograph no. 8. Washington, D.C.: Association of American Geographers, 1976.

Harper, Robert D. "Wright Morris's 'Ceremony in Lone Tree': A Picture of Life in Middle America." *Western American Literature* 11 (1976): 199–213.

Hart, James D. *The Popular Book: A History of America's Literary Taste.* London: Oxford University Press, 1950.

Hart, John F. "The Middle West." *Annals of the Association of American Geographers* 62 (1972): 258–82.

Hicks, John D. *The Populist Revolt.* Minneapolis: University of Minnesota Press, 1931.

Hudson, John C. "Yankeeland in the Middle West." *Journal of Geography* 85 (1986): 195–200.

Jackson, John B. *American Space: The Centennial Years, 1865–1876.* New York: W. W. Norton, 1972.

———. *The Necessity for Ruins and Other Topics.* Amherst: University of Massachusetts Press, 1980.

Jakle, John A. *Images of the Ohio Valley: A Historical Geography of Travel, 1740 to 1860.* New York: Oxford University Press, 1977.

———; Stanley Brunn; and Curtis C. Roseman. *Human Spatial Behavior: A Social Geography.* North Scituate, Mass.: Duxbury Press, 1976.

Kollmorgen, Walter M. "The Woodsman's Assaults on the Domain of the Cattleman." *Annals of the Association of American Geographers* 59 (1969): 215–39.

Kramer, Frank R. *Voices in the Valley: Mythmaking and Folk Belief in the Shaping of the Middle West.* Madison: University of Wisconsin Press, 1964.

La Follette, Robert. "Interstate Migration and Indiana Culture." *Mississippi Valley Historical Review* 16 (1929): 347–58.

Lavender, David. "The Petrified West and the American Writer." In *Western Writing,* edited by Gerald W. Haslam, pp. 143–56. Albuquerque: University of New Mexico Press, 1974.

Leland, Lorrin, ed. *The Kansas Experience in Poetry.* Lawrence: University of Kansas, Division of Continuing Education, 1978.

Lendt, David L. *Ding: The Life of Jay Norwood Darling.* Ames: Iowa State University Press, 1979.

Lewis, R. W. B. *The American Adam: Innocence, Tragedy, and Tradition in the Nineteenth Century.* Chicago: University of Chicago Press, 1955.

Littlefield, Henry W. "The Wizard of Oz: Parable on Populism." *American Quarterly* 16 (1964): 47–58.

Love, Glen A. "New Pioneering on the Prairies: Nature, Progress, and the Individual in the Novels of Sinclair Lewis." *American Quarterly* 25 (1973): 558–77.

Lowenthal, David. *The Past Is a Foreign Country.* New York: Cambridge University Press, 1985.

Lynch, William O. "The Influence of Population Movements on Missouri before 1861." *Missouri Historical Review* 16 (1922): 506–16.

McAvoy, Thomas T., ed. *The Midwest: Myth or Reality?* Notre Dame, Ind.: University of Notre Dame Press, 1961.

McCandless, Perry. *A History of Missouri.* Vol. 2: *1820–1860.* Columbia: University of Missouri Press, 1972.

McGiffert, Michael, ed. *The Character of Americans: A Book of Readings.* Rev. ed. Homewood, Ill.: Dorsey Press, 1970.

Malin, James C. "Kansas: Some Reflections on Culture, Inheritance, and

Originality." *Journal of the Central Mississippi Valley American Studies Association* 2 (Fall, 1961): 3–19.

Marshall, Howard W. *Folk Architecture in Little Dixie: A Regional Culture in Missouri.* Columbia: University of Missouri Press, 1981.

Marx, Leo. *The Machine in the Garden: Technology and the Pastoral Ideal in America.* London: Oxford University Press, 1964.

Mather, Cotton. "The Midwest: Image and Reality." *Journal of Geography* 85 (1986): 190–94.

Meeks, Harold A. *Time and Change in Vermont: A Human Geography.* Chester, Conn.: Globe Pequot Press, 1986.

Meinig, D. W. "The Continuous Shaping of America: A Prospectus for Geographers and Historians." *American Historical Review* 83 (1978): 1186–1205.

———. "The Mormon Culture Region: Strategies and Patterns in the Geography of the American West, 1847–1964." *Annals of the Association of American Geographers* 55 (1965): 191–220.

———. "Symbolic Landscapes: Some Idealizations of American Communities." In *The Interpretation of Ordinary Landscapes: Geographical Essays,* edited by D. W. Meinig, pp. 164–92. New York: Oxford University Press, 1979.

———. "Three American Northwests: Some Perspectives in Historical Geography." Paper read at the annual meeting of the Association of American Geographers, Apr. 1, 1957, at Cincinnati, Ohio. Abstract published in *Annals of the Association of American Geographers* 47 (1957): 170–71.

Meyer, Douglas K. "Southern Illinois Migration Fields: The Shawnee Hills in 1850." *Professional Geographer* 28 (1976): 151–60.

Meyer, Roy W. *The Middle Western Farm Novel in the Twentieth Century.* Lincoln: University of Nebraska Press, 1965.

Milton, John R. *South Dakota: A Bicentennial History.* New York: W. W. Norton, 1977.

Morgan, Howard W., and Anne H. Morgan. *Oklahoma: A Bicentennial History.* New York: W. W. Norton, 1977.

Novak, Barbara. *Nature and Culture: American Landscape Painting, 1825–1875.* New York: Oxford University Press, 1980.

Nye, Russel B. *Midwestern Progressive Politics: A Historical Study of Its Origins and Development, 1870–1958.* East Lansing: Michigan State University Press, 1959.

Power, Richard L. *Planting Corn Belt Culture.* Indianapolis: Indiana Historical Society, 1953.

———. "Wet Lands and the Hoosier Stereotype." *Mississippi Valley Historical Review* 22 (1935): 33–48.

Reed, John Shelton. *The Enduring South: Subcultural Persistence in Mass Society.* Chapel Hill: University of North Carolina Press, 1974.

Relph, E. *Place and Placelessness*. London: Pion, 1976.

Rickard, Timothy J. "The Great Plains as Part of an Irrigated Western Empire, 1890–1914." In *The Great Plains: Environment and Culture*, edited by Brian W. Blouet and Frederick C. Luebke, pp. 81–98. Lincoln: University of Nebraska Press, 1979.

Rooney, John F., Jr.; Wilbur Zelinsky; and Dean R. Louder, eds. *This Remarkable Continent: An Atlas of United States and Canadian Society and Cultures*. College Station: Texas A & M University Press, 1982.

Rose, Gregory S. "Hoosier Origins: The Nativity of Indiana's United States–Born Population in 1850." *Indiana Magazine of History* 81 (1985): 201–32.

————. "South Central Michigan Yankees." *Michigan History* 70 (Mar./ Apr., 1986): 32–39.

————. "Upland Southerners: The County Origins of Southern Migrants to Indiana by 1850." *Indiana Magazine of History* 82 (1986): 242–63.

Rundell, Walter, Jr. "Concepts of the 'Frontier' and the 'West.'" *Arizona and the West* 1 (1959): 13–41.

Shi, David E. *The Simple Life: Plain Living and High Thinking in American Culture*. New York: Oxford University Press, 1985.

Shortridge, James R. "Changing Usage of Four American Regional Labels." *Annals of the Association of American Geographers* 77 (1987): 325–36.

————. "Cowboy, Yeoman, Pawn, and Hick: Myth and Contradiction in Great Plains Life." *Focus* 35 (Oct., 1985): 22–27.

————. "Vernacular Regions in Kansas." *American Studies* 21 (Spring, 1980): 73–94.

Slotkin, Richard. *The Fatal Environment: The Myth of the Frontier in the Age of Industrialization, 1800–1890*. New York: Atheneum, 1985.

————. *Regeneration through Violence: The Mythology of the American Frontier, 1600–1860*. Middletown, Conn.: Wesleyan University Press, 1973.

Smith, Henry Nash. *Virgin Land: The American West as Symbol and Myth*. Cambridge, Mass.: Harvard University Press, 1950.

————. "The West as an Image of the American Past." *University of Kansas City Review* 18 (1951): 29–40.

Stegner, Wallace. "Born a Square: The Westerner's Dilemma." *Atlantic Monthly* 213 (Jan., 1964): 46–50.

———— "History, Myth, and the Western Writer." *American West* 4 (May, 1967): 61–62, 76–79.

Steiner, Michael C. "Regionalism in the Great Depression." *Geographical Review* 73 (1983): 430–46.

Suckow, Ruth. "Middle Western Literature." *English Journal* 21 (1932): 175–82.

Taylor, Joshua C. *America as Art*. New York: Harper & Row, 1976.

Tuan, Yi-fu. "Place: An Experiential Perspective." *Geographical Review* 65 (1975): 151–65.

———. *Space and Place: The Perspective of Experience*. Minneapolis: University of Minnesota Press, 1977.

Turner, Frederick Jackson. *The Frontier in American History*. New York: Henry Holt, 1920.

Viles, Jonas. "Sections and Sectionalism in a Border State." *Mississippi Valley Historical Review* 21 (1934): 3–22.

Webb, Walter Prescott. *The Great Plains*. New York: Ginn, 1931.

Wertenbaker, Thomas J. "The Molding of the Middle West." *American Historical Review* 53 (1948): 223–34.

Wilhelm, Hubert G. H. "The Origin and Distribution of Settlement Groups: Ohio, 1850." Mimeographed ms., Department of Geography, Ohio University, 1982.

Wilkins, Wynona H. "The Idea of North Dakota." *North Dakota Quarterly* 39 (Winter, 1971): 5–28.

Worster, Donald E. *Dust Bowl: The Southern Plains in the 1930s*. New York: Oxford University Press, 1979.

Zelinsky, Wilbur. *The Cultural Geography of the United States*. Englewood Cliffs, N.J.: Prentice-Hall, 1973.

———. "North America's Vernacular Regions." *Annals of the Association of American Geographers* 70 (1980): 1–16.

Index

193